The Anatomy of the Holocaust

Vermont Studies on Nazi Germany and the Holocaust

Editorial Committee:
Jonathan D. Huener, University of Vermont
Francis R. Nicosia, University of Vermont
Susanna Schrafstetter, University of Vermont
Alan E. Steinweis, University of Vermont

The University of Vermont has been an important venue for research on the Holocaust since Raul Hilberg began his work there in 1956. These volumes reflect the scholarly activity of UVM's Miller Center for Holocaust Studies. They combine original research with interpretive synthesis and address research questions, interdisciplinary investigations, and international interests.

Medicine and Medical Ethics in Nazi Germany: Origins, Practices, Legacies
Edited by Francis R. Nicosia and Jonathan Huener

Business and Industry in Nazi Germany
Edited by Francis R. Nicosia and Jonathan Huener

The Arts in Nazi Germany: Continuity, Conformity, Change
Edited by Jonathan Huener and Francis R. Nicosia

Jewish Life in Nazi Germany: Dilemmas and Responses
Edited by Francis R. Nicosia and David Scrase

The Law in Nazi Germany: Ideology, Opportunism, and the Perversion of Justice
Edited by Alan E. Steinweis and Robert D. Rachlin

The Germans and the Holocaust: Popular Responses to the Persecution and Murder of the Jews
Edited by Susanna Schrafstetter and Alan E. Steinweis

Nazism, the Holocaust, and the Middle East: Arab and Turkish Responses
Edited by Francis R. Nicosia and Boğaç A. Ergene

The Anatomy of the Holocaust: Selected Works from a Life of Scholarship
Raul Hilberg; edited by Walter H. Pehle and René Schlott

Raul Hilberg

The Anatomy of the Holocaust

Selected Works from a Life of Scholarship

Edited by
Walter H. Pehle
and
René Schlott

Published in 2020 by
Berghahn Books
www.berghahnbooks.com

English-language edition © 2020 Berghahn Books

Originally published in German as
Anatomie des Holocaust: Essays und Erinnerungen
© S. Fischer Verlag GmbH, Frankfurt am Main, 2016

All rights reserved. Except for the quotation of short passages
for the purposes of criticism and review, no part of this book
may be reproduced in any form or by any means, electronic or
mechanical, including photocopying, recording, or any information
storage and retrieval system now known or to be invented,
without written permission of the publisher.

Owing to limitations of space, reprint credits can be found on pages vii–viii.

Library of Congress Cataloging-in-Publication Data

Names: Hilberg, Raul, 1926–2007, author. | Pehle, Walter H., 1941– editor. | Schlott, René, 1977– editor.
Title: The Anatomy of the Holocaust: Selected Works from a Life of Scholarship / Raul Hilberg, edited by Walter H. Pehle and René Schlott.
Other titles: Anatomie des Holocaust. English
Description: First edition. | New York; Oxford: Berghahn Books, 2020. | Series: Vermont studies on Nazi Germany and the Holocaust; vol 8 | "Originally published in German as Anatomie des Holocaust: Essays und Erinnerungen, © S. Fischer Verlag GmbH, Frankfurt am Main, 2016"— title page verso. | Includes bibliographical references and index.
Identifiers: LCCN 2019033792 (print) | LCCN 2019033793 (ebook) | ISBN 9781789203554 (hardback) | ISBN 9781789204896 (paperback) | ISBN 9781789203561 (ebook)
Subjects: LCSH: Holocaust, Jewish (1939–1945) | Holocaust, Jewish (1939–1945)—Historiography. | Hilberg, Raul, 1926–2007.
Classification: LCC D804.3 .H5413 2020 (print) | LCC D804.3 (ebook) | DDC 940.53/18—dc23
LC record available at https://lccn.loc.gov/2019033792
LC ebook record available at https://lccn.loc.gov/2019033793

British Library Cataloguing in Publication Data

A catalogue record for this book is available from the British Library

ISBN 978-1-78920-355-4 hardback
ISBN 978-1-78920-489-6 paperback
ISBN 978-1-78920-356-1 ebook

Contents

Acknowledgments	vii
Introduction *Walter H. Pehle and René Schlott*	1

I. Research and Scholarship

1. The Anatomy of the Holocaust	13
2. German Motivations for the Destruction of the Jews	23
3. The Bureaucracy of Annihilation	50
4. The Significance of the Holocaust	70
5. Incompleteness in Holocaust Historiography	79

II. Controversies and Debates

6. Bitburg as Symbol	99
7. The Ghetto as a Form of Government	113
8. The *Judenrat*: Conscious or Unconscious "Tool"	133
9. I Was Not There	147

III. Memories and Memoirs

10. The Holocaust Mission: 29 July to 12 August 1979	159

Contents

11. In Search of the Special Trains   178

12. Working on the Holocaust   195

13. The Development of Holocaust Research:
    A Personal Overview   225

Indexes   238

Acknowledgments

The editors and publisher wish to thank the following for granting reprint permissions:

3. "The Bureaucracy of Annihilation" from *Unanswered Questions*, edited by François Furet, translated by Benjamin Ivry, translation copyright © 1989 Penguin Random House LLC. Used by permission of Schocken Books, an imprint of the Knopf Doubleday Publishing Group, a division of Penguin Random House LLC. All rights reserved. The same material is used with the additional permission of Éditions du Seuil, publisher of the French edition of the anthology *L'Allemagne nazis et le genocide juif. Colloque de l'Ecole des Hautes Etudes en Sciences Sociales*, © Éditions du Seuil, 1985.

6. "Bitburg as Symbol," from *Bitburg in Moral and Political Perspectives*, ed. Geoffrey Hartman © 1986. Reprinted with permission of Indiana University Press.

7. "The Ghetto as a Form of Government," from *The Annals of the American Academy of Political Social Science* 450, no. 1 © 1980. Previously published by SAGE Publications.

8. "The *Judenrat*: Conscious or Unconscious 'Tool,'" from *Pattern of Jewish Leadership in Nazi Europe 1933–1945* © 1979. Reprinted with permission of Yad Vashem Publications.

9. "I Was Not There," from *Writing and the Holocaust*, ed. Berel Lang © 1988. Reprinted with permission from Berel Lang.

10. "The Holocaust Mission: 29 July to 12 August 1979," from *St. Johns Review* 34, no. 1 © 1982–83.

12. "Working on the Holocaust," from *The Psychohistory Review* 14, no. 3 © 1986. Originally printed and edited by Sangamon State University; reprinted with permission of University of Illinois Springfield.

13. "The Development of Holocaust Research: A Personal Overview," from *Holocaust Historiography in Context*, ed. David Bankier and Dan Michman © 2008. Reprinted with permission of Yad Vashem Publications.

Introduction
Walter H. Pehle and René Schlott

I am not a man who gives in.
Raul Hilberg in Weimar, 1995

Anyone who investigates the persecution and murder of the Jews during National Socialism and World War II knows the name of Raul Hilberg. His work, *The Destruction of the European Jews*, remains indispensable even today. There are many other texts, however, in which Raul Hilberg offers important contributions to various debates in this field. A few of these still relatively inaccessible texts are now published together in one collection in their original language.

This volume of Hilberg's texts also invites interested readers and Holocaust researchers to trace the development of his scientific work over more than five decades. The thirteen texts presented here were published between 1965, just a few years after the appearance of *The Destruction of the European Jews*, and 2007, the year Hilberg died. In them, Raul Hilberg not only reflects on the results of his research and the controversies it generated, but also describes his perception of the ways the Holocaust is remembered. And, finally, the texts recount Hilberg's own memories of archival visits gathering material for his research work. They convey a sense of how the true extent of what was then known as the "Final Solution" was only gradually understood through the difficult process of digesting tens of thousands of administrative and court files after World War II. They show how the Holocaust became the subject of academic study and how this research developed into its current, highly professionalized form.

Hilberg's scientific engagement with the Holocaust did not attract much interest from either the public or historians in its first few decades.[1] Hilberg sometimes grew frustrated, even bitter, about the international ignorance, but he never gave up his dedication to the research.

Only in the mid-1970s did attention to the Holocaust increase, first in the United States and then in Western Europe, and it was not until 1990, when the German paperback edition of *The Destruction of the European Jews* came out, that an international boom in Holocaust research began that lasted through the next decades up to the present. In recent years, a number of research centers have been founded all around the world, e.g., in Germany with Munich's Center for Holocaust Studies at the Institute of Contemporary History and with the creation of a chair for Holocaust research at Johann Wolfgang Goethe University in Frankfurt. The founding of the internationally renowned research department of the Washington Holocaust Museum really propelled Hilberg forward, himself a long-time member of the United States Holocaust Memorial Council.

This selection by the editors from the multitude of his published texts focuses on Hilberg's intellectual interests as a Holocaust researcher. Among other topics, they deal with the bureaucracy of the Holocaust, the number of victims, the role of the *Judenräte* (Jewish councils), and the function of the railway and the police in the extermination process. The scholarly impulses extending from Hilberg's work remain remarkable and virulent almost a decade after his death.[2] They deserve to be readily accessible in one place to historians and the interested public in the new compilation offered here. Many of the debates influenced by Hilberg are not yet resolved. The texts presented can be quite revealing in light of these controversies.

Hilberg's work has had a lasting effect on Holocaust research, even if the field has grown significantly more international and refined over time.[3] Nevertheless, the groundwork still needs to be deepened, a task taken up in the ambitious project *Die Verfolgung und Ermordung der europäischen Juden durch das nationalsozialistische Deutschland 1933–1945*, whose volumes are now available in English (*Persecution and Murder of the European Jews by Nazi Germany 1993–1945*) as well. This benchmark source edition will serve as a complement to Hilberg's source-saturated main work,[4] whose sources are chosen in accordance with Hilberg's triad of *perpetrators, victims,* and *bystanders*.[5] Hilberg, who constantly referred to his sources and who himself brought forth in 1971 a collection of sources that had never been translated into other languages,⁶ promoted this large edition in the planning phases of its publication, but did not live to see the appearance of the first volumes.

Raul Hilberg died in August 2007 after a short, severe illness. In April of the same year, he gave his last public address at his local synagogue in South Burlington, Vermont, and reviewed his research on the destruction of the European Jews that he had begun in 1948 and continued through to the end of his life. On 1 September 2019 he would have celebrated the eightieth anniversary of his arrival in the United States as a young Jewish-Austrian refugee. To commemorate this occasion this book is a tribute to Raul Hilberg's life work, which helped to lay the foundation for Holocaust research, and highlights his six decades of scholarly engagement with the National Socialists' murder of the Jews.

Isaac Deutscher doubted in 1968 that Hitler, Auschwitz, Majdanek, and Treblinka could ever be explained. Raul Hilberg helped to dispel that doubt somewhat, in his own words, by writing "footnotes after Auschwitz" (see chapter 9), that is, by approaching the subject analytically using strict scientific methods. And yet: "At the end, nothing remains but despair and doubt about everything, because for Hilberg there is only recognition, perhaps also a grasp, but certainly no understanding."⁷ In his parliamentary speech on the seventieth anniversary of the end of the war on 8 May 1945, German historian Heinrich August Winkler emphasized the particular significance of Raul Hilberg and included him in a list of distinguished Holocaust researchers: "Decades had to go by in Germany before the Holocaust was seen as the central fact of German history of the twentieth century, not least thanks to the groundbreaking research of Jewish scholars such as Joseph Wulf, Gerald Reitlinger, Raul Hilberg and Saul Friedländer."⁸

The Texts

This book starts with an essay published in 1980, "The Anatomy of the Holocaust," which gave the volume its programmatic title. Research into the aim, form, and structure of the Holocaust was a lifelong scholarly engagement for Raul Hilberg, traceable throughout his body of work. As a political scientist, Hilberg was always focused on the *how* of the National Socialists' genocide of the European Jews, in order to reveal the mechanisms that allowed a decimation of such magnitude, and to grasp the bureaucratic functioning of the perpetrator apparatus. His dissertation, submitted in 1955 to Columbia University and published in 1961, "The Destruction of the European Jews," was inspired by the work of his teachers Hans Rosenberg and Franz Neumann and analyzes the "machinery of destruction" as divided into different phases. In this volume's first text, Hilberg discusses the importance of Neumann's work for his own understanding, and presents his three-phase model of *definition, concentration*, and *physical extermination*, a model influential even today.

Only once did Hilberg grapple with the *why* of the Holocaust. The second work in this collection was originally written for a volume that was never published, commemorating his dissertation advisor Franz Neumann who died in a car accident in Switzerland in 1954. In it, Hilberg explores the ultimately unconvincing attempts to explain the Holocaust that resorted to blaming the essential qualities of the victims and perpetrators. Hilberg announced after his dissertation that he was planning to put forth a volume covering the reasons for the destruction of the Jews, but nothing appeared after the first essay came out in 1965.

Hilberg was much more interested in the interpretation of the Holocaust as an administrative process and added new categories to his analysis of the bureaucratic annihilation apparatus and the characters of its bureaucrats. Two examples are the railway and the police, whose roles he analyzed at a conference in Paris in 1980—his paper is the third text in this collection. Christopher Browning was also present at the conference and learned about the role of the police in the murder of the Jews from Hilberg's presentation. In 1992, he put forward his groundbreaking study *Ordinary Men* about a German police battalion in Poland. Aside from his historical engagement with the Holocaust, Hilberg always tried to explain the meaning of the event and its consequences for the present day, for instance in his 1980 essay "The Significance of the Holocaust" (the fourth chapter here), which comes from a presentation given at the San José conference in 1979. At the end of his scientific career, Hilberg was aware that his historiographic work on the Holocaust was destined to remain incomplete and that the research process was more a journey than a destination, as he expressed in the fifth chapter here. US President Ronald Reagan's controversial 1985 visit to the Bitburg soldiers' cemetery prompted Hilberg to submit a contribution to an anthology (see chapter six) in which he contemplated not only the national memorial culture in

Germany, but also the participation of the German army in the destruction of the Jews—a good decade before the "army exhibition" (*Wehrmachtsausstellung*) visualizing this theme was to spark a great public debate in the country.

Hilberg himself also incited controversies with his work, some of which are ongoing. In addition to his skepticism of the Jewish resistance in the Holocaust, particularly his view of the *Judenräte* as "instruments" of the Germans in the murder of the Jews is hotly debated. In a discussion of Isaiah Trunk's fundamental work *Judenrat: The Jewish Councils in Eastern Europe under Nazi Occupation*, which came out in the United States in 1972, Hilberg modified his previously staunch position. In this essay (chapter 7 of this book), he points again to the diary kept by Adam Czerniaków, chair of the Judenrat in the Warsaw ghetto from 1939 to 1942, whose records Hilberg published in an English translation in 1979.[9] Contributors to the edition besides Hilberg included a Polish-speaking colleague from the University of Vermont, Stanislaw Staron, and Josef Kermisz, who worked for Israel's Yad Vashem, the World Holocaust Remembrance Center.

Although Hilberg's relationship with his Israeli colleagues was initially quite tense, not least because his dissertation was rejected there[10] and ultimately torn up in a review after its publication,[11] the relationship gradually improved later on. In 1977, Hilberg first participated in a conference in Jerusalem, where he spoke about the *Judenräte*, their "illusions," and their roots in Jewish history—the eighth chapter in this volume. In terms of content, Hilberg's position was still light years away from that of the historians at Yad Vashem, and Hilberg was subjected to harsh criticism at the conference from Gideon Hausner, former chief prosecutors at the trial of Adolf Eichmann and then chairman of the council of Yad Vashem. The adversaries were thus nevertheless now on speaking terms.

Although Hilberg, who experienced the "Anschluss" of Austria in his hometown Vienna at the age of eleven and the November Pogrom of 1938 and was thus in a certain sense himself a survivor of the Nazi terror, he remained skeptical with regard to the source value of survivor reports—an attitude still debated. In 1988, he expanded upon his reservations for the volume *Writing and the Holocaust*, the ninth chapter here, in which he contemplated both the sources and the language with which the murder of the Jews was described.

In 1979, Hilberg returned to Yad Vashem, this time as a member of a delegation led by Elie Wiesel, who was commissioned by US President Jimmy Carter to develop a concept for a Holocaust Museum in the United States. To this end, the commission traveled to a number of places, including Poland and the Soviet Union, where Hilberg saw for the first time the actual places of extermination and in Warsaw found the grave of Czerniaków. In 1982, he published his very personal memories from this trip—the tenth text here.

Although by the end of the war Hilberg had decided for at least four decades not to set foot again on German soil, he traveled to West Germany in 1976 to access files for his research. The Jewish exile and former US soldier Hilberg's ambivalent relationship to the Germans at this time can be seen in the travel report that he published three years after the trip in the Jewish opinion magazine *Midstream*, found here as the eleventh chapter.

The twelfth text presents the minutes from a discussion circle on psychohistory. The well-regarded US psychiatrist Robert Lifton (b. 1926) had invited Hilberg to his summer house in Wellflet on Cape Cod, Massachusetts. On this occasion, Hilberg, almost sixty at the time, spoke for the first time about his own biography and reflected on his life as a Holocaust researcher.

The collection concludes with a presentation that Hilberg gave at a conference in 2005 at Yad Vashem. In it, he examines the historiographic history of the Holocaust and reviews the results of his lifelong research. He ends with the words, "And, looking back, I am extremely gratified that we are making a far greater effort than I ever imagined possible."[12]

Remarks from the Editors

This collection of texts by Raul Hilberg is based on the original English-language versions. The majority of them are presentations that were later printed as part of conference publications. Because Hilberg tended to speak without written remarks, the texts are based on his notes, and he reviewed the articles before they went to press. The language and structure correspond to that of an oral presentation; a few, therefore, have no notes or references.

Marginalia present in the original documents, such as typographical or punctuation errors in proper names and transposed numerals, were corrected without notation in the text. The correct Polish spelling of places like Łódź or Bełżec was not used in this book because during the German occupation their names appear without special characters: e.g., Belzec was a German death camp close to but different from the Polish village of Bełżec. Deviations from the academic norm that were obviously intended by Hilberg were kept as they were. All editorial changes to the text are noted in brackets. These include, but are not limited to, updates and completions of the citations and bibliographical entries. Additional information given by the editors is marked with an asterisk in the lower margins.

The direct language and at times laconic tone with which Hilberg talked about the Holocaust are still recognizable, however. He himself once explained that his idiosyncratic writing style made up of short, consecutive sentences was inspired by the Bible.[13]

The chapters are organized following a loosely structured thematic grouping. The various rubrics are named according to the main theme of the texts in each group. The volume is not laid out such that the chapters build on each other or follow an overarching plotline. The interested reader can open the book to any section and begin reading. Repetitions of episodes or arguments in the various chapters were therefore consciously preserved without alteration. They may appear redundant over the course of the entire book, but they have their place in each chapter. The reader can thus in many different ways be impressed and challenged by the thematic breadth and intellectual depth of Hilberg's thought.

Thanks

The editors wish to thank the Hilberg family, especially Raul Hilberg's widow Gwendolyn, for her support of the German edition of this compilation that appeared in 2016 commemorating what would have been the ninetieth birthday of Raul Hilberg. Gwen Hilberg died two years later and this English edition is dedicated to her.

Thanks also to Anne-Sophie Kruppa and Viktor-Emanuel zu Sachsen who took over the compilation of the index that would have been so important to Raul Hilberg, as his lifelong desire was the scholarly use and development of his research.

Finally, we thank the Leibniz Centre for Contemporary History in Potsdam (Leibniz-Zentrum für Zeithistorische Forschung – ZZF) and the Miller Center for Holocaust Studies at the University of Vermont—two important research institutions that made this publication possible.

Walter H. Pehle was born in 1941, studied in Cologne, Bonn, and Düsseldorf, and holds a doctorate in history. From 1977 to 2011, he was the editor for historical texts at the German publisher S. Fischer Verlag. Since 1988, he has served as the acquisitions editor for S. Fischer Verlag's series "The Age of National Socialism," which to date includes over 250 books. His own publications include, as volume editor, the anthology *November 1938: From "Reichskristallnacht" to Genocide* (Berg, 1991) and, together with Wolfgang Benz, *Encyclopedia of German Resistance to the Nazi Movement* (Continuum, 1997). He is an honorary professor at the University of Innsbruck.

René Schlott is a historian and researcher at the Leibniz Centre for Contemporary History in Potsdam and teaches history at the universities of Potsdam and Berlin. He received his PhD in 2011 from the University of Giessen and is currently working as a postdoc on the first biography covering the life, work, and legacy of Raul Hilberg. In 2017, he was awarded a three-year scholarship (*Habilitationsstipendium*) from the Konrad-Adenauer-Stiftung for his research project.

Notes

1. See Nicolas Berg, "Phantasie der Bürokratie," describing Raul Hilberg's pioneer study on the destruction of the European Jews, in *50 Klassiker der Zeitgeschichte*, ed. Jürgen Danyel, Jan-Holger Kirsch, and Martin Sabrow (Göttingen, 2007), 71–75. Nicolas Berg, "Der Holocaust und die westdeutschen Historiker: Erforschung und Erinnerung," *Moderne Zeit*, 3, (Göttingen, 2003 [Diss. Freiburg, 2001]).
2. This is clearly the case, as shown in the latest "inventory" of Holocaust research and the frequency of references to Raul Hilberg's works contained therein. Frank Bajohr and Andrea Löw, eds., *Der Holocaust: Ergebnisse und neue Fragen der Forschung* (Frankfurt am Main, 2015).
3. See Frank Bajohr and Andrea Löw, "Tendenzen und Probleme der neueren Holocaust-Forschung: Eine Einführung," in *Der Holocaust: Ergebnisse und neue Fragen der Forschung*, ed. Frank Bajohr and Andrea Löw (Frankfurt am Main, 2015), 9–30.
4. Lorenz Jäger, "Die Sache selbst. Zum Forschungsstand: Hilberg, Aly und die Vernichtungspolitik," in *Frankfurter Allgemeine Zeitung*, 27 January 2005.
5. Ulrich Herbert refers to this connection in an interview in *tageszeitung (taz)*, 25 January 2008. Raul Hilberg, *Täter, Opfer, Zuschauer: Die Vernichtung der Juden 1933–1945* (Frankfurt am Main, 1992).

6. Raul Hilberg, ed. *Documents of Destruction. Germany and Jewry 1933–1945* (Chicago, 1971).
7. H. G. Adler, cited in Raul Hilberg, *The Politics of Memory: The Journey of a Holocaust Historian* (Chicago 1996), 203.
8. Deutscher Bundestag, "Rede von Prof. Dr. Heinrich August Winkler zum 70. Jahrestag Ende des Zweiten Weltkrieges 8. Mai 2015," retrieved on 9 January 2019 from https://www.bundestag.de/dokumente/textarchiv/2015/kw19_gedenkstunde_wkii_rede_winkler/373858.
9. Raul Hilberg, Stanislaw Staron, and Josef Kermisz, eds. *The Warszaw Diary of Adam Czerniakow: Prelude to Doom* (New York, 1979).
10. See René Schlott, "Der lange Weg zum Buch. Zur Publikationsgeschichte von Raul Hilbergs *The Destruction of the European Jews*," in *Zeiträume: Potsdamer Almanach des Zentrum für Zeithistorische Forschung 2015*, ed. Frank Bösch and Martin Sabrow (Göttingen, 2015), 146–47.
11. Nathan Eck, "Historical Research or Slander," *Yad Vashem Studies* 6 (1967): 385–430.
12. Raul Hilberg, "The Development of Holocaust Research: A Personal Overview," in this volume.
13. Raul Hilberg, *The Politics of Memory: The Journey of a Holocaust Historian* (Chicago 1996), 46.

Bibliography

Bajohr, Frank, and Andrea Löw, eds. *Der Holocaust: Ergebnisse und neue Fragen der Forschung*. Frankfurt am Main: Fischer Verlag, 2015.
Berg, Nicolas. "Der Holocaust und die westdeutschen Historiker: Erforschung und Erinnerung." In *Moderne Zeit*, 3. Göttingen, 2003 (Diss. Freiburg, 2001).
———. "Phantasie der Bürokratie." In *50 Klassiker der Zeitgeschichte*, ed. Jürgen Danyel, Jan-Holger Kirsch, and Martin Sabrow, 71–75. Göttingen: Vandenhoeck & Ruprecht, 2007.
Eck, Nathan. "Historical Research or Slander." *Yad Vashem Studies* 6 (1967): 385–430.
Hilberg, Raul, ed. *Documents of Destruction: Germany and Jewry 1933–1945*. Chicago: Quadrangle Books, 1971.
———. *Perpetrators Victims Bystanders: the Jewish Catastrophe, 1933–1945*. New York: Aaron Asher Books, 1992.
———. *The Politics of Memory: The Journey of a Holocaust Historian*. Chicago: Ivan R. Dee, 1996.
Hilberg, Raul, Stanislaw Staron, and Josef Kermisz, eds. *The Warszaw Diary of Adam Czerniakow: Prelude to Doom*. New York: Madison Books, 1979.
Jäger, Lorenz. "Die Sache selbst. Zum Forschungsstand: Hilberg, Aly und die Vernichtungspolitik." *Frankfurter Allgemeine Zeitung*, 27 January 2005.

Schlott, René. "Der lange Weg zum Buch: Zur Publikationsgeschichte von Raul Hilberg's *The Destruction of the European Jews*." In *Zeiträume: Potsdamer Almanach des Zentrum für Zeithistorische Forschung 2015*, ed. Frank Bösch and Martin Sabrow, 143–52. Göttingen: Wallstein, 2015.

I

Research and Scholarship

1

THE ANATOMY OF THE HOLOCAUST
(1980)

IN THE MIDDLE OF THE war a remarkable man by the name of Franz Neumann, who worked in the Office of Strategic Services and the Department of State, wrote a book about Nazi Germany called *Behemoth*. The first edition came out in 1942, the second in 1944. Each edition was written without the benefit of any original documents, any of the captured materials which became available after the collapse of Germany and which constitute the major source of our knowledge about the destruction process. Franz Neumann worked from newspapers, from published decrees, from journal articles that were somehow transmitted across the ocean, through Switzerland to the United States. He worked intuitively, and he analyzed the structure of the Nazi regime with singular insight. He called Germany a "non-state," a "behemoth" but not a state. He identified four hierarchical groupings as operating virtually independently of one another, and occasionally coming together to make what he sarcastically called "social contracts." Those four hierarchies were the veritable pillars of modern Germany, as they have occasionally been described by German constitutional lawyers and historians: the German civil service, the German army, the

---

Originally published in *The Holocaust: Ideology, Bureaucracy, and Genocide*, ed. Henry Friedlander and Sybil Milton (Millwood, NY: Kraus International Publications, 1980), 85–94.

later emergent industrial conglomeration of various giant enterprises, and finally, the Nazi Party and its machinery.

Several years later, when the war crimes trials were begun in Nuremberg, most particularly after the very first one, more and more documents were turned up here and there, a paper residue of a vast bureaucracy. The primary problem was to make a few piles of them so that one could at least break down this mass of tens of thousands and even hundreds of thousands of materials into manageable quantities. The records were labeled roughly by subject matter: "NG," "NI," "NO," and "NOKW." "NG" stands for Nazi government, in the main correspondence produced by the civil service; "NI" is Nazi industry; "NO," Nazi organizations, that is to say, Party documents; and "NOKW" stands for Nazi *Oberkommando der Wehrmacht*, the high command of the armed forces. Independently of Franz Neumann, the archivists and researchers preparing the Nuremberg trials had developed the identical scheme of things as they looked at these documents. They, too, concluded that there were four major hierarchies.

Fortunately, I came under Neumann's influence very early, while I was a beginning graduate student at Columbia University. Neumann was not a very approachable man, and I did not want to tell him that I was about to embark on the study of the destruction of the Jews. Therefore I said that I wanted to investigate the role of the German civil service in that destruction. He nodded his head, and that was as much conversation as he made because he was hard of hearing. Actually, I was preparing to do more—I was going to write about all the other hierarchies as well, because somehow I felt that each was involved in the destruction process in some way. And then I realized that I would have to write four stories paralleling one another. That wouldn't do. Consequently, I had to come upon another scheme, another anatomy, to describe that development. At that very moment I came across an analysis by an extraordinarily shrewd observer who was in Hungary during the war. Rudolf Kastner, a Jew who made audacious attempts to negotiate with the Germans in 1944 for ransoming the Jews of Hungary (efforts that, by and large, failed), wrote an affidavit on his experiences and perspectives at Nuremberg right after his liberation. In that eighteen-page summation he said words to the effect: For years, we sat there in Hungary surrounded by other Axis countries. We watched the Jews disappear in Germany. We watched them disappear in Poland. We watched them disappear in Yugoslavia and many other places. And then we noticed—meaning in essence *he* noticed—that everywhere the same events seemed to be happening, that certain steps followed in sequence. In a crude way, he outlined these steps. And it suddenly occurred to me that the destruction of the Jews was a process.

In the administrative process, the path of a bureaucracy is determined, not by blueprints or strategies, but by the very nature of the undertaking. Thus, a group of people, dispersed in a larger population over an entire continent, will not be concentrated or seized until after they have been identified and defined. One step at a time, and each step dependent on the preceding step. The destruction of the Jews transpired in this manner; it had an inherent logic, irrespective of how far ahead the perpetrators could see and irrespective of what their plans were. They could have stopped at any one moment and at any one place, but they could not have omitted steps in the progression or "escalation" of the process. They had to traverse all of these routines. They had to sever, one by one, the relations and ties of the Jewish community with the surrounding population in every region of German-dominated Europe. Step one, in the analytical scheme of things, was thus the undertaking of defining Jews as such. It would appear to have been a simple matter, but it was not. There is a Jewish definition of the term "Jew," but that would not serve the Germans. To them, an adherence to the Jewish religion or descent from a Jewish mother was not decisive because there might have been recent converts to Christianity, or half-Jews with a Jewish father who were not Jewish in Jewish eyes but who could not be German in the Third Reich. Above all, if Jewry were defined in accordance with religious criteria alone, Jews might convert overnight and, by doing so, immunize themselves from the effects of the destruction process, a medieval approach adequate enough in an earlier age, but one that was not proper in a racial environment. Yet everyone knew that Jews could not be identified in every case by physiognomy. Definition could not rest on measurements of faces. The whole notion of race had an ideological tinge, but very little administrative utility.

It was an official in the Interior Ministry (originally in the customs administration) who wrote the final version of the definition decree that we associate with the Nuremberg Laws. The original Law, the very first in which measures were taken against Jews, the Law for the Restoration of the German Civil Service, had specified "non-Aryan." The phrase had come down from the nineteenth century. It resulted in a protest by the Japanese government, which felt insulted. The Germans replied, "Wait. We do not mean that different races are necessarily different in quality. They are just different in kind." But even with this explanation, that concept was in trouble.

Non-Aryan, at any rate, was any person with a single Jewish grandparent. That grandparent only had to belong to the Jewish religion. A person with a Jewish grandparent could be dismissed from a post in the civil service or from the teaching profession. Yet in the escalating destruction process, such a definition, embracing individuals who were three-quarters German, was too harsh. It was up to Bernhard Lösener, the customs official transferred to the Interior Ministry, to define the term Jew. He had to do so urgently because at Nuremberg a law had been issued, a criminal law, in which "Jews" were forbidden to marry Germans, and "Jews" were forbidden to have extramarital intercourse with Germans, and "Jews" were forbidden to employ in their household German women under the age of forty-five. And Jews were not defined in that criminal law.

Thus, an implementation decree had to be issued that would contain that missing definition. It was to provide that a person was to be considered Jewish if he had three or four Jewish grandparents. That person was Jewish regardless of his own religious adherence. He could have been brought up as a Christian, his parents might have been Christians, but if most of his grandparents were Jewish by religion, then he was Jewish in accordance with this new definition. If an individual had two Jewish grandparents, he would be classified as Jewish only if he himself belonged to the Jewish religion at the time of the issuance of the decree, or if—at that moment—he was married to a Jewish person. The critical factor in every case was in the first instance the religion of the grandparents. That is the reason for a new profession that came into being all over Germany, the *Sippenforscher*, specialists in genealogy who were providing evidence of the religion of grandparents by means of records found in state offices or baptismal certificates furnished by churches.

The definition decree had the effect of targeting the Jews automatically in that it precluded them from doing anything at all to change their status and thereby to escape from the impact of all the destructive measures that were to come. The very next step in the unfolding destruction process was economic, primarily the expropriation of Jewish business firms, a process known as "Aryanizations."

At the beginning, the "Aryanizations" were "voluntary." German companies, aided by regulations of the Economy Ministry, would bid for Jewish enterprises, always at levels below market value. Still, we can clearly see a struggle being waged by Jewish owners attempting to obtain a meaningful price, and by German interests competing for Jewish property against each other, attempting to enlarge their overall strength or influence in a sector of the economy. However, this phase of acquisition came to an end, by and large, at the end of 1938 when the synagogues were set on fire. At that point, the Aryanizations were no longer voluntary but compulsory. Jewish firms could be sold or liquidated by German "trustees" and Jewish employees in these concerns lost their jobs.

The very next step was concentration, the physical separation and the social isolation of the Jewish community from the German. Actually, the very first Nuremberg decree prohibiting new marriages between Jews and Germans was an initial step in that direction. There followed others, including measures that placed the machinery of the Jewish community under German command. Henceforth, in the Reich as well as in newly conquered territory, the Germans would employ Jewish leaders and Jewish community personnel for housing segregation, personal property confiscation, forced labor, and even deportations. In the wake of the violence and the arrest waves of November 1938, Hermann Göring and several other Nazi personalities discussed the question of whether one ought to form ghettos inside Germany. The idea was rejected, most particularly by that expert policeman Reinhard Heydrich, who was to head the German Security Police and Security Service, on the ground that so long as the Jews were not inside a wall, out of sight of the German population, every German could act as an auxiliary policeman, every German could watch the Jews, every German could keep track of them.

Less than one year after that conference, war broke out. Poland was invaded, and several million additional Jews came under German jurisdiction. A concentration process in Poland began almost immediately; the medieval ghetto came into existence once more. The largest was the Warsaw ghetto, the second largest was the ghetto of Lodz, and there were hundreds of others. All were captive city-states, with a variety of functions including mundane as well as extraordinary tasks. That is a history so varied, so diversified, so complex as to demand attention in and of itself. In the great work of Isaiah Trunk, *Judenrat*, you may discover the history not only of the Jewish Councils, but of the entire structure of the ghettos, their social, economic, and political problems under the Nazis.

There was an ambiguity in the very formation of the ghettos. What was going to happen to the Jews inside the walls? The death rates slowly began to climb. We have detailed statistics from Lodz and from Warsaw, though not from most of the other ghettos. Because those two ghettos were very different, the Lodz ghetto having been stratified and centralized under a kind of Jewish dictatorship, even as the Warsaw ghetto remained laissez-faire with private enterprise, it is instructive to note that in both starvation and illness they were roughly comparable, and that the death rates rose at an almost uniform rate to 1 percent of the population per month.

By 1940, the Germans attacked the western countries: France, Belgium, Holland. They won a quick, decisive victory on the ground and contemplated a peace treaty with England. Were that treaty to have come into being, it would automatically have been made also with France, and France was to have ceded the African island of Madagascar to the Germans. That island was to have been governed by the police, and all the Jews of Europe would have been shipped there. Such, at least, was the fantasizing in certain sections of the German Foreign Office. But the British did not make peace. When that fact began to sink in toward the end of 1940, there was a transition period of greatest importance in German thinking. Up to that moment there had really only been two policies in all history against the Jews, the first was the conversion of the Jews to Christianity, the second was the expulsion of the Jews from a country in which they lived. Expulsion was now becoming impossible. In the middle of a war, millions of people cannot be expelled. Forced emigration was no longer feasible. Hence the idea of "a territorial solution" emerged. How? What form was it to take? That was not spelled out in 1940 or even in early 1941. Everyone was waiting with some anticipation for a decision.

Then came the planning of "Barbarossa" (the attack on the Soviet Union). The onslaught was being contemplated in a military conference held as early as 22 July 1940, and plans were taking shape in directive after directive, order of battle after order of battle, and in negotiations with Axis partners. In the course of these preparations, a document was being drafted in the High Command of the Armed Forces. The order contained a cryptic sentence to the effect that the armed forces would be accompanied by special units of the SS and Police, which were to carry out certain state-political tasks in occupied territory. That was the beginning of the first massive killing operation. It has its origin in a social contract, as Neumann would have called it, between the German army and the SS and Police. The arrangement was hammered out in a series of agreements between the Quartermaster General of the German Army, Edward Wagner, and representatives of the Security Police, particularly Heydrich and Walter Schellenberg. On 22 June 1941, when the German armies spilled into Russia, the Security Police units—called *Einsatzgruppen*—also moved in and started killing Jews on the spot.

The *Einsatzgruppen* sent daily reports to Berlin. In consolidated form, this revealing material was routed to many recipients, but only one set of copies was discovered after the war. As for the original reports from the field, very few are still around. From the Soviet Union came one report of a single commando that operated in Lithuania. A commando was a company-sized unit augmented by native helpers. The commando of which I speak killed 135,000 Jews in its area between June 1941 and January 1942.

The occupied territories of the U.S.S.R. were the scenes of massacre after massacre. Sometimes the *Einsatzgruppen* commanders would return to the same place again and again, shooting Jews en masse. In White Russia, a substantial number of victims fled to the woods; few were the survivors of roundups and shootings in the Ukraine.

But shooting operations had their problems. The Germans employed the phrase *Seelenbelastung* ("burdening of the soul") with reference to machine-gun fire or rifle fire directed at men, women, and children in prepared ditches. After all, the men that were firing these weapons were themselves fathers. How could they do this day after day? It was then that the technicians developed a gas van designed to lessen the suffering of the perpetrator. It was simply a vehicle, or a van, strictly speaking, with an exhaust pipe turned inward so the carbon monoxide would kill the seventy people inside even while they were being driven to their graves. The gas vans began operating in the east for women and children, but the unloading was very dirty work.

In 1941, some six weeks after the attack on the Soviet Union, a letter was written by Hermann Göring to Reinhard Heydrich, charging Heydrich with the Final Solution of the Jewish problem in Europe. I have always regarded that letter as the signal for the total destruction of European Jewry, the decisive step across the threshold. Although Göring was not specific about the time or manner in which his directive was to be implemented, his words implied finality and irreversibility.

How was the killing set into motion? As of November 1941, there was some thinking about deporting Jews to the *Einsatzgruppen* so they could be killed by these experienced shooters. That is why German Jews were transported to Minsk, Riga, and Kovno. In the long run, however, the shooting of millions would be an insurmountable problem; there would be too many witnesses, too many bodies, too many soul-burdened members of the SS and Police. Some of the deportees were consequently sent to the crowded ghettos of Poland. The ghettos themselves were to be dissolved soon. In various parts of the occupied Polish territory, the Germans were erecting facilities for the silent killing of Jews—the gas chambers. There were pure killing centers, including Kulmhof, Treblinka, Sobibor, and Belzec, the object of which was nothing except the gassing of people on arrival. A more complex camp was Auschwitz because it had industry as well as killing facilities. At Auschwitz, death was administered by hydrogen cyanide. The crystals were poured from a canister by an SS man wearing a gas mask with a special filter. In the crowded chamber the solid material became a gas.

The Jews had to be transported from all over Europe, always to the "East." We now know of the very expensive preparations that were required for these deportations. The Foreign Office negotiated and actually made treaties with satellite countries promising, as it were, that the Jews would be leaving for good, but that their property would be left behind. Some of the countries allied with Germany would not agree. The Romanians, although at first very enthusiastic killers in Russia, balked, and by the fall of 1942 rescinded an agreement to hand over their Jews, while Bulgaria procrastinated, allowing the deportation of Jews from Bulgarian occupied territories in Yugoslavia and Greece, but not permitting the deportation of Jews from Bulgaria itself.

The French Vichy regime adopted a compromise: negotiations were conducted with a view to protecting Jews of French nationality, while foreign Jews were surrendered to the Germans. "How can an occupied country," said French Premier Pierre Laval, "be a country of asylum?" The Italians not only did not deport their Jews, they refused to allow the deportation of Jews under Italian jurisdiction in other Mediterranean regions, including France, Greece, and Yugoslavia. The Germans never let up. You may find correspondence about twelve Jews in Liechtenstein. "What are they doing there?" Or Monaco. Several hundred Norwegian Jews were being deported from Oslo and Trondheim; they were gassed in Auschwitz.

It was wartime, and transport itself was a problem. Movement to killing centers took place by railroad for the most part, occasionally over long distances, as in the case of deportations from southern France or southern Greece. For the Transport Ministry, the movement of the Jews was a financial as well as an operational matter. In principle, each passenger transport had to be paid for. Jews were "travelers" and the Gestapo paid the railroads one-way fare (third class) for each deportee, half price for each transport of more than four hundred. The railroads were accommodating that way. The Gestapo for its part attempted to collect the necessary funds from the Jewish communities themselves. Although such "self-financing" took place in contravention of normal budgetary procedure, the Finance Ministry acquiesced in the practice.

The operational problem was even more complex. For each death transport, central and regional railway offices had to assign scarce rolling stock and time on tracks. Yet these transports seldom had a priority rating. A classification would have identified them for what they were. Instead they were being dispatched whenever possible. The timetables, written for each of them, placed them behind and ahead of regularly scheduled trains. Thus it was with the intensification of the war, and even after the climax of Stalingrad, the Germans were pursuing ever more relentlessly and ever more drastically the one operation they were bound and determined to finish. They were going to solve the Jewish problem in Europe once and for all.

By the end of 1942, the death camp of Belzec had fulfilled its mission and was dismantled. Six hundred thousand Jews had died in Belzec; there was but one known survivor. At Sobibor and Treblinka there were uprisings. The survivors numbered in the dozens, but the dead of these two camps were about one quarter of a million and three-quarters of a million, respectively.

The one camp that remained in operation throughout was Auschwitz. It was the farthest west, not in the path of the advancing Red Army. It was maintained, and even built up, in 1944. The year 1944 is of interest to us because no one could pretend not to know what was going on at that moment. The Jews knew. The Germans knew. The British knew, the Americans knew, everyone knew. There had already been escapes from the Auschwitz camp, and information was gathered also by the War Refugee Board in the United States. Despite that dissemination, no serious ransom negotiations were attempted by the Allies, no strategy of psychological warfare was developed, and no bombs were dropped on gas chambers.

The Germans continued to destroy the European Jews, even under bombing, even while the Soviet forces were breaking into Romania and eastern Poland, and even as Allied landings were begun in France.

To the end, we see the alignment of the German army, the German SS, the German Transport Ministry, the German Foreign Office, as well as financial agencies, all completing the work of solving the "Jewish problem" in Europe. Now we see the results. Here they are in plain statistics.

I believe the Jewish death toll to be slightly above five million. I arrive at this figure not by subtracting the postwar population from the prewar figures, but by adding numbers that I find in German documents, and extrapolating from them the unreported data. The deaths in camps were roughly three million: Auschwitz had over a million dead; Treblinka, on the order of seven hundred to eight hundred thousand; Belzec, about six hundred thousand; Sobibor, two hundred to two hundred fifty thousand; Kulmhof, one hundred fifty thousand; Lublin (also known as Maidanek) some tens of thousands. In addition, tens of thousands of Jews were shot by the Romanians in camps between the Bug and Dniester rivers, thousands of Jews were killed at Semlin and other places in Yugoslavia. There were a number of additional camps where Jews suffered heavy losses, but in Holocaust statistics, thousands and even tens of thousands may be lost in footnotes.

About one million four hundred thousand Jewish victims were shot or died in mobile operations of one sort or another. Six hundred thousand died in ghettos.

The heavy concentration of dead is in Eastern Europe. Polish Jewry has virtually disappeared; three million are dead. Soviet Jewry, which was subject to shooting, lost seven hundred thousand within pre-1939 boundaries of the Soviet Union and another two hundred thousand in the Baltic area. In Western Europe, the number of dead was proportionally smaller—in France, Belgium, and Italy, the survival rate was relatively high.

Today, the distribution of Jews is radically changed. The United States now has the largest Jewish population in the world, followed by almost equally sized Jewish communities in Israel and Russia.* In these three countries live three-quarters of all the Jews remaining in the world. Europe is, for Jewry, a graveyard, and this, after a presence, on that continent, going back to the Roman Empire, of some two thousand years. That is the anatomy. And that is the statistic.

---

* These numbers have significantly changed since the text was published in 1980. Currently the largest Jewish population in the world lives in Israel. The US has the largest Jewish population outside of Israel (based on estimations). The number of Jews in Russia and other former Soviet states have decreased enormously since the 1990s.

2
GERMAN MOTIVATIONS FOR THE DESTRUCTION OF THE JEWS
(1965)

DURING THE NAZI REGIME, ONE of the most drastic acts in history was fashioned by German hands: the Jews of Europe were annihilated. In conception and execution, it was a unique occurrence. When Adolf Hitler came to power in 1933, a modern bureaucracy set out for the first time to destroy an entire people. Step by step and blow by blow, more than five million Jews were driven to their deaths.* Few operations could have been more efficient than this bewildering deed in the midst of a general war.

Twenty years have gone by and grass is growing over the riddled and charred remains of the European Jewish community. One question, however, has lingered unaltered and unanswered through the passage of time. Why were these people killed? What sort of mind produced such an act? The question persists, if only because it yields not discoveries but inferences, not answers but definitions and categorizations.

Originally published in *Midstream: A Quarterly Jewish Review* 11, no. 2 (1965): 23–40.
* The estimated number of six-million murdered Jews is more common. Hilberg himself calculated "the Jewish death toll ... slightly above five million" (see chapter 1).

The German mind has to be reconstructed from the impact which it had. To ask what kind of mind brought forth this act is to ask what kind of act it was. The portrayal of that motivational pattern is derived from a characterization of the event. We shall reproduce the principal descriptions in the pages below. In ordering these conceptualizations, we will attempt to place them under headings that most closely delimit their content and meaning. We should then observe that they fall into a continuum from the most familiar but least appropriate to the most compelling but least explicable.[1]

The search for German motivations has proceeded from two directions. One orientation seeks to account for the holocaust in something that is rooted in the victim; the other looks to the perpetrator for the underlying clues. Let us consider each in turn.

Provocation

Every hypothesis focused upon Jewry contains an assumption of provocation: the Jews brought their fate upon themselves; they had, in a sense, invited the blow.

Provocation is implied by the very shape of Jewish life in the diaspora, the durability of hostility toward the Jews and the uniformity of reactions against them. The Jews of Europe have been incessantly hounded, perpetually persecuted, recurrently slaughtered. They were not immune in Spain; they were not sheltered in England and France; they were not safe in Russia. That history suggests a set of reasons why Jewry was hunted down.

There have been two emphases in studies of Jewish behavior. One is an ascription to Jewry of an excessive accumulation of negative qualities; the other sees in the Jews an overdose of positive accomplishments.

The portrait of negativism rests essentially on three components: the unassimilability of the Jews, their ambivalence, and their marginality. These factors deserve a brief examination.

The survival of the Jewish substance over thousands of years has involved a rejection of precepts and aims which governed the life of the gentile majority. The Jewish historian Jacob Katz asserts that while Jews have prayed for the welfare of their Christian rulers, they harbored at the same time "deep reservations as to the ultimate significance of secular States which, seen in the perspective of the messianic hope, were but ephemeral."² Viewed in long range, we might well discern such reservations. That famous Jewish apartness nevertheless shrinks in importance when measured in the Germany of the early twentieth century. There, and by that time, Jews had become German in greater proportion and to a greater extent than almost anywhere else. On the eve of World War I, Walther Rathenau called upon them to remove their remaining "correctable peculiarities,"³ and in the war that followed, Jews died for Germany in masses.

Ambivalence has been the second factor in observable Jewish life. Jews have frantically assimilated without assimilating. The German philosopher Eduard von Hartmann described them at the end of the nineteenth century as both "eclectically acquisitive" and "skeptically negative."⁴ Throughout its history, Jewry has been confronted by impossible choices, evading laws and customs under which it could not live, and invoking rules and principles without which it could not survive. During the Middle Ages, the paramountcy of "danger to the community" dictated reliance upon the emperor for protection against local authority, while in modern times, Jews have appealed to the interfering power of foreign states or international organizations in conflicts with their governments. Nowhere, however, was anxiety smaller and trust greater than in modern Germany.

The Jews in most recent times have become successful competitors. Working out of marginal areas, they have occupied powerful economic and cultural positions. Often, the question is asked: Just how much power had passed into the hands of the Jews? A Nazi researcher during the war asked himself that very question, and after exhaustive research, published his results in 1944 in a book that was not circulated. His basic conclusions are not without interest in an exploration of the phenomenon:⁵

1. The high point of Jewish economic power in Europe was reached in 1913.

2. The Jews were among the hardest hit by the economic results of World War I. Jewish influence resting upon bank capital in Berlin and Vienna was virtually destroyed in 1931.

3. Prewar "Judaization" of the economy increased from West to East. It was highest in Silesia, Hungary, etc. At the same time, the size of Jewish industrial undertakings decreased in the same direction.

Major questions may be raised by the close and the limits of that development. The successful competitor was not taking over Germany after all. Moreover, the advancement of the Jew was not guided by Jewry alone. Its paths were determined by exclusions practiced for centuries. It is almost as if Jewry was charged with doing what it was forced to do.[6] In that sense, the problem becomes an inquiry into the extent to which the provocation was the work of those who were provoked.

Not all of the commentators who seek the basis of the German assault in the behavior of its victims portray the Jews with repugnant features: there are observers who see an irritant element in a constellation of Jewish merits and perfections.

Two mechanisms may render virtues provocative. The first is jealousy: the majority attempts to be like the minority, but does not quite succeed. Failing, it withdraws into rejection and hostility. "To the anti-Semite," states Jean-Paul Sartre, "intelligence is Jewish."[7]

A more subtle effect is distraction. For centuries, the two communities have existed side by side, two philosophies, two thought patterns, two ways of life, sometimes deceptively alike, on occasion completely enmeshed, at times hopelessly entangled, but never wholly grown together. The Jewish culture is the older one and its age is magnetic to newer nations, drawing them out of their grooves into a more finished civilization. It is for this reason that, in Oswald Spengler's words, "he who belongs inwardly affirms in the last analysis also where he destroys, while he who is inwardly a stranger negates even where he seeks to build."[8] In all these years, then, the European has continually sought to retain his identity and, failing, attacked his distractors.[9]

What, precisely, is virtuous in Jewry? Much has been said about this subject, but in essence the outstanding qualities attributed to the European Jews may be classified in three areas.

First of all, the Jews have been identified with freedom of the individual and protection of his thought. They do not seek dictatorial rule; they will not thrive under censorship. The Jewish spirit, to quote Max Lerner, has "depended on individuality and skepticism. It has depended on the right to be a Jeremiah, the right to be a prophet, lamenting the inequities of society. It has depended on the right to be nobody's rubber stamp..."[10] Jews are iconoclasts. They will not worship idols. In the nineteenth century, the rise of the titanic Jewish idol-smashers, Marx, Freud, and Einstein, jarred the Western world into disequilibrium and quandary. "The Europeans found themselves on quicksand everywhere. Some, most of them, have resisted the onslaught and sought to reconquer the solid ground of former convictions; but in the process, the Jewish people have suffered the most abominable of the persecutions they have known in their long and painful history."¹¹

Jewish commitment is seen as embracing, along with a rejection of tyranny, a marked abstention from illegality, injustice, and immorality. The Jews are the people of the law. The Jewish people gave to Christianity its moral code. Jewry will forever be a witness and a reminder of the divine commandments. "Do you know," wrote Walther Rathenau, "why we were born into this world? To summon every human countenance to Sinai. You won't go? If I don't call you, Marx will call you; if Marx doesn't call you, Spinoza will call you. If Spinoza doesn't call you, Christ will call you."¹² Viewed in that role, the Jews are the conscience of the world. They are the father figures, stern, critical, and forbidding. Hence, the succession of uprisings against them. The Jewish policemen of the highest law become the primary target of the basest mutiny in Christendom.¹³

Finally, the Jews are like mortar between the bricks of society. At times, they have held it together. In their long history, they have pitted themselves repeatedly against death, dissipation, and debauchery. They are even now preservers of life, guardians of wealth, exponents of beauty. They are the doctors, the merchants, and the performers of the arts. In their everyday functions, they satisfy special wants. The Jews are catalysts and quicken reaction to challenge. "They act as yeast to other peoples," and this role too has contributed to their undoing, for yeast "must remain but a small percentage of the dough."¹⁴

In the last analysis, however, even the quintessence of Jewish accomplishments is not so overwhelming in the land of the Germans. That nation has not usually stood still at the sight of the performance of others, and the "Judaization" of Germany is but minute in comparison with the Germanization of the Jews.

If Jewish traits, bad or good, have provoked destructive reactions, they must have had a significance transcending their apparent scope. Three arguments may be advanced in underscoring this possible effect.

The first is salience. The Jewish character pattern "stands out." Jewish behavior is "deliberate"; it touches the nerve centers of nations. The Jewish people possess a large component of "normality," but the ordinariness of Jewry is a zero quality; its quiescent periods do not count. The peculiarities of the Jews will still be decisive, no matter how few the provocateurs, how intermittent their activities, or how subtle their effects. The slightest deviation will register; the weakest disturbance is felt.

The salience of Jewish characteristics is multiplied as soon as there is an increase of contacts between Jews and the Christian world. The principle underlying the contact theory is that group conflicts arise on the periphery. Given a latently hostile situation, the danger to the minority is increased as soon as it loses geographic and social compactness. In the ghetto, people deal with each other, and their relations with the surrounding population are few. At the onset of emancipation, however, this static condition is upset and the scattering of the concentrated mass causes agitation outside. The result is a multiplication of collisions and the heightened provocation of the gentile majority. When Jewry left its sheltered ghettos, it maximized the tension field, and when Jewish penetrations were recorded in the farthest sectors, the threshold of destruction was reached.[15]

The third dimension of the Jewish configuration is its invariance. The Jews are said to have behaved in an identical manner since the days of antiquity. "They behaved in Hellenistic times," said Freud, "as they do today."[16] The provocations in that case would have become cumulative. Throughout their suffering, the Jews have persisted in their action and clung to their ways. Their stubbornness could therefore have become fatal. The cataclysmic reaction felled the Jews of Europe. To the Nazis, it was the "final solution"; to the Jews, it was the last of their martyrdoms.

What, then, can we make of Jewish behavior? The first consideration is that Jewish conduct in all of its intensification, ramification, and magnification, falls manifestly short of those dimensions that alone could have resulted the actions that struck them. Jews had been defined, expropriated, and concentrated before, but the German destruction process escalated into something more vehement and total. The systematic shootings and gassings virtually emptied entire countries and regions of their Jewish inhabitants; the annihilation of Jewish men, women, and children was implemented in an area extending from Russia to France, and from Norway to Greece. What sort of threat was being eliminated here?

All the documents show that the Jews on the eve of their doom were as harmless as they were impotent. The German Nazis themselves understood the nature of Jewish allegiance, the incidence of Jewish sacrifices, the extent of Jewish productivity. The extollers of Jewish righteousness have the record of Jewry's desperate attempts to survive on any terms in Adolf Hitler's Europe. Jewry at its worst was no danger to a growing Germany; Jewry at its best was no obstacle to Nazi plans.

When the totality of the Jewish "challenge" is ranged against the magnitude of the German response, there is consequently a problem of disparity. It is one thing to be provoked. It is something else to be provoked into the killing of five million people. The difference was apparent to so fierce a proponent of Jewish provocation as Josef Goebbels who spoke of the "judgment" visited upon the Jews as "barbaric."[17]

Another complication intrudes upon provocation analysis: the German reaction to other groups. If Jewry has had other persecutors, Germany has also had other victims. Gypsies were shot and gassed along with Jews; sterilization experiments were conducted with a view to eliminating the Slavic populations; consideration was given to the killing of convicted German criminals whose photographs showed that the prospective victims were ugly. If we should rely upon the provocation theory in the case of the Jews, we should be able to construct similar hypotheses about a variety of other groups, some of them inconspicuous, others far from the German scene, still others new "enemies" of Germandom. Even if we could lend to such formulations some measure of plausibility, we would nevertheless have to take note of a simple fact: the diversified elements that fell into the orbit of Nazi destruction did share a single attribute. Their common denominator was weakness; their outstanding characteristic was helplessness. Their vulnerability itself was a "provocation." This consideration raises the question as to whether Nazi Germany had reasons for taking advantage of helplessness as such. The next problem then is to find a possible set of such reasons.

Perpetration

In provocation analysis, we have looked for anomalies among the Jews without examining the makeup of the Germans who performed the act. We have instead assumed that these Germans belonged to the normal world and conformed to its practices. Now we have to reverse that assumption and, without regard to the identity of the victim, seek out and specify the special characteristics of the participants in the destruction process. Investigations of this kind may be classified as perpetration theories. The procedures we must follow in that undertaking are a little more complex.

When we consider the Jewish victim, we think Jewry as a whole, for the target of destruction was Jewry as such, and in German plans a maximum number of them were to be killed. In speaking about the German perpetrator, however, we will be concerned primarily with those men who were involved in the destructive work, and often this work was performed by a minimum number of personnel. Hence, there appears to be a choice. One may consider the perpetrators as a group of people with independent motives who sought in the destruction of Jewry the attainment of ends of their own. The principal task in such an exploration is therefore the specification of individual aims that could be realized through action against Jews. But one may also view the active Germans as agents of German society. An assumption of this kind leads to a probe in the German collectivity for the mainsprings of the destructive upheaval. That is, in essence, a postulation of mass-eruption.

Self-Gratification

The possibility of self-gratification in the process of destruction arose from the circumstance that Nazi Germany's bureaucratic apparatus was basically anarchic. The administrative machine consisted of a *Führer* and a far-flung network of offices in the party, the ministries, business, and the army. In each of these power structures, there were capabilities for initiating and implementing a variety of measures. Functionaries could thus move freely, in isolation or in clusters, until restrained by superiors, checked by competitors, or subverted by subordinates. In the permissive atmosphere of the anti-Jewish campaign, these bureaucrats hurled stake after stake into new jurisdictional territory, extending their "work spheres" into areas never touched before. Among the vanguards in this outpouring, one may discern three types of personalities with special goals: the opportunists, the profiteers, and the sadists.

The opportunists were interested in power. There were two levels of that interest; one was the attempt to maintain the Nazi system as a whole, the other was the narrower tendency to preserve or extend control within a particular organization. The first was primarily a concern of the "usurpers"—the Nazi party and its formations. The second was a general phenomenon in German administration.

The usurpers could employ two mechanisms to stay at the top. Since they had made promises, they could be expected to have used the Jews as a scapegoat for their failures. Anti-Jewish measures, in this sense, could be employed as substitutes for substantive action not realized in other spheres: thus, the "Aryanization" of Jewish property in place of a nationalization of German firms, the decimation of Eastern Jewry in lieu of the destruction of Soviet partisans, the annihilation of European Jewry instead of the winning of the war.[18] They could also be timed to deflect attention from problem areas or mobilize excitement during inactivity.[19] Shock-waves of anti-Jewish attacks did come during such lulls, for example, the Nuremberg laws that had to be ready for a party rally in 1935, or the pogroms in 1938 organized between invasions. Neither the substitutions nor the deflections, however, were more than manipulations within a multipronged destructive process planned continuously and pushed relentlessly into ever more drastic phases. In its growing complexity, the agitators were unable to steer its course; with its spreading secrecy, they lost all opportunity to publicize their doings.

While the Jews could no longer serve as a scapegoat during the later stages of the operation, the annihilation of Jewry did lend itself to another kind of control mechanism, for now the party men could implicate widening sections of the bureaucracy in a thickening bloodguilt. Those who had killed would not desert.[20] The bloodguilt had its difficulties, if only because the party and the SS had to set an "example"—in the "euthanasia" stations, the mobile killing units, the major killing centers. More importantly, these efforts do not explain why other groups whose power base was not dependent on the survival of Nazism should have participated to such an extent.

Opportunism, to be sure, manifested itself also in sheer bureaucratic self-preservation and self-extension. Within the German bureaucracy non-participation in Jewish affairs could mean a shrinkage of relative power, if not an absolute loss of functions. In that connection, one might mention officials whose hold over jurisdiction was at times precarious: the diplomats, the military administrators, and the judiciary. The party itself had offices and formations whose functions were derived in large part from anti-Jewish activities: the Race-Political Office, the propagandists, the SS industries. Much may be said about these preoccupations and their implications, they do not account for the actions of those large hierarchical conglomerations that had been pillars of the German state for generations and had too little to gain from the destruction of the Jews to have contributed so much to its success: the Ministries of Interior, Economy, Finance, Labor, and Agriculture, which laid the foundations of the destruction process, the Order Police that guarded Jews in large parts of Nazi-occupied Europe, the German railroads that transported most of the victims to their deaths.

If opportunism was not all-encompassing, there were elements even less decisive: profiteering and sadism. The profit motive was a twofold spur to destructive activity: Jewry had to be suppressed so that its possessions could be seized, and it had to be eliminated so that gains from these seizures could be kept. Those who gained the most—powerful corporate entities who dealt as equals with the party and the civil service—soon swallowed the choicest morsels. They were followed by a phalanx of lower middle-class and low-class characters who operated on the smallest scale and on the lowest level. One may cite a number of "Aryan" partners and debtors of Jewish businessmen, the "eastern helpers" including ethnic Germans and Balts who pitched in during the shootings and then helped themselves to the possessions of the dead, the SS families and bombed-out Germans who received furniture and clothing of deported Jews. Although there were many such operations, their importance is nevertheless limited. The destruction process was governed, however imperfectly, by the overriding principle of "all profits to the Reich," and those violating that rule were frequently on the defensive, always under suspicion, sometimes prosecuted, often harassed. It would be difficult to prove that any major segment in the machine of destruction was dominated by these people or even that it depended on them.

The third group in the destructive vanguard consisted of sadists prone to use their positions of power to revel with immunity in the orgy of blood. They included, to cite but well-known examples, (1) the perverts in the field, such as Obersturmbannführer [Eduard] Strauch, Commander of Security Police and SD in White Russia, who paraded wounded Jews bleeding from their heads through the streets of Minsk, or Oberscharführer [Otto] Moll at Auschwitz who smashed babies' heads against pavements and walls, or Brigadeführer [Oskar] Dirlewanger who, as commander of a labor camp in Poland is reported to have undressed comely Jewish women, injected them with strychnine, cut them into pieces, and tossed the remains into boiling water to prepare a brew of soap, (2) the experimenters in the camps, like Dr. [Josef] Mengele of Auschwitz who tortured twins with a view to discovering the secrets of multiple birth, and his colleague Dr. Carl Clauberg who operated on Jewish women in a vain attempt to perfect a method of sterilization, and (3) the zealots in Berlin who were intoxicated with destructive words and statistics of death, among them the Foreign Office's Martin Luther and the Gestapo's deportation expert Adolf Eichmann, or the party's race expert Dr. Walter Gross who wanted to mate unmarried quarter-Jews in the hope that the offspring from such unions might show a sufficient accumulation of Jewish characteristics to make them eligible for "extermination."

However large the crowd of opportunists, profiteers, and sadists, their presence does not explain the coherence of the destruction process, its efficiency, and its success. It appears almost as if these men were the inevitable byproducts of such an operation rather than its essential cause. To view the outburst in its totality, we should, therefore, explore in what way it might have been formed and furthered by the very character of the German nation itself.

Mass-Eruption

In 1933, the Jews were an old, established community. Its roots were complex and deep; its strands reached far into the institutions and associations of its neighbors. The German administrative machine cut those links one by one, dissolving "Aryan"-Jewish relations, establishing "Jew-houses" and ghettos, regulating food rations and working conditions for Jews, confiscating bank accounts, pensions, and personal belongings. The intricacies of that task required the application of every skill and specialization. No class or profession, no agency or office was unrepresented in or exempted from that process. The destruction of the Jews was shaped and fashioned by the organization of an entire society. That is why the perpetrator cannot be distinguished, in his background or makeup, from the Germany of his day. All of his actions stemmed ultimately from a ubiquitous, all-encompassing readiness.

The German nation is a large and difficult area of study. Nevertheless, not a few researchers have already delved into that subject, some coming to the conclusion that the destruction process was the result of a fault in German society that threw it out of gear and caused it to run wild, others perceiving in the outbreak the presence of a special factor, peculiar to German history and thought, propelling the perpetrator into unique and irrevocable paths. The first assume a malfunction; the second propose a fixation.

Malfunction

Broadly speaking, three kinds of breakdowns have been proposed in malfunction theory: an intellectual failure, a cultural disruption, and a psychic disturbance. Propagandistic fabrications, upsetting a rational order of thought, may lead to indoctrination; the floundering of a culture may result in regression; personality disorders, produced by a series of frustrations, may yield abnormal behavior with compulsive, paranoid, masochistic, or anxiety-driven manifestations.

The history of anti-Jewish propaganda in Germany is conspicuous because of its duration, volume, and nature. Anti-Jewish sentiments have been voiced in German-speaking lands for centuries. They were poured out in pamphlets and newspapers and codified by political movements and parties. In its contents, much of that propaganda left all bounds of observation. It became hallucinatory and fantastic, devoid of any factual basis whatsoever.[21] The presence of that anti-Semitic tradition, largely unopposed by the German intelligentsia that at times abetted and supported it, has led a number of observers to the view that the population at large picked up an anti-Jewish bias and that, provided with a hostile goal, it struck out in the direction of that target as a matter of "logical consequence."[22]

There is at least some oblique evidence for the contention that the continuous bombardment of propaganda had left a haze of anti-Jewish sentiment in Germany. In a poll conducted by the *Institut für Demoskopie* twelve years after the events, respondents were asked what they thought of the Jews: 23 percent gave "anti-Semitic" answers and 15 percent replied "cautiously." A second question was phrased in terms of whether National Socialism had increased anti-Jewish tendencies in Germany (*die gefühlsmässige Einstellung gegen die Juden verstärkt*). Sixty-five per cent said yes. The third inquiry was put to elicit an opinion about the "fundamental cause" of anti-Semitism: was it the character of the Jewish people, their religion, anti-Semitic propaganda, or something else? Respondents, who were permitted to list several reasons, divided as follows: "characteristics of the Jewish people" 53 percent, the "Jewish religion" 12 percent, "anti-Semitic propaganda" 30 percent, other grounds 8 percent, undecided 14 percent.[23]

We must, nevertheless, suspect two major limits to the effectiveness of propaganda. One concerns the implantation of beliefs; the other affects their power to induce action. In regard to actual convictions, there are indications that the perpetrators themselves did not really believe their own words. Thus, the German plenipotentiary in Denmark, Best, explained to the Foreign Office in 1943 that his charges of Jewish sabotage were without any "concrete foundation." The chief of military administration in Serbia, Staatsrat Harald Turner, writing to the Higher SS and Police Leader in Danzig, admitted that "if one had to be exact about it" the hostages in the camps should have been Serbs rather than Jews. Reichsführer SS Heinrich Himmler instructed Security Police Chief Ernst Kaltenbrunner to manufacture ritual murder stories. When ranking perpetrators caught after the war, it turned out that many, including camp commanders like Rudolf Höss, had disdained to read publications like *Der Stürmer* and that none of the major war criminals was acquainted with Alfred Rosenberg's *The Myth of the Twentieth Century*.[24]

The anti-Jewish make-believe is coupled with another difficulty: the effect of actual anti-Jewish convictions. This problem was illustrated by two curious statements cited by the Dutch historian Louis de Jong. One reads in part as follows:

> We did not like the Jews.... Even as children we were impressed by the strange, very peculiar atmosphere of Jewish family life.

The other is more elaborate:

> Aren't the Jews pretty well unbearable? That cannot be denied; they are completely different from us, they are of a different kind, in type a different race. One is conscious of this as soon as one comes into contact with them: we have good reason to speak of "Jewish tricks." They are indeed importunate and domineering; we always had to be on our guard against them in business; they were often incalculable and unreliable.

The first quotation was from a Dutchman in the rural northeast who had risked his life for Jews during the occupation, the second from a Dutch clergyman who had spent time in the concentration camp Amersfoort for sheltering two Jews.[25] One might well wonder then about the essentiality of beliefs as a motivation for destruction: for Germans, they were not sufficiently necessary; for Dutchman, they were not necessarily sufficient.

How may we account, then, for the strength and persistence of an anti-Jewish atmosphere in Germany? The answer is that German propaganda did not exist so much for the purpose of indoctrination as for the maintenance of rationalizations. Anti-Jewish words were required less for an inducement to action than for its justification. The words and their volume varied with the pace of activity. This may also explain why Jewry was unable to convince its tormenters of its good qualities. Germany's beliefs were ultimately not founded on perception. They could not be shaken or altered by logical proof, for they stemmed from a psychological need which they were designed to shield and protect. With the passing of that undercurrent of guilt, the rationalizations should gradually decay and disappear.

More basic than the assumption of intellectual impairment is the possibility of a *cultural* malfunction. Two forms of this hypothesis have emerged in literature. One is the notion of a backslide into the Middle Ages, the other the postulation of a split into modern-technological and archaic-primitive components. Although both of these theories refer to a regression, their contents and implications are quite different.

The idea of a reversion to an earlier period in German development is backed by Germany's comparatively recent accession to Christianity and Roman civilization. Germany was "badly Christened," said Freud, and the philosopher Hans Weil points out that the civilizing influence of Rome had stopped too far west of the Rhine and south of the Danube. When Christianity crossed these rivers, the ancient gods did not disappear. The Teutonic deities who had populated Germany's woods and meadows were turned into dark and satanic larvae; the German pantheistic view was transformed into a pandemonic one.[26] In centuries to follow, that dualism of divine and devilish forces has persisted, and the overthrow of the gods was repeated. Several writers saw in the Nazi movement a peculiar "manichean" quality:[27] its redeemer—total in his power, perfect in his decisions—Adolf Hitler, the evil incarnate—the Jew.[28] Thus it came about that Jewry was offered in a great auto-da-fé as a human sacrifice to the Nordic gods.[29] Hitler, the supreme usurper, is now gone—a new devil banished to the Teutonic deities that long preceded him, and the new German turns once more with Christian reparation and homage to the mother religion, Israel.

A dichotomy of another kind appears in a comparison between the sudden demands of a technological age with the moral restraints of Western civilization. The technical culture has accelerated so rapidly that moral criteria cannot be widened fast enough to cover complex, modern decision-making. The result is "schizophrenia" or organized behavior with technical tools obeying rules that no longer resemble earlier teachings still applicable to direct relations in private life. The machine-like bureaucrat, sheltered and impersonal, can now engage in "primordial narcissism" or "unrestrained aggression" against any and all. As technocratic decision-maker, he has become "innocent" in the original sense; he literally "knows not" what he is doing.[30] Not unnaturally, in war crimes trials and denazification proceedings, he would approach the bench somewhat bewildered and dazed.

We shall not deal *in extenso* with these basic, but difficult formulations of regression. There is, however, one fact we must note. The perpetrator was not altogether unaware of the nature of his acts. He did not fail to see the reach of his decisions. His intelligence was not confined to the mere operation of a machine; he understood that operation and his part as a cog in it. All this is bared by the elaborate psychological defenses the bureaucracy set up and that pervaded its offices and correspondence. In euphemisms, the bureaucrats sought to blot out the deed, in anti-Jewish accusations they attempted to rationalize it on a massive scale. They wanted to, but could not escape from fundamental moral norms. They did not, therefore, forget the law; rather they chose to defy it.

Malfunction theory contains, along with explanations stressing distortions of perceptions or an imbalance in the culture, a large body of writings that emphasize a *psychic* breakdown. Indeed, even before the onset of Nazism, the German was thought to be a frustrated individual. While there is surprisingly little evidence for the oft-mentioned harshness in German upbringing,[31] it is conceivable that institutional organization as a whole should accentuate deprivation and discipline to the point of producing a stringent society in which the freedom of all of its members is continuously apportioned, rationed, controlled, or withheld. Such a society may take on the symptoms of psychic disorders, functioning until skewed and tilted it crashes into the domain of neighboring nations.[32]

The Germans have developed a number of behavior patterns symptomatic of psychological disturbance. Some of its primary characteristics are: (1) rank consciousness or ego preoccupation tending to paranoia, (2) rigidity to the extent of compulsion, (3) romanticism to the point of self-inflicted suffering and masochism, and (4) endless philosophizing betraying a persisting and irremovable anxiety.

The paranoid structure emerges from an aggregation of habits and peculiarities that take the form of suspiciousness, the lack of a sense of humor, non-toleration of criticism, the notion of "insult" and its corollary "honor," self-reference, emphasis on status, medals, language referring to "enormity" and "immensity," astronomical terminology in general, the non-admissibility of defeat (*Niederlage*), and the substitution of a "collapse" (*Zusammenbruch*) or "catastrophe" (*Katastrophe*), plus revenge (*Rache*).³³

Two features particularly noticeable in anti-Jewish activity were megalomania and projective accusation. The perpetrator clamored to be recognized. Once the world found out what he had in store for it, he would never again be ignored. In one of his speeches, Hitler said these words:³⁴

> In my life I have often been a prophet and most of the time I have been laughed at. During the period of my struggle for power, it was in the first instance the Jewish people who received with laughter my prophecies that someday I would take over the leadership of the state and thereby of the whole people. . . . I believe that in the meantime that the hyena-like laughter of the Jews of Germany has been smothered in their throats.

Having embarked on a path of destruction, the German administration attributed to its victims the very characteristics it had made its own. Jewry was bent upon "world conquest." It was "criminal" and killed children. In its very existence, it was "parasitic," feeding upon the resources of the community it sought to weaken, adapt, and destroy. These projections were a feedback device. The very attempt at justification called for additional measures. The perpetrator could never really stop. He was always "behind" the victim in the severity and destructiveness of his deeds. When he awoke, after the end, to the nature of his act, he stood like Ajax before his slaughtered sheep.

More pronounced even than the paranoid indication was the compulsive one. Germany was—and to an extent still is—the land of titles, ranks, duty, order. In their actions, Germans are given to meticulousness, cleanliness, and also squeamishness.³⁵ All this was displayed in the destruction of the Jews. Viewed as an administrative development, it was consistent, complete, uncompromising. A German commentator applied to it the term *Folgerichtigkeit*—a chain of sequential steps in a single direction.³⁶

The annihilation of Jewry became compulsive in the very manner of its implementation. The persecutions of earlier epochs had generated classifications, restrictions, and ghettoizations, only to stop at the brink. The Nazi movement crossed the threshold to a "final solution." In this advance, the discriminatory measures of the past had found their logical conclusion. The act, once done, was also the last; death rendered the process irreversible. The second compulsion was the translation of words into deeds. Hitler "prophesied"; he committed himself by announcement. On 30 January 1939, well over a year after the Hoßbach conference during which he had enunciated his plan for attacking Czechoslovakia and France, he said: "If international finance Jewry inside and outside of Europe should succeed once more to plunge nations into another world war, then the consequence will not be the Bolshevization of the earth and thereby the victory of Jewry, but the annihilation of the Jewish race in Europe." A third manifestation was speed. In the words of a Nazi party circular dated 1942, the "problem" had to be solved by the "present generation." It was. The activities of the perpetrators during the crucial years 1941 through 1944 were marked by haste and feverish completion. Finally, the German administration reached for a "total solution." Deportation experts were active in satellites all over Europe. Infants were killed, half-Jews were liable unless Christian or intermarried, and older people, no longer capable of reproduction, were shoved into gas chambers if they had not received high decorations or severe wounds in World War I. The protected and exempted Jews were a thorn in the eye of the bureaucrat and he sought to destroy them.

If the paranoid-compulsive pattern was salient and conspicuous, the masochistic tendency was more subtle and submerged. Thomas Mann, in a classic essay on the nature of Germany, pointed to its romanticism. It was especially difficult for him, who loved romanticism to the core, to accept Goethe's "laconic dictum" that the classic form was "healthy" and the romantic "sick." Yet, romanticism was classicism in excess and dissolution—the revolt of intellectualism against rationalism, music against literature, mysticism against clarity.[37] It was a painful process, self-reinforcing and perpetuating, even accelerating to the abyss. The German, observed an English specialist, is "abnormally sentimental and melancholy; incurably romantic, overserious and mystical, pessimistic to the point of the 'death-wish.'"[38] These were qualities that revealed themselves also in the destruction process.

One of the strangest symptoms of the perpetrator was his "suffering." He suffered with official approval. Himmler would not have liked it if German men did such things "gladly." The doubts, sleeplessness, nausea, and breakdowns, were to a degree protected. One of the more remarkable SS men, General Erich von dem Bach-Zelewski, suffered a nervous collapse, complete with hallucinations of dying Jews only to return to duty as chief of the anti-partisan command to kill some more. As a matter of policy, the SS men were to derive satisfaction, comfort, and even solace from their psychological burdens. The damage was to steel and harden them, it was to bring them greater strength. In Himmler's words to his generals: "Most of you know what it means when 100 corpses are lying there, or 500 or 1,000. . ."*

Perhaps the most basic, if also least obvious, of the psychic malfunctions was a characteristically German confrontation with existence. In that contemplation, there was real fear. The German expression for existence is *Dasein*, and Martin Heidegger, deconstructing the word, rendered it *Da-sein*, or "being here." The opposite, "not being here," is to become "homeless," literally *un-heim-lich*. Agglutinated, this word is *unheimlich*, the German for "weird."[39]

The glimpse of non-existence is unsettling; all hold is lost. Germans, overcome by the tension, grasped for mastery of life by extinguishing it.[40] That mastery, as even the perpetrators could see, was but an apparition. The perpetration became a cosmic joke. At the death camp of Treblinka, the guards had mounted a Star of David on the roof of a gas chamber as an expression of a little humor. In 1945, Eichmann remarked that, having killed five million enemies of the Reich, he would jump into his grave laughing. Hitler himself thought of the total destruction process as a trick. Giving vent to the thought, he called his victims "stupid."

Those who were closest to the killing operations were often prone to refer to their work as their "fate." They knew the war was lost. During all of their doings, they could watch the constricting and narrowing circle of Adolf Hitler's Reich and of their own lives in their entrapment.

The psychic malfunctions and their effects are distinctly visible in the history of German behavior, but this was not a case of illness in a conventional sense. These were symptoms distributed among seventy million people and observable in the continuous action of masses of them. The magnification of any one of these tendencies would have instantly obstructed all possibility of cooperative performance. True

---

* Hilberg cited here the so-called Posen speeches by Heinrich Himmler held in the beginning of October 1943 in the occupied Polish town Posen and each before an audience of Nazi officials.

paranoia would have undermined trust and confidence within the administrative apparatus; extreme compulsion could have easily been extended to prohibitively wasteful consumption of administrative energy; excessive masochism would have been turned inward into self-destruction; pronounced anxiety would have brought the bureaucracy to the border of chaos. In fact, these propensities were almost always under control. They were channeled into bureaucratic assignments and directed at Jewish target groups. They were "nationalized" into a sublimated, sloganized philosophy and promulgated as official virtues. Thus, paranoia was reserved for the perception of "threats" to the German people; compulsion was to spur a sense of "duty" and the accomplishment of "difficult" tasks; masochism became "sacrifice" for the nation; and anxiety was turned into a psychic force propelling the bureaucracy into an unknown from which there was no return. While the destruction process may thus have fed upon and utilized these disorders, it would have disintegrated under an overdose. Whichever way that quantity of disturbance may possibly be ascertained, its measurement will register within "normal" limits.

When we view the malfunction theories as a whole, we may note that in their ultimate formulation the perpetrator is the sufferer. The destruction process is happening to him. He is stricken by intellectual failure, cultural disruption, or psychic afflictions. He is a delinquent, an animal, or a patient. He has to be reformed, humanized, or cured. In fact, the perpetration was something more than a series of outgrowths of such malfunctions. It was a concerted act with a unified structure and a definite configuration.

Fixation

When one examines the administrative unfolding of the destruction process, one may note that it consisted of the diverse activities of a sprawling bureaucratic machine. In spite of decentralization, there was purposeful action with few interruptions and little waste. One can see a striking pathfinding ability in the absence of blueprints or programs, congruous activity when there were no express directives, common understanding without explicit reports. That kind of integration had to be the product of a conception that had directional and structuring capability.

Let us give specifications for this thought pattern. It was old, for it had meaning to all Germans. It was basically simple, since it was grasped in all the strata of the bureaucracy. It was unfinished, because it was actualized in a new technological environment. Substantively, the whole formation is dimly discernible in three familiar fixations: the will to make "history," an elevation of "blood," the passing of almost supernatural "tests."

The mobilization of these images was begun in the streets. During the 1930s, a wave of demonstrations and pageantry swept Germany. Flags, drums, torches, and voices of command conveyed the nearness and immanence of what was to come.[41] Thus, from the first days of the Hitler regime, people could sense that Germany stood on the threshold of events that would have "world-historical" significance.

To that population, Nazism was not so much a system of government as a movement (*Bewegung*) that would cross geographic and psychological boundaries as they had not been trod over before. The German idea of history was to shake mankind to its foundations. The bureaucrats in particular stood at the helm of that historical march. The German shadow covering Europe was cast from their height. As wearers of the uniform and the holders of titles, all Europe was to stand in awe of them. By 1939, Germans understood that the banner of the swastika was a pointer to an attack that would stop nowhere and spare no one. The understanding was not always easily put into words. Charged with that job, German Security Police Personnel Chief Bruno Streckenbach explained to the assembled commanders of the mobile killing units about to move into Russia that they were expected to proceed ruthlessly there (*dass dort rücksichtslos durchgegriffen werden müsste*). The Jews were half of Germany's civilian victims, the largest community to be crushed by that movement, the group most completely annihilated.

It was in 1941 that an emphasis on finality and irreversibility crept into secret correspondence and open speech on the "solution of the Jewish problem." Blood was to be shed. This act—this work—was never to be undone. It was not to be forgotten. A landmark in history, it was cast in "monumental" proportions. Who would henceforth be able to overlook the disappearance of one of the oldest historical people in the West? This was no episode. It was a deed.

In the middle of the end, a final cognition was felt. The perpetrator was gazing upon a forbidden vista. Under the murky huts of Auschwitz, Germans stood alone as they lined up their victims, herding them into gas chambers. These guards were living through something ultimate. Experience (*Erlebnis*) was reaching its outer limits. The act had become knowledge, and that knowledge was unique, for the sensation of a first discovery is not repeatable.

The thoughts that had drawn these men to such polar ends were present long before their realization. G. W. F. Hegel had spoken of a world-historical unfolding and of world-historical men who comprehended that which was ripe for their time. In Goethe, there is a pact of blood with a "demonically intoxicated" professor to delve into experiences never before witnessed by man.[42] Nietzsche preached transcendence and Heidegger intoned "become what you are" (*Werde was du bist*).[43] We know, of course, that Hegel had no "Führer," Goethe no "special treatment," Nietzsche no "subhuman." The German bureaucrat used ponderous and cumbersome language. But when the imagery of German philosophy, poetry, mythology, and music is lined up against the totality of the German destruction process, there is nevertheless a resemblance. The likeness is thematic. The old words and the new deeds are photographs of the same mind, mirrors of the same thoughts, expressions of the same idea.[44]

The Nazi revolution was a technological concretization of the old ideational material. Coming upon the conclusion of the greatest outpouring of the German arts, it duplicated in a layout of administrative acts that series of verbal, tonal, and color creations. It reproduced their content, rhythm, and atmosphere. Indeed, there were moments when the German perpetrator was prone to look back upon his handiwork as an aesthetic accomplishment. Thus, the very enormity of the conception endowed the deed with dimension. The flow of blood gave it its own peculiar permanence. Its unprecedented character lent to the event a quality of uniqueness.

The destruction of the Jews was a tour de force. An alignment of all the motivation theories against the available facts yields that conclusion as a residue. We are thus left with a crude contour of the hypothetical German mind. It is the image of a German who walked with fleeting phantasms. Frustrations nurtured and reinforced them. In a technological bureaucracy he found an impersonal medium for their realization. Obscure memories of a medieval heritage shrouded him with protective symbols. Propaganda supplied him with rationalizations. Ambitions spurred him on. And below, a helpless victim, twitching in pain, was ready for the fatal blow.

Notes

1. Theoretical works are cited here to be representative, not exhaustive. Factual material is drawn mainly from my book, *The Destruction of the European Jews* (Chicago, 1961). This essay was begun with a small grant from the University of Vermont for eventual inclusion in a Franz L. Neumann memorial volume. Since the volume was not published, the article is hereby dedicated to his memory.
2. Jacob Katz, *Exclusiveness and Tolerance: Studies in Jewish-Gentile Relations in Medieval and Modern Times* (Oxford, 1961), 51.
3. Walther Rathenau, *Zur Kritik der Zeit*, 4th ed. (Berlin, 1912), 220.
4. Eduard von Hartmann, *Das Judentum in Gegenwart und Zukunft* (Berlin, 1885), 162.
5. Wolfgang Höfler, *Untersuchungen über die Machtstellung der Juden in der Weltwirtschaft: I. England und das Vornationalsozialistische Deutschland* (Vienna, 1944), in the library of the University of Vermont through the courtesy of Dr. S. A. Goudsmit. On the proportional decrease of Jewish economic power from the nineteenth century to the twentieth, see also Bernard W. Weinryb, "The Economic and Social Background of Modern Antisemitism," in *Essays on Antisemitism*, ed. Koppel S. Ponson (New York, 1946), 17–34. As for the paucity of Jewish control in the sensitive area of the press, see Oron J. Hale, *The Captive Press in the Third Reich* (Princeton, NJ, 1964), 2–3.
6. See the striking parallels with Huguenots in Warren C. Scoville, *The Persecution of Huguenots and French Economic Development 1680–1720* (Berkeley, CA, 1960), particularly 133, 145–50.
7. Jean-Paul Sartre, *Anti-Semite and Jew* (New York, 1948), 23.
8. Oswald Spengler, *Der Untergang des Abendlandes: Umrisse einer Morphologie der Weltgeschichte* (Munich, 1922), 2:395.
9. Three focal points of distraction in history are Christianity, the capital economy, and the city. Both Nietzsche and Marx saw particularly in Christianity a Judaization of the world. Friedrich Nietzsche, "Zur Genealogie der Moral," in *Werke* Karl Schlechta edition (Munich, 1954), 2:778–82, 2:795–97. Karl Marx and Siegried Landshut, *Die Frühschriften* (Stuttgart, 1953), 171–207, particularly 178, 184–85, 201, 206. On capitalism, see Werner Sombart, *Die Juden und das Wirtschaftsleben* (Leipzig, 1911). The city is stressed by Spengler, *Untergang*, 2:389, 2:390–91. It is mentioned also by Franz Neumann: "The modern theater, atonal music, expressionism in painting and literature, functional architecture, all these seemed to constitute a threat to the conservatives whose cultural outlook was basically rural, and who thus came to identify the city and its culture, its economics, and its politics with the Jew." *Behemoth: The Structure and Practice of National Socialism, 1933–1944*, 2nd ed. (New York, 1944), 123.
10. Max Lerner, *The Role of the American Jew* (New York, undated postwar pamphlet).
11. Salvador de Madariaga, *Portrait of Europe* (New York, ca. 1955), 200.

12. From a letter by Rathenau dated 20 February 1919, as quoted by Hermann Rauschning, *The Redemption of Democracy: The Coming Atlantic Empire* (New York, 1941), 223. Rathenau, a Jew, was Germany's foreign minister after World War I. He was assassinated. For an observation very similar to Rathenau's, see Erich Kahler, *Die Verantwortung des Geistes: Gesammelte Aufsätze* (Frankfurt, 1952), 164–65.
13. See Henry Loeblowitz-Lennard, "The Jew as Symbol," *Psychoanalytic Quarterly, XVI* 21, no. 2 (1947): 36.
14. Madriaga, *Portrait*, 202. The biological term "symbiosis" has been introduced to characterize the usefulness of Jewry in a Christian environment. See Robert Ezra Park, *Race and Culture* (Glencoe, IL, 1950), 353–54. Also, Adolf Leschnitzer, *The Magic Background of Anti-Semitism: An Analysis of the German-Jewish Relationship* (New York, 1956). Similarly, the notion of a "cultural pair" by Rudolph M. Loewenstein, *Christians and Jews: A Psychoanalytic Study* (New York, 1951), 181–99.
15. See Werner J. Cahnman, "Socio-Economic Causes of Antisemitism," *Social Problems*, 5, no. 1 (1957): 21–29.
16. Sigmund Freud, *Moses and Monotheism* (New York, 1967), 134. A German theologian adds: their "peculiar power of life" already struck the pagans as "weird" (*unheimlich*). Franz Köhler, "Wurzeln des Antisemitismus," pamphlet of *Landeszentrale für Heimatsdienst in Niedersachsen, Reihe A, Heft 8* (Duderstadt, 1958), 30. Invariance, to the extent that it exists, is somewhat localized. It does not imply that Indian Jews, North African Jews, and European Jews are alike.
17. Louis Lochner, ed., *The Goebbels Diaries 1942–1943* (Garden City, NJ, 1948), 147–48.
18. "Racism and anti-Semitism are substitutes for the class struggle." Neumann, *Behemoth*, 125. The party interpreted its nationalization clause away by restricting its applicability to Jews. In reports from occupied Russia, Jews were often referred to as bandits, partisan helpers, etc. On the substitution of the destruction process for the war, see Hitler's political testament, Nuremberg document PS-3569.
19. Neumann, *Behemoth*, 121.
20. Göring spoke of a "burning of bridges." Lochner, *Goebbels Diaries*, 266, entry for 2 March 1943. The phenomenon was noted by Neumann in the 2nd ed. of *Behemoth* (1944), 552, and by Leo Alexander, "War Crimes and Their Motivation," *Journal of Criminal Law and Criminology* 39 (1948): 298–326.
21. See Paul Massing, *Rehearsal for Destruction: A Study of Political Anti-Semitism in Imperial Germany* (New York, 1949); Waldemar Gurian, "Antisemitism in Modern Germany," in *Essays on Antisemitism*, ed. Koppel S. Pinson (New York, 1946), 218–65; and Peter G. J. Pulzer, *The Rise of Political Anti-Semitism in Germany and Austria* (New York, 1964).
22. See the comment by Erich von dem Bach-Zelewski, "Das Leben eines SS-Generals," *Aufbau*, 30 August 1946, 40. The general, a highly intelligent man, killed many thousands of Jews. See also Gerhart Saenger, *The Social*

Psychology of Prejudice: Achieving Intercultural Understanding (New York, 1953), 139.
23. Questions and statistics quoted in *Aufbau*, 18 October 1957, 18. Not indicated are sample area and sample sizes.
24. It would seem that the crude propagandist has not been respectable in Germany for quite some time. Nietzsche had expressed contempt for the anti-Semites of his day and even the Nazis looked down on Streicher.
25. Louis de Jong, "Jews and Non-Jews in Nazi-Occupied Holland," in *On the Track of Tyranny*, ed. Max Beloff (London, 1960), 139–55.
26. See the essay by Heinrich Heine, "Zur Geschichte der Religion und Philosophie in Deutschland," written in 1834, in his collected works. Also, R. L. Sedgwick, "The German Character," *Blackwood's Magazine* (June 1962): 537–47.
27. Sartre, *Anti-Semite and Jew*, 43. Hans G. Adler, *Theresienstadt 1941–1945* (Tübingen, 1955), 643–44.
28. Adler, *Theresienstadt*, 650. For the medieval antecedents of the satanization of Jewry, see Joshua Trachtenberg, *The Devil and the Jews* (New Haven, CT, 1943).
29. Leschnitzer points to the apparent "interchangeability" of witch burnings and anti-Jewish outbursts in German history. See his *Magic Background*.
30. See primarily Ernst Simmel, "Anti-Semitism and Mass Psychopathology," in *Anti-Semitism: A Social Disease*, ed. Ernst Simmel (New York, 1946), 33–78, and Günther Anders, "Reflections on the H Bomb," in *Voices of Dissent: A Collection of Articles from Dissent Magazine* (New York, 1958), 359–68.
31. See the anthropological study at Bremen by David Rodnick, *Postwar Germans* (New Haven, CT, 1948), 17: "The German child comes into the world wanted..." and note also patterns of family life in such neighboring countries as Denmark, Holland, and Switzerland.
32. See Richard M. Brickner, Margaret Mead, and Edward A. Strecker, *Is Germany Incurable?* (New York, 1943), 135–36: "It looks as if it were theoretically possible to develop a more or less stable culture out of practically any set of emotional postulates."
33. Brickner, Mead, and Strecker, *Is Germany Incurable?*, 63, 67, 196, 215, 246, 248. Also, Gerhard Nebel, *Die Not der Götter—Welt und Mythos der Germanen* (Hamburg, 1957), 14, 54, 93, 216.
34. Hitler speech, 30 January 1939, German press.
35. Compulsion is the symptom that appears to show up most consistently in psychological tests. See David C. McClelland, "The United States and Germany: A Comparative Study of National Character," in *The Roots of Consciousness* (Princeton, 1946), 62–92, and Henry V. Dicks, "Personality Traits and National Socialist Ideology," *Human Relations* 3, no. 2 (1950): 111–54.
36. Rudolf Hagelstange, "Metamorphosen des Antisemitismus," *Deutsche Rundschau* 80 (1954): 1, 260.
37. Thomas Mann, "Deutschland und die Deutschen," in *Sorge um Deutschland: Sechs Essays* (Frankfurt, 1957), 73–93.
38. Sedgwick, "The German Character," 539.

39. Martin Heidegger, *Sein und Zeit* (Tübingen, 1957), 142–48, 184–91.
40. See Eric Fromm, *Escape from Freedom* (New York, 1941), 183–84. Franz L. Neumann, "Anxiety and Politics," in *The Democratic and the Authoritarian State* (Glencoe, IL, 1957), 270–300. On the choice of Jewry as the stand-ins for God, see Hans Ornstein, *Der antijüdische Komplex* (Zurich, 1949), 43–44.
41. The mechanics in a single German town are described in detail by William Sheridan Allen, *The Nazi Seizure of Power: The Experience of a Single German Town, 1930–1935* (Chicago, 1965).
42. Thomas Mann rendered that figure the German of our time. See his essay, "Deutschland," 78.
43. Heidegger, *Sein und Zeit*, 145.
44. See Morris Ginsburg, *Reason and Unreason in Society: Essays in Sociology and Social Philosophy* (London, 1948), 143; William S. Schlamm, *Die Grenzen des Wunders* (Zurich, 1959), 65–66; Walter Hofer, *Geschichte zwischen Philosophie und Politik* (Basel, 1956), 32–34; Thomas Mann, "Nietzsche's Philosophy in the Light of Recent History," in *Last Essays* (New York, 1959), 141–77; and particularly William S. Bossenbrook, *The German Mind* (Detroit, MI, 1961).

Bibliography

Adler, Hans G. *Theresienstadt 1941–1945*. Tübingen: Mohr Siebeck, 1955.

Alexander, Leo. "War Crimes and Their Motivation." *Journal of Criminal Law and Criminology* 39 (1948): 298–326.

Allen, William Sheridan. *The Nazi Seizure of Power: The Experience of a Single German Town, 1930–1935*. Chicago: Quadrangle Books, 1965.

Anders, Gunther. "Reflections on the H Bomb." In *Voices of Dissent: A Collection of Articles from Dissent Magazine*, 359–368. New York: Grove Press, 1958.

Bach-Zelewski, Erich von dem, "Das Leben eines SS-Generals." *Aufbau*, 30 August 1946, 40.

Bossenbrook, William S. *The German Mind*. Detroit, MI: Wayne State University Press, 1961.

Brickner, Richard M., Margaret Mead, and Edward A. Strecker. *Is Germany Incurable?* New York: Lippincott, 1943.

Cahnman, Werner J. "Socio-Economic Causes of Antisemitism." *Social Problems* 5, no. 1 (1957): 21–29.

Dicks, Henry V. "Personality Traits and National Socialist Ideology." *Human Relations* 3, no. 2 (1950): 111–54.

Freud, Sigmund. *Moses and Monotheism*. New York: Vintage Books, 1967.

Fromm, Eric. *Escape from Freedom*. New York: Farrar & Rinehart, 1941.

Ginsberg, Morris. *Reason and Unreason in Society: Essays in Sociology and Social Philosophy*. London: Publication for the London School of Economics and Political Science, University of London by Longmans, Green, 1948.

Gurian, Waldemar. "Antisemitism in Modern Germany." In *Essays on Antisemitisim*, ed. Koppel S. Pinson, 218–65. New York: Conference on Jewish Relations, 1946.
Hagelstange, Rudolf. "Metamorphosen des Antisemitismus." *Deutsche Rundschau* 80 (1954): 1, 255–60.
Hale, Oron J. *The Captive Press in the Third Reich* (Princeton, NJ: Princeton University Press, 1964).
Hartmann, Eduard von. *Das Judentum in Gegenwart und Zukunft*. Berlin: Friedrich, 1885.
Heidegger, Martin. *Sein und Zeit*. Tübingen: Niemeyer, 1957.
Heine, Heinrich. "Zur Geschichte der Religion und Philosophie in Deutschland." (1834) In *Heinrich Heines Über Deutschland, Essays und Pamphlete. Ausgewählte Werke IV: Die romantische Schule*, ed. Joerg K. Sommermeyer, Norderstedt: Books on Demand, 2019.
Hilberg, Raul. *The Destruction of the European Jews*. Chicago: Quadrangle Books, 1961.
Hofer, Walter. *Geschichte zwischen Philosophie und Politik*. Basel: Basel, 1956.
Höfler, Wolfgang. *Untersuchungen über die Machtstellung der Juden in der Weltwirtschaft: I. England und das Vornationalsozialistische Deutschland*. Vienna: A. Holzhausens, 1944.
Jong, Louis de. "Jews and Non-Jews in Nazi-Occupied Holland." In *On the Track of Tyranny*, ed. Max Beloff, 139–55. London: Vallentine, Mitchell, 1960.
Kahler, Erich. *Die Verantwortung des Geistes: Gesammelte Aufsätze*. Frankfurt: Fischer, 1952.
Katz, Jacob. *Exclusiveness and Tolerance: Studies in Jewish-Gentile Relations in Medieval and Modern Times*. Oxford: Oxford University Press, 1961.
Köhler, Franz. "Wurzeln des Antisemitismus." Pamphlet of *Landeszentrale für Heimatsdienst in Niedersachsen, Reihe* A, *Heft* 8. Duderstadt, 1958.
Lerner, Max. *The Role of the American Jew*. New York: American Jewish Congress, n.d.
Leschnitzer, Adolf. *The Magic Background of Modern Anti-Semitism: An Analysis of the German-Jewish Relationship*. New York: International Universities Press, 1956.
Lochner, Louis, ed. *The Goebbels Diaries 1942–1943*. Garden City, NJ: Doubleday, 1948.
Loeblowitz-Lennard, Henry. "The Jew as Symbol." *Psychoanalytic Quarterly, XVI* 21, no. 2 (1947): 32–38.
Loewenstein, Rudolf M. *Christians and Jews: A Psychoanalytic Study*. New York: International Universities Press, 1951.
Madariaga, Salvador de. *Portrait of Europe*. New York: Roy Publishers, ca. 1955.
Mann, Thomas. "Deutschland und die Deutschen." In *Sorge um Deutschland: Sechs Essays*, 73–93. Frankfurt: S. Fischer, 1957.
———. "Nietzche's Philosophy in the Light of Recent History." In *Last Essays*, 141–77. New York: Knopf, 1959.
Marx, Karl., and Siegried Landshut. *Die Frühschriften*. Stuttgart: Verlag, 1953.
Massing, Paul. *Rehearsal for Destruction: A Study of Political Anti-Semitism in Imperial Germany*. New York: Harper, 1949.

McClelland, David C. "The United States and Germany: A Comparative Study of National Character." In *The Roots of Consciousness*, 62–92. Princeton, NJ: Nostrand, 1964.

Nebel, Gerhard. *Die Not der Götter—Welt und Mythos der Germanen*. Hamburg: Hoffman und Campe, 1957.

Neumann, Franz L. *Behemoth: The Structure and Practice of National Socialism, 1933–1944*, 2nd ed. New York: Oxford University Press, 1944.

———. "Anxiety and Politics." In *The Democratic and the Authoritarian State*, 270–300. Glencoe, IL: The Free Press, 1957.

Nietzsche, Friedrich Wilhelm, and Karl Schlechta. "Zur Genealogie der Moral." In *Werke*, 2nd ed. 778–82. Munich: C. Hanser, 1954.

Ornstein, Hans. *Der antijüdische Komplex*. Zurich: Gestaltung, 1949.

Park, Robert Ezra. *Race and Culture*. Glencoe, IL: The Free Press, 1950.

Pulzer, Peter G.J. *The Rise of Political Anti-Semitism in Germany and Austria*. New York: J. Wiley & Sons, 1964.

Rathenau, Walther. *Zur Kritik der Zeit*. 4th ed. Berlin: S. Fischer Verlag, 1912.

Rauschning, Hermann. *The Redemption of Democracy: The Coming Atlantic Empire*. New York: Alliance Book, 1941.

Rodnick, David. *Postwar Germans*. New Haven, CT: Yale University Press, 1948.

Saenger, Gerhart. *The Social Psychology of Prejudice: Achieving Intercultural Understanding*. New York: Harper and Row, 1953.

Sartre, Jean-Paul. *Anti-Semite and Jew*. New York: Schocken Books, 1948.

Schlamm, William S. *Die Grenzen des Wunders*. Zurich: Europa Verlag, 1959.

Scoville, Warren C. *The Persecution of Huguenots and French Economic Development 1680–1720*. Berkley: University of California Press, 1960.

Sedgwick, R. L. "The German Character." *Blackwood's Magazine* (June 1962): 537–47.

Simmel, Ernst. "Anti-Semitism and Mass Psychopathology." In *Anti-Semitism: A Social Disease*, ed. Ernst Simmel, 33–78. New York: International Universities Press, 1946.

Sombart, Werner. *Die Juden und das Wirtschaftsleben*. Leipzig: Leipzig Duncker & Humblot, 1911.

Spengler, Oswald. *Der Untergang des Abendlandes: Umrisse einer Morphologie der Weltgeschichte*. Munich: C.H. Beck'sche Verlagsbuchhandlung, 1922.

Trachtenberg, Joshua. *The Devil and the Jews*. New Haven, CT: Yale University Press, 1943.

Weinryb, Bernard W. "The Economic and Social Background of Modern Antisemitism." In *Essays on Antisemitism*, ed. Koppel S. Ponson, 17–34 (New York: Jewish Social Studies, 1946).

3

The Bureaucracy of Annihilation
(1985/1989)

WE ARE, ALL OF US who have thought and written about the Holocaust, accustomed to thinking of this event as unique. There is no concept in all history like the Final Solution. There is no precedent for the almost endless march of millions of men, women, and children into gas chambers. The systematization of this destruction process sets it aside from all else that has ever happened. Yet if we examine this event in detail, observing the progression of small steps day by day, we see much in the destruction of Jewry that is familiar and even commonplace in the context of contemporary institutions and practices. Basically, the Jews were destroyed as a consequence of a multitude of acts performed by a phalanx of functionaries in public offices and private enterprises, and many of these measures, taken one by one, turn out to be bureaucratic, embedded in habit, routine, and tradition. It is almost a case of regarding the whole upheaval in all of its massiveness as something incredible, and then observing the small components and seeing in them very little that one could not expect in a modern

---

Originally published in French as "La bureaucratie de la solution finale," in *L'Allemagne nazie et le genocide juif*, ed. École des Hautes Études en Sciences Sociales (Paris: Seuil, 1985), 219–235. Subsequently published in English in *Unanswered Questions: Nazi Germany and the Genocide of the Jews*, ed. François Furet (New York: Schocken Books, 1989), 119–33.

society. One can go further and assert that it is the very mundaneness and ordinariness of these everyday official actions that made the destruction process so crass. Never before had the total experience of a modern bureaucracy been applied to such an undertaking. Never before had it produced such a result.

The uprooting and annihilation of European Jewry was a multi-pronged operation of a highly decentralized apparatus. This was no perpetration by a single department staffed with specialists in destruction. Germany never had a commissariat of Jewish affairs. The machinery of destruction was the organized German society, its ministries, armed forces, party formations, and industry.[1] In democratic countries we are accustomed to thinking of legislatures as devices that control administrative units, infuse them with power and money, authorize them to undertake action, and by implication, of course, apportion jurisdiction between them. In Nazi Germany there was no legislature that, like the US Congress, could create an agency and abolish it. In Nazi Germany every organization moved on a track of self-assertion. To some of us this may seem like anarchy. How much more remarkable then that this congeries of bureaucratic agencies, these people drawn from every area of expertise, operating without a basic plan, uncoordinated in any central office, nevertheless displayed order, balance, and economy throughout the destruction process.

The apparatus was able to advance unerringly because there was an inner logic to its measures. A decree defining the term "Jew," expropriations of Jewish property, the physical separation and isolation of the victims, forced labor, deportations, gassings—these were not random moves. The sequence of steps was built-in; each was a stage in the development. By 1941, the participating decision-makers themselves became aware that they had been traveling on a determined path. As their assault took on gestalt, its latent structure became manifest. Now they had an overview that allowed them to see a beginning and an end and that prompted them to demand of indigenous administrations in occupied and satellite countries that the "Nuremberg" principle be adopted in the definition of Jews and that other precedents laid down in Germany be followed in the appropriate order for the accomplishment of a "final solution."[2]

Nothing, however, was simple. Neither the preliminary nor the concluding phases of the destruction process could be traversed without difficulties and complications. The Jewish communities had all been emancipated and they were tied to the Gentile population in countless relationships, from business contacts, partnerships, leases, and employment contracts, to personal friendships and intermarriages. To sever these connections one by one, a variety of measures were necessary, and these actions were taken by specialists who were accountants, lawyers, engineers, or physicians. The questions with which these men were concerned were almost always technical. How was a "Jewish enterprise" to be defined? Where were the borders of a ghetto to be drawn? What was to be the disposition of pension claims belonging to deported Jews? How should bodies be disposed of? These were the problems pondered by the bureaucrats in their memoranda, correspondence, meetings, and discussions. That was the essence of their work.

No organized element of German society was entirely uninvolved in the process of destruction. Yet this very fact, which is virtually an axiom, has been extraordinarily hard to assimilate in descriptions and assessments of the Nazi regime. It is much easier to visualize the role of a propagandist or some practitioner of violence than to appreciate the contribution of a bookkeeper. For this reason the principal spotlight in postwar years has been placed on the SS and the Gestapo. There is some awareness also of the military, particularly where, as in occupied France, it had made itself conspicuous. Similarly unavoidable was the discovery that an enterprise like I. G. Farben had established branches in Auschwitz. Much less well known, however, are the activities of such faceless components of the destructive machine as the Ministry of Finance, which was engaged in confiscations, or the armed forces network of armament inspectorates, which was concerned with forced labor, or German municipal authorities that directed or participated in the creation and maintenance of ghettos in eastern Europe. Two large bureaucracies have remained all but obscure, even though they operated at the very scene of death: the German railroads and the Order Police. This omission should give us pause.

Trains and street police have been common sights in Europe for more than a century. Of all the agencies of government these two organizations have always been highly visible to every inhabitant of the continent, yet they have been overlooked in the analysis of the Nazi regime. It is as if their very size and ubiquity deflected attention from the lethal operations in which they were so massively engaged. What *was* the function of the German railroads in the annihilation of the Jews? What tasks did the Order Police perform?

Case I: The Indispensability of the Railroads

In the chain of steps that led to the extinction of millions of Jewish victims, the Reichsbahn, as the German railways were known, carried the Jews from many countries and regions of Europe to the death camps, which were situated on occupied Polish soil. The Jews were passed from one jurisdiction to another: from the civil or military authorities who had uprooted and concentrated them, to the Security Police who was in charge of rounding them up, to the Reichsbahn that transported them to the camps where they were gassed. Reichsbahn operations were a crucial link in this process and their significance is underscored by their magnitude. Camps account for most of the Jewish dead, and almost all of the people deported there were moved by rail. The movement encompassed 3 million Jews.

Of course, these transports were but a small portion of the Reichsbahn's business. At its peak the railway network stretched from Bordeaux to Dnepropetrovsk and points east, and its personnel consisted of half a million civil servants and almost twice as many other employees.[3] In the Reich itself (including Austria, Polish incorporated territory, and the Białystok district), some 130,000 freight cars were being assembled for loading every day.[4] Germany depended on its railroads to carry soldiers and civilians, military cargo and industrial products, throughout the war. A complex functional and territorial division of labor was required to administer these transport programs.

The transport minister, Julius Dorpmüller, held the office from 1937 to the end of the war. The *Staatssekretär* (state secretary) responsible for railways in the Ministry was at first Wilhelm Kleinmann and, from the spring of 1942, Albert Ganzenmüller, a young, capable engineer and consummate technocrat who was to transport what Albert Speer was to produce.[5] Ganzenmüller's central divisions, labeled E (for *Eisenbahn*, or railway) included E 1 (Traffic and Tariffs), E 2 (Operations), and L (*Landesverteidigung*, or Defense of the Land, meaning military transport). The Traffic Division dealt with financial matters, E 2 with operational considerations, and L with military priorities. Within E 2, the following breakdown should be of interest:[6]

E 2 *(Operations)*	Max Leibbrand (from 1942: Gustav Dilli)
21 (Passenger Trains)	Paul Schell
211 (Special Trains)	Otto Stange

Stange administered the transport of Jewish deportees. He received the requests for trains from Adolf Eichmann's office in the Security Police and channeled them to financial and operational offices in the Reichsbahn.[7] The position and designation of 211 on the organization chart point to two important features of the deportation process. The first is that the Jewish deportees were always booked as people, even though they were carried in boxcars. The passenger concept was essential, in order that the Reichsbahn could collect the fare for each deported Jew in accordance with applicable tariffs and to preserve internal prerogatives and divisions of jurisdiction; the passenger specialists would remain in control. The second characteristic of Stange's office is indicated by the word "special." He dealt only with group transports, each of which had to be planned.

Passenger trains were either regular (*Regelzüge*), moving at hours stated in published schedules, or special (*Sonderzüge*), assembled and dispatched upon demand. Jews were deported in *Sonderzüge* and the procurement and scheduling of such trains was a lengthy and involved procedure that had to be administered at the regional level, particularly in the Generalbetriebsleitung Ost (General Directorate East), one of three such *Leitungen* in Nazi Germany. *Ost* was concerned with trains directed to Poland and occupied areas farther to the east, and hence Jewish transports from large parts of Europe were channeled through this office. An abbreviated chart of the Generalbetriebsleitung would look as follows:[8]

Generalbetriebsleitung Ost	Ernst Emrich
I. (Operations)	[Albert] Eggert (Philipp Mangold)
L (Wehrmacht)	[Erich] Bebenroth
P (Passenger Schedules)	[Wilhelm] Fröhlich
PW (Passenger Cars)	[Karl] Jacobi
II. (Traffic)	[Alfred] Simon (Ernst Hartmann)
III. (Main Car Allocation Office for Freight Cars)	[Johannes] Schultz

In this array of officials, it is primarily Wilhelm Fröhlich and Karl Jacobi who dealt with Jewish train movements. Conferences were called and dates were fixed for transport programs aggregating forty or fifty trains at a time: ethnic Germans, Hitler Youth, laborers, Jews—all were on the same agenda.[9] The actual schedules were written locally, in the Reichsbahndirektionen, or in the Generaldirektion der Ostbahn, the railway network in central Poland that dispatched Jews on short hauls from ghettos to death camps nearby.[10] The Reichsbahndirektionen were also responsible for the allocations of cars and locomotives. Only then were transports assembled for the Jews loaded, sealed, dispatched, emptied, and cleaned, to be filled with new, perhaps altogether different cargoes, in the circulatory flow. The trains moved slowly and most were overloaded. The norm in western Europe or Germany was 1,000 persons per train.[11] During 1944, transports with Hungarian Jews averaged 3,000.[12] In Poland, such numbers were often exceeded. One train, fifty cars long, carried 8,205 Jews from Kolomea to the death camp of Bełżec.[13] Unheated in the winter, stifling in the summer, the cars, filled with men, women, and children, were death traps in themselves. Seldom would a transport arrive without 1 or 2 percent of the deportees having died en route.

One thinks of railroads as providing a service. What they produce is "place utility," and in this case they contributed their industriousness and ingenuity to the possibility of annihilating people, by the thousands at a time, in places where gas chambers had been installed. Like the Reichsbahn, the Order Police was a major apparatus of the Third Reich and was needed over a long period of time in a wide geographic area, and its utility manifested itself in several stages of the destruction process, from concentration to killings.

Case II: The Indispensability of the Order Police

Nazi Germany was, in essence, a "police state," a type of regime that implies limitless power over the population. Under Heinrich Himmler, the offices and units of the SS and Police were welded into an organization that was a symbol of much that Nazism stood for: arrests and concentration camps, racism and destruction. The police components of this power structure were grouped under two main offices: Security Police, directed by Reinhard Heydrich, and Order Police, commanded by Kurt Daluege, organized thusly:[14]

Security Police (Sicherheitspolizei, or Sipo)
    Gestapo, ca. 40,000 to 50,000 men
    Criminal Police (Kripo), ca. 15,000

Order Police (Ordnungspolizei, or Orpo)
   Stationary (Einzeldienst), ca. 250,000, including reservists
      Cities: Schutzpolizei (Schupo)
      Rural: Gendarmerie
   Units (battalions and regiments), ca. 50,000, including reservists
   Indigenous personnel in occupied territory of the USSR:
      Schutzmannschaft (Schuma), ca. 100,000, including Einzeldienst and Schuma battalions
   Other offices (technical services, volunteer fire departments, etc.)

Comparing the Security Police and the Order Police, we may note two differences between them. The Security Police, in which the Gestapo was the predominant element, could be regarded as a new institution, whereas the conventional Order Police was old and established in Germany. Security Police—spread out over a continent—were relatively few; Order Police were clearly more numerous. Even so, the Ordnungspolizei was strained by the extent and variety of its assignments.

The Einzeldienst, a term denoting stationary duty that could be performed by a single individual, was significant mainly in the Reich and annexed territories, while mobile formations (battalions and regiments) were important primarily outside of home or incorporated regions. In most of the occupied countries, including France and the General Government of Poland, where German Order Police personnel served only in units, an indigenous police force remained in place to carry out its own tasks and to assist the Germans in theirs.

The areas wrested from the USSR were covered by a thin layer of Order Police, composed of both Einzeldienst and units. Einzeldienst, stationed in large urban centers as well as in many rural zones, reached a total of close to 15,000 at the end of 1942; battalions not fighting at the front contained a similar number of men.[15] To augment this German police establishment, a native Schutzmannschaft was created that, by 1 July 1942, had already grown to 42,708 in Einzeldienst within cities and on the land, and to 33,270 in Schuma battalions.[16] The so-called rural districts in Latvian, Lithuanian, White Russian, and Ukrainian regions included small towns with many Jewish residents as well as villages with purely Baltic or Slavic populations. Such a district (*Gebiet*), generally with around 250,000 inhabitants, was garrisoned by a German Gendarmerie platoon and its native helpers.

The fairly typical rural *Gebiet* of Brest-Litovsk in occupied Ukraine was controlled by 26 Gendarmerie men (15 of them older reservists) and 308 Ukrainian Schuma.[17] If all of these figures appear to be small, they should be juxtaposed with the numerical strength of the Security Police. Gestapo and Criminal Police in the entire occupied USSR were barely a few thousand, and when a Security Police post was placed in a rural area, it would contain around a half dozen men.

The sheer geographic expanse of the Order Police is in fact the principal clue to its function in destructive operations. The Orpo was the ever-present standby force that could be drawn upon whenever Jews had to be concentrated or killed. In Amsterdam, Order Police contingents were needed to round up Jews for deportation.[18] In eastern Europe, Order Police guards were posted near the walls and at the gates of ghettos. For example, in Warsaw, a company of a police battalion was steadily engaged in ghetto supervision.[19] Similarly, in Riga, eighty-eight Schuma were assigned to this duty.[20] And so on, for hundreds of ghettos. Order Police detachments were also guarding laborers outdoors. One Order Police battalion and seven Schuma battalions were deployed along Durchgangsstrasse IV, a thousand-kilometer road construction project from the Danube estuary to Taganrog, on which many Jews worked and died.[21] Furthermore, Order Police routinely accompanied the special trains to their destinations.[22] To put it simply, what the victim saw from a ghetto fence, a labor camp, or a box car, were the rifles of ordinary policeman.

The Order Police could not be dispensed with in killing operations themselves. A police battalion (the 9th in 1941 and the 3rd in 1942) was divided among the four *Einsatzgruppen* of the Security Police that followed the German armies into the USSR to shoot Jews and Communists.[23] Two Order Police detachments in Kiev assisted Einsatzkommando 4a of *Einsatzgruppe* c in the massacre of Babi Yar.[24] An Order Police contingent was similarly engaged in herding Jews to shooting sites near Riga.[25] A Lithuanian Schuma battalion was stationed in Majdanek,[26] and German Order Police from Łódź were transferred to the death camp at Chełmno (Kulmhof).[27] Often, officers of the Order Police were all but in charge of the killings. During the summer of 1942, when an attempt was made to annihilate the Jews in each of several dozen rural *Gebiete* of the occupied USSR, the local *Gendarmerieführer*, deploying his Germans and native helpers, would surround a small-town ghetto with guards standing approximately twenty meters apart, round up the Jews inside, and supervise the shootings in ditches nearby.[28] To the west of the USSR, in the improvised killing centers of the General Government, Order Police personnel with previous experience in "euthanasia operations" were serving not only as guards, but also as commanders. Such was the career of Franz Stangl, commander of Sobibór and, thereafter, Treblinka.[29]

To be sure, neither the railroads nor the Order Police fit any preconceived notion of an ideological vanguard. For that very reason, however, their heavy participation in relentless acts of mass destruction should engage our attention. If nothing else, this history should tell us that if an Adolf Hitler and his Nazi movement of party offices and SS formations were essential for the destruction of the Jews, so was, at least in equal measure, the readiness—in the fullest sense of the word—of ordinary agencies to engage in the extraordinary tasks inherent in the Final Solution.

Bureaucratic Preparedness

The all-encompassing readiness for action of the diverse machinery of public and private agencies is one of the key phenomena of the bureaucratic destruction process. It resulted, in the case of several professions, in complete reversals of time-honored roles. An obvious example is furnished by the physician who performed medical experiments in camps, or who, as public-health officials, urged the creation of hermetically sealed ghettos for the ostensible purpose of preventing the spread of typhus from Jewish inhabitants to the surrounding population, or who, as specialists in psychiatry, administered the euthanasia program, which was transformed in the *General Government* into a network of camps to kill approximately 1.5 million Polish Jews. Indeed, one of the euthanasia physicians, Dr. Irmfried Eberl, was the first commander of Treblinka.[30] A second illustration of such negation is the planning by offices in occupied Poland, labeled "Population and Welfare," of deportations of ghetto Jews to death camps.[31] Yet a third instance of goal transformation may be glimpsed in the efforts of civil engineers or architects to construct the ultimate antithesis of a shelter or home the concentration camp, especially the installations designed for controlled, efficient mass annihilation.[32]

What prompted such a sprawling bureaucratic machine to involve itself so profoundly in a single direction toward death and more death? There were, of course, leaders who gave orders, for this was, after all, the state that utilized the *Führerprinzip*, the leadership principle. Clearly, if orders had been disregarded or evaded, the destruction of the Jews could not have been carried out.[33] Scarcely less important, however, is the fact that the process could not have been brought to its conclusion if everyone would have had to wait for instructions. Nothing was so crucial as the requirement that the bureaucrat had to understand opportunities and "necessities," that he should act in accordance with perceived imperatives, and most especially so when it was not easy to enunciate them in plainly written words. The German historian Uwe Dietrich Adam has shown that, even before the war, there was a pronounced tendency to dispense with laws and other formal enactments. Laws (*Gesetze*) in particular were to be held to a minimum. "Implementary decrees" no longer carried into effect the laws to which they referred and, like the 11th Ordinance to the Reich Citizenship Law that dealt with confiscations, contained entirely new subject matter.[34] Decree-making gave way to government by announcement, as in the case of a Himmler order of December 1938 to deprive Jews of their driver's licenses that was published in newspapers directly without first appearing in the appropriate legal gazette.[35] This administrative evolution continued with more and more reliance on internal directives, first written, then oral. An order by Hitler to annihilate European Jewry was almost certainly given only in oral form.[36] In the final phases, not even orders were needed. Everyone knew what had to be done, and no one was in doubt about directions or goals.

The bureaucracy itself was the source of much that was to transpire. Ideas and initiatives were developed by experts in its ranks. They were submitted as proposals to supervisors and returned as authorizations to their originators. The foremost example is the famous Göring directive at the end of July 1941 charging Heydrich with organizing the "final solution of the Jewish question" in Europe.[37] It was drafted by Eichmann at the request of Heydrich and presented to Göring ready for signature (*unterschriftsfertig*).[38] Every word, including an opening reference to an earlier directive for expediting Jewish emigration, was carefully chosen. The substantive paragraph, with its euphemism about a "final solution," was designed to assure the necessary backing for maximum freedom of action.

Not surprisingly, a constant reliance on bureaucratic initiation eventually brought about the existence of experts accustomed to dealing with Jewish matters in particular. Many agencies had one or more of these specialists: Bernhard Lösener and Hans Globke in the Ministry of the Interior, Walter Maedel in the Ministry of Finance, Franz Rademacher in the Foreign Office, Erhard Wetzel in the Ministry for the Occupied Eastern Territories, Otto Stange in the Reichsbahn, and Adolf Eichmann in the Security Police. This kind of specialization also emerged in the field. The organization chart of the Finance Office of the Reichskommissar in the Ostland shows an official assigned to Jewish property.[39]

Occasionally, there were enthusiasts who were not constantly preoccupied with Jewish matters in the normal course of their activities, but who would not relinquish an opportunity to go out of their way to leave their imprint on the annihilation process. One of these men was the army's Major General Otto Kohl who, until 15 June 1942 was in charge of transport, civilian and military, in the occupied zone of France.[40] On 13 May 1942, he met for an hour and a half with an SS captain, the deportation specialist Theodor Dannecker to assure him: "When you tell me 'I want to transport 10,000 or 20,000 Jews from France to the East,' you can count on me to provide the necessary rolling stock and locomotives." Kohl explained that he regarded the rapid solution of the Jewish question in France a vital necessity for the army of occupation, and therefore he would always maintain a radical point of view, even if some people might regard him as "raw."[41] Most participants, however, were aware of the fine line between volunteering one's services, as Kohl had done, and acting, when the time came, in the full use of one's office. Although they avoided an appearance of rawness or reality, they did not have to be goaded to destroy human lives.

Viewing the makeup of the administrative machine as a whole, we must conclude that there was very little prodding or purging of the German bureaucracy. The Reichsbahn or the Order Police could hardly have been pressured in any case. No one but a railroad man could dispatch a train, and no one but the Schutzpolizei and the Gendarmerie could provide police garrisons in the farthest corners of Europe. Within the entire system, internal directives were, if anything, few and sparse. The fact is that the initiators, formulators, and expediters, who at critical junctures moved the bureaucratic machine from one point to the next, came from within that apparatus. Overburdened as they often were, they contributed their share to the destruction of the Jews as a matter of course.

The Preservation of Procedures

Even as the bureaucracy of annihilation consisted in large part of regular personnel in well-established agencies, so the methods of destruction were to a great extent the traditional means of administrative action. Normal procedures were employed also in abnormal situations, as if extreme decisions were not being made, and there were no discernible differences between everyday government functions and the Final Solution.

Let us take the example of setting up a concentration camp. When Auschwitz was being expanded, condemnation proceedings were launched to acquire public and private property with a view to bringing about land transfers,[42] and when barracks were being built and cyanide gas was being procured, the acquisition of materials was subject to the allocation mechanisms of Speer's Ministry for Armaments.[43]

The routines were being followed with even greater perseverance in financial matters. Fiscal integrity was not to be impaired in the destruction process. Heinrich Himmler himself once had to consider the case of an SS lieutenant who in a previous role as a "trustee" of real estate had been obliged to manage the property for the benefit of the Reich until it could be sold to a new owner but who had "prematurely" terminated leases of Jewish tenants with resulting losses of rent. Had the officer violated his fiduciary responsibility?[44]

A larger quandary faced the German municipal officials of Warsaw after the sudden mass deportations of the ghetto's Jews had begun in July 1942. Utility bills for electricity and gas had not been paid, and how was this debt going to be covered?[45] A similar dilemma was generated for the chief of the Finance Division of the Generalkommissariat Latvia (Dr. [Willy] Neuendorff) who discovered that taxes owed by dead Jews could not be collected without transfer to his office of money realized from disposals of their confiscated property.[46]

One of the biggest problems was the financing of transport. The Reichsbahn derived its income from clients, that is, people, corporations, or agencies requiring space on its equipment for personal travel or for shipments of cargo. The client for a death train was the Gestapo and the travelers were Jews. The fare, payable by Gestapo offices, was calculated at the passenger rate, third-class, for the number of track kilometers, one-way only, with reductions for children. For guards, the round trip price was charged.[47] If at least four hundred Jews were deported, group rates were applicable.[48] Arrangements could be made directly or through the official travel bureau (*Mitteleuropäisches Reisebüro*).[49] The Gestapo, however, had no budget for transport and it would have been awkward to present a bill for the deportations to the Ministry of Finance. Accordingly, a policy of "self-financing" was instituted, whereby the funding burden was shifted to authorities in foreign areas where Jewish property had been expropriated or to Jewish communities themselves. In the satellite state of Slovakia, for example, the Foreign Office argued that the Slovak government should pay for the "resettlement," and that, in exchange, the Jews would not be returned.[50] In Germany, the Gestapo directed the official Jewish community organization, the Reichsvereinigung der Juden in Deutschland, to collect cash "contributions" from deportees at the point of their departure to help defray the costs of their future existence in the "east."[51] Such levies were deposited in special accounts "W," which the Gestapo could control. The Ministry of Finance, which discovered the stratagem, considered it an evasion of the basic principle that only the ministry could collect funds for the Reich and disburse them to agencies as needed, but it acquiesced in the practice.[52] Even more complex was the payment for transports leaving Holland or France, Italy or Greece, for Auschwitz. These trains passed not only through various countries, but also through several currency zones, and in this traversal the balance of payments had to be considered every time a border was crossed.[53] So costly and difficult were all of these funding requirements that at one point consideration was given to the possible erection of a death camp in western Germany for Jews from western countries.[54]

"Self-financing" was involved also for projects other than transport, such as the building of the Warsaw Ghetto wall. The chairman of the ghetto's Jewish council, Adam Czerniaków, protested to the German ghetto commissar against this burden on the community's treasury, arguing that, since the ghetto had been created for the stated purposes of protecting the non-Jewish population from the spread of epidemics, the assessment was tantamount to asking the pharmacist to pay the bill for the medicine.[55]

The legal procedures and accounting routines were the essential tools of a decentralized apparatus that was attempting to preserve non-Jewish rights at every turn and to balance the books at all times. By these means, the bureaucrat would satisfy himself that his actions were appropriate and proper. He could equate correctness with rightness and accuracy with accountability. The culmination of this way of thinking may be observed in the reporting system, particularly the regular flow of daily, monthly, or annual reports from regional or local offices. Just as there were no special agencies or extraordinary operating funds for the destruction of the Jews, so there was no separate reporting channel or segregated record-keeping in matters of annihilation.[56] Frequently, offices and units in the field would therefore make references to the Final Solution only in long summaries of diverse activities. Such reports, with their markings denoting authorship and distribution, followed a rigid format, maintained a single perspective, and were cast in a laconic, matter-of-fact style. Typical is a sentence from the war diary of the Armament Inspectorate in the Netherlands for November 1942: "The accelerated implementation of the de-Jewification action by the commander of the Security Police is being accompanied by unavoidable disturbances in fur and clothing enterprises under contract with the armed forces."[57] For many of these officials, the Jews became a subheading. We see it in rubrics: Wages—Jews, Rations—Jews, Taxes—Jews, Production—Jews. The Jews are absorbed in the daily passage of events, and there is seldom any disconcerting emphasis on their ultimate fate.

Even secrecy could be abandoned in record management. Railroad timetable orders were being dispatched without stamps calling attention to their sensitivity,[58] and in Riga a bureaucrat noted in 1942 that correspondence about the Jewish "estate" (*Nachlass*) in the Trusteeship Division of the German administration of Latvia was no longer classified for security purposes.[59] In a sense, nonlabeling became the ultimate camouflage.

The Perpetrator

What sort of man then was the perpetrator? The very structure and practices of the German bureaucracy should provide us with indications of his character. He valued his competence and efficiency to surmount innumerable obstacles and adverse conditions. He knew what to do without having to ask for directives. Political platforms and campaigns provide little specific content for bureaucratic action, and Nazi Germany was no different in this respect. The public utterances of leaders and propagandists, the flags, torches, and drums, all these were acts of psychological mobilization that gave theme, form, and pace to the physical measures that were to follow. The bureaucrat, however, was not a creation of the Nazi Party, nor was he an old-fashioned indoctrinated anti-Semite. Julius Streicher's *Stürmer* was not his literature. When the war ended, he would assert that he had never hated Jews, and in any nineteenth-century sense, he did not harbor such feelings in actual fact. He had stood above the small issues to face the larger challenge, though he would not talk in such terms any more than he would have written the word "kill" in an order or report.

Some observers have already recognized that the diffuse machine that destroyed the Jews was staffed by people who would not be recognized for what they were if one talked to them in a living room or some other quiet place. Their social mores were not atypical and their family life and personal concerns were completely commonplace. To one commentator this was "banality."* Another, noting the rote manner of bureaucratic action, may find that the most salient trait of German officialdom was a kind of stupefaction, a vast indifference to the nature and consequence of one's acts. Yet we must beware of veneers. There is nothing that appears banal in Eichmann and his many colleagues as soon as they are seen in their acts of destruction. Nor can we describe them as robots when we recall how they deliberated about definitions and classifications, gains and costs. To be sure, they left unsaid much that they thought, for they were breaking barriers and crossing thresholds in ways that bureaucrats seldom attempt. What they did was designed to make history and they were aware of their roles in this undertaking. In the basement of the Nuremberg Traffic Museum, secluded from the gaze of casual visitors, there is a railway map. It shows the network of lines under German control in 1942, the year of its greatest extent.

---

* Hilberg avoided calling the "commentator" by her name. It was his "rival" Hannah Arendt. On Hilberg's difficult relationship with Arendt, see his autobiography: *The Politics of Memory: The Journey of a Holocaust Historian* (Chicago 1996), 147–157.

Notes

1. These four hierarchical structures, and their roles as independently operating conglomerates, were first recognized by Franz Neumann, *Behemoth: The Structure and Practice of National Socialism, 1933–1944* 2nd ed. (New York, 1944), 467–70. The US prosecution at Nuremberg classified its evidentiary material under four headings: NG, NOKW, NO, and NI, corresponding to the four groups identified by Neumann.
2. Negotiations (by the Foreign Office and SS representatives attached to German embassies and legations) were conducted with Vichy France, Italy, Croatia, Slovakia, Bulgaria, Romania, and Hungary, not always successfully. For characteristic criticism of a Slovak law defining the term "Jew," see *Donauzeitung* (Belgrade), 10 December 1941, 3.
3. Dokumentationsdienst der DB, *Dokumentarische Enzyklopädie V—Eisenbahn und Eisenbahner zwischen 1941 und 1945* (Frankfurt am Main, 1973), 110.
4. Eugen Kreidler, *Die Eisenbahnen im Machtbereich der Achsenmächte während des Zweiten Weltkrieges* (Göttingen, 1975), 278–89.
5. Kreidler, *Eisenbahnen*, 205–6. Albert Speer, *Inside the Third Reich* (New York, 1970), 222–25. Prosecution at Düsseldorf to Landgericht Düsseldorf, 16 March 1970, transmitting indictment of Ganzenmüller, File No. 3 Js 430/67, in Zentrale Stelle der Landesjustizverwaltungen, Ludwigsburg, and in Landgericht Düsseldorf. Statement and answers to questions by Ganzenmüller, 7 October 1964, Case Ganzenmüller, vol. 5, 216–27.
6. See the annual *Verzeichnis der obersten Reichsbahnbeamten*, particularly for 1941 and 1943.
7. Statement by Franz Novak, 19 October 1966, Strafsache gegen Novak 1416/61, Landesgericht für Strafsachen Wien, vol. 16, 33.
8. See *Verzeichnis* and undated statement by Philipp Mangold, Verkehrsarchiv Nürnberg, collection Sarter, folder aa. Generalbetriebsleitung West was involved in processing transports from France, Belgium, and Holland. Leibbrand to West, Ost, Wehrmachtverkehrsdirektionen Paris and Brussels, Plenipotentiary in Utrecht, and Reichsbahndirektion Oppeln (arrival jurisdiction for Auschwitz), 23 June 1942, Case Ganzenmüller, vol. 4, pt. 3, 57.
9. Directives by Jacobi, 8 August 1942 and 16 January 1943, Institut für Zeitgeschichte, Munich, Fb 35/2, 217 and 206.
10. For example, Reichsbahndirektion Königsberg, timetable instruction no. 62, 13 July 1942, ibid., 260, and Generaldirektion der Ostbahn, timetable instruction no. 567, 26 March 1943, Zentrale Stelle Ludwigsburg, Polen 167, Film 6, 192–93.
11. Summary of Reich Main Security Office IV B 4 conference in Düsseldorf, under chairmanship of Eichmann, March 1942, Case Novak, vol. 17, 203–7.
12. Report by Lt. Col. Ferenczy (Hungarian gendarmerie), 9 July 1944, Case Novak, vol. 12, 427.
13. Reserve lieutenant of Schutzpolizei (Wessermann?) to Kommandeur of Ordnungspolizei for Galician district in Lwów, 14 September 1942, Zen-

trale Stelle Ludwigsburg, UdSSR, vol. 410; 508–10. About two hundred of the Jews were dead on arrival.
14. Affidavit by Walter Schellenberg (Security Police), 21 November 1945, Nuremberg document PS-3033. Kurt Daluege (chief of Order Police) to Karl Wolff (chief of Himmler's personal staff), 28 February 1943, Nuremberg document NO-2861. Daluege was the only Order Police general who began his career in the SS.
15. Daluege to Wolff, 28 February 1943, NO-2861.
16. Order Police strength report (*Stärkenachweis*) of Schuma for 1 July 1942, Bundesarchiv R 19/266. Firemen and auxiliaries not included in the figures. Year-end data given by Daluege to Wolff, 28 February 1943, NO-2861. By December, the Schuma (without firemen or auxiliaries) was well over 100,000.
17. Gendarmeriegebietsführer in Brest-Litovsk (Lt. Deuerlein) to Kommandeur of Gendarmerie in Lutsk, 6 October 1942. National Archives microfilm T 454, roll 102.
18. SS Sturmbannführer Zöpf to Judenlager Westerbork, 10 May 1943, Israel Police Eichmann trial document 590. Otto Bene to Foreign Office, 25 June 1943, NG-2631.
19. The 304th Battalion, replaced in 1941 by the 61st. Zentrale Stelle Ludwigsburg, Polen 365 d and e, passim.
20. Instructions by Captain Kompa, 22 June 1942, T 459, roll 21. The original force was larger. Instructions by Major of Schutzpolizei Quasbarth, 24 April 1942, T 459, roll 21. The men belonged to the 20th Latvian (Guard) Battalion.
21. The German battalion was set up in Berlin for this purpose. Schuma included the 4th, 7th, and 8th Lithuanian battalions, the 17th, 23rd, 27th, and 28th Latvian battalions. Hans-Joachim Neufeldt, Jürgen Huck, and Georg Tessin, *Zur Geschichte der Ordnungspolizei 1936–1945* (Koblenz, 1957), pt. II (by Tessin), 51–68, 101–9. Daluege to Wolff, 28 February 1943, NO-2861.
22. Order by Daluege, 24 October 1941, PS-3921.
23. Tessin, *Ordnungspolizei*, 97. Helmut Krausnick and Hans-Heinrich Wilhelm, *Die Truppe des Weltanschauungskrieges* (Stuttgart, 1981), 146–47.
24. Reich Main Security Office IV A 1 Operational Report USSR no. 101, 2 October 1941, NO-3137.
25. Text of Soviet interrogation of Friedrich Jeckeln (Higher SS and Police Leader in Ostland), 14 and 15 December 1945, Krausnick and Wilhelm, *Truppe*, 566–70.
26. Strength Report of Schutzmannschaft, 1 July 1942, R 19/266, and Friedrich-Wilhelm Kruger to Himmler, 7 July 1943, Himmler Files, folder no. 94, Library of Congress.
27. Adalbert Rückerl, *NS-Vernichtungslager* (Munich, 1977), 262–64.
28. Orchestration of the killings remained in the hands of the Security Police, whose representatives would usually appear on the local scene a few days before an operation. See Deuerlein report, 6 October 1942, T 454, roll 102. Also, statement by Zeev Sheinwald (survivor of Luboml, Ukraine), Yad Vashem Oral History document O-3/2947.

29. Stangl's life was reconstructed in detail by Gitta Sereny, *Into that Darkness* (New York, 1974).
30. On Eberl, see Sereny, *Darkness*, 77, 85, 86, and 160, and Lothar Gruchmann, "Euthanasie und Justiz in Dritten Reich," *Vierteljahrshefte für Zeitgeschichte* 20, no. 3 (1972): 250.
31. See, for example, report by Richard Türk (Population and Welfare Division, Lublin District) for March 1942, Jüdisches Historisches Institute Warschau, *Faschismus-Getto-Massenmord* (Berlin, 1960), 272–73.
32. Note the career of the architect Walter Dejaco. See Friedrich Brill, "Sie hatten nichts gewusst!" *Aufbau* 8, no. 5 (1942): 5. Dejaco was a body disposal expert in Auschwitz. Report by Untersturmführer Dejaco, 17 September 1942, NO-4467.
33. One of the most telling examples is the attitude of Italian officials and army officers. See Daniel Carpi, "The Rescue of Jews in the Italian Zone of Occupied Croatia," in *Rescue Attempts during the Holocaust: Proceedings of the Second Yad Vashem International Historical Conference, Jerusalem, 8–11 April 1974*, ed. Israel Gutman and Efraim Zuroff (Jerusalem, 1977), 465–525.
34. Uwe Dietrich Adam, *Judenpolitik im Dritten Reich* (Düsseldorf, 1972), esp. 108–13, 240–46, 292–302.
35. Order dated 5 December 1938, in *Völkischer Beobachter*, PS-2682. Also Adam, *Judenpolitik*, 213, 244.
36. The issuance of an oral order from Hitler to Himmler is reported by Eichmann in his autobiography, *Ich, Adolf Eichmann* (Leoni am Starnberger, 1980), 176–79, 229–31. See also affidavit by Albert Speer, 15 June 1977, facsimile in Arthur Suzman and Denis Diamond, *Six Million Did Die* (Johannesburg, 1977), 109–12.
37. Göring to Heydrich, 31 July 1941, PS-710.
38. Eichmann, *Ich*, 479.
39. Organization plan of Reichskommissar Ostland II (Finance), 17 August 1942, T 459, roll 2. His deputy was Bruns.
40. Hans Umbreit, *Der Militärbefehlshaber in Frankreich 1940–1942* (Boppard am Rhein, 1968), 243–44. On that date, the Reichsbahn took over civilian traffic. Directive of Transport Minister (Dorpmüller), 13 June 1942, in Kreidler, *Eisenbahnen*, 356–57.
41. Text in Serge Klarsfeld, ed., *Die Endlösung der Judenfrage in Frankreich Deutsche Dokumente 1941–1944* (Paris, 1977), 36–37.
42. Land transfer conferences, 3 November and 17–18 December 1942, under chairmanship of Oberfinanzpräsident Dr. Casdorf, PS-1643.
43. Speer to Himmler, 5 April 1943, Himmler Files, folder no. 67. On gas, see affidavit by Dr. Gerhard Peters, 16 October 1947, NI-9113, and testimony by Joachim Mrugowski, Nuremberg doctors case (*U.S. v. Brand*), transcript 5403–4.
44. Correspondence in T 175, roll 60.
45. Durrfeld (*Dezernat* 3 of German city administration in Warsaw) to SS and Police Leader von Sammern, 10 August 1942, and memorandum by Kunze

(*Dezernat* 4), 13 August 1942, Zentrale Stelle Ludwigsburg, Polen 365 d, 275–77.
46. Neuendorff to Generalkommissar/Trusteeship (Kunska), 4 June 1942, T 459, roll 21.
47. Deutsche Reichsbahn/Verkehrsamt, Łódź, to Gestapo in city, 19 May 1942, enclosing bill for twelve trains, facsimile in *Faschismus-Getto-Massenmord*, 280–81, and directive of Reichsverkehrsdirektion Minsk, 27 January 1943, Fb. 82/2, among others.
48. Paul Treibe (E 1) to Reichsbahndirektionen, copies to Generaldirektion der Ostbahn, Protectorate railways, and Mitteleuropäisches Reisebüro, 26 July 1941, Case Ganzenmüller, special vol. 4, pt. 3, 47–55.
49. Reichsbahndirektion Vienna (signed Dr. Bockhonn) to Slovak Transport Ministry, copies in house and to Dresden, Oppeln, and Mitteleuropäisches Reisebüro, 27 April 1942, Yad Vashem document M-5/18 (1).
50. Luther (Foreign Office/Division Germany) via Trade Political Division to Staatssekretär Weizsäcker, 29 January 1943, NG-5108. Ludin (German minister in Slovakia) to Foreign Office, 18 April 1942, NG-4404. Representative of Transport Ministry in Slovakia to Slovak Transport Ministry, 1 March 1945, M-5/18 (I).
51. Reichsvereinigung directive of 3 December 1941, Israel Police document 738.
52. Maedel to Mayer and Kallenbach (all in Finance Ministry), 14 December 1942, Bundesarchiv R 2/12222.
53. Rau (E 1/17) to High Command of the Army, 1 March 1944, and subsequent correspondence in Bundesarchiv R 2/14133.
54. SS Standartenführer Dr. Siegert (budget specialist in the Reich Main Security Office) to Finance Ministry, 17 August 1942, Bundesarchiv R 2/12158. The precipitating factor was the heavy transport cost from France to Auschwitz.
55. Entry by Czerniaków in his diary, 2 December 1941, in Raul Hilberg, Stanislaw Staron, and Josef Kermisz, eds., *The Warsaw Diary of Adam Czerniakow* (Briarcliff Manor, NY, 1979), 304.
56. In Eichmann's office there were ca. 200,000 open and 30,000–40,000 secret folders. He states that destruction of the records was ordered at the end of January 1945. Eichmann, *Ich*, 155, 449. On Stange's files, see statement by Reichsbahn specialist Karl Heim, 18 April 1969, Case Ganzenmüller, vol. 18, 98–103. By their very nature, such records were filled with Jewish affairs.
57. Armament Inspectorate Netherlands (Vizeadmiral Reimer), War Diary, summary for 1942, Wi/IA 5.1. German records located in Alexandria, Virginia, during postwar years.
58. Statement by Erich Richter, 11 June 1969, Case Ganzenmüller, vol. 19, 5–12. Interrogation of Walter Stier, 16 March 1963, Case Novak, vol. 16, 355 ff. Richter and Stier were Reichsbahn specialists in Krakow.
59. Notation by Kunska (Generalkommissar of Latvia/Trusteeship), 27 June 1942, on copy of directive from Reichskommissar's Trusteeship Office, 30 April 1942, T 459, roll 21.

Bibliography

Adam, Uwe Dietrich. *Judenpolitik im Dritten Reich*. Düsseldorf: Droste Verlag, 1972.

Brill, Friedrich. "Sie hatten nichts gewusst!" *Aufbau* 8, no. 5 (1942).

Carpi, Daniel. "The Rescue of Jews in the Italian Zone of Occupied Croatia." In *Rescue Attempts during the Holocaust: Proceedings of the Second Yad Vashem International Historical Conference, Jerusalem, 8–11 April 1974*, ed. Israel Gutman and Efraim Zuroff, 465–525. Jerusalem: Yad Vashem, 1977.

Dokumentationsdienst der DB. *Dokumentarische Enzyklopädie V—Eisenbahn und Eisenbahner zwischen 1941 und 1945*. Frankfurt am Main: Redactor Verlag, 1973.

Eichmann, Adolf, and Rudolf Aschenauer. *Ich, Adolf Eichmann*. Leoni am Starnberger: Druffel-Verlag, 1980.

Gruchmann, Lothar. "Euthanasie und Justiz in Dritten Reich." *Vierteljahrshefte für Zeitgeschichte* 20, no. 3 (1972): 235–79.

Hilberg, Raul, Stanislaw Staron, and Josef Kermisz, eds. *The Warsaw Diary of Adam Czerniaków*. Briarcliff Manor, NY: Stein & Day, 1979.

Jüdisches Historisches Institute Warschau. *Faschismus-Getto-Massenmord*. Berlin: Rutten & Loening, 1960.

Klarsfeld, Serge, ed. *Die Endlösung der Judenfrage in Frankreich. Deutsche Dokumente 1941–1944*. Paris: Centre de Documentation Juive Contemporaine, 1977.

Krausnick, Helmut, and Hans-Heinrich Wilhelm. *Die Truppe des Weltanschauungskrieges*. Stuttgart: Deutsche Verlagsanstalt, 1981.

Kreidler, Eugen. *Die Eisenbahnen im Machtbereich der Achsenmächte während des Zweiten Weltkrieges*. Göttingen: Musterschmidt Verlag, 1975.

Neufeldt, Hans-Joachim, Jürgen Huck, and Georg Tessin. *Zur Geschichte der Ordnungspolizei*. Koblenz: Breuer, 1957.

Neumann, Franz L. *Behemoth: The Structure and Practice of National Socialism, 1933–1944*. 2nd ed. New York: Oxford University Press, 1944.

Rückerl, Adalbert. *NS-Vernichtungslager*. Munich: Deutscher Taschenbuch Verlag, 1977.

Sereny, Gitta. *Into that Darkness*. New York: McGraw-Hill, 1974.

Speer, Albert. *Inside the Third Reich*. New York: Macmillan, 1970.

Suzman, Arthur, and Denis Diamond. *Six Million Did Die*. Johannesburg: South African Jewish Board of Deputies, 1977.

Umbreit, Hans. *Der Militärbefehlshaber in Frankreich 1940–1942*. Boppard am Rhein: Harald Boldt Verlag, 1968.

4

THE SIGNIFICANCE OF THE HOLOCAUST
(1980)

My topic is the significance of the Holocaust for Western civilization. This is quite an assignment. I know that many Holocaust researchers, compartmentalized in their own academic disciplines, have not been in touch with one another. Only in recent years have theorists turned to history and have asked themselves in more detail, "What happened?" By the same token, empiricists like me, who have always been concerned with concrete questions, are now becoming more contemplative as we address the larger issue of meaning. Still, it would be difficult, if not impossible, to spell out the import of the Holocaust in an evening. Perhaps it could be defined and even refined in that time, but the task would not be finished in a lifetime. Understanding of these matters comes slowly and sometimes not at all. Thus, I will try only to present an outline, one which, incidentally, I have never before attempted. Let us characterize this event in three ways. My approach may sound a little professorial, but it helps to reduce the awesomeness of the topic so that one may, in a certain sense, confront it.

The first consideration, and the foremost one, is the obvious—or perhaps not so obvious—fact that the Holocaust was irreducibly distinct from any other historical event or phenomenon. One cannot

---

Originally published in *The Holocaust: Ideology, Bureaucracy, and Genocide*, ed. Henry Friedlander and Sybil Milton (Millwood, NY: Kraus International Publications, 1980), 95–102.

explain it in terms of anything else. One cannot submerge it in the campaigns of World War II or in the aims of the Germans in that war. One cannot drown it in scapegoat theories of government. The Holocaust was *sui generis*. That is the reason it cannot be simply a part of a study of persecutions or dictatorships. It demands its own literature and its own sources. We must always remember that the Holocaust was pursued relentlessly by its perpetrators from 1933 to 1945, it had its own momentum, and it was pressed to its logical conclusion even after it had become evident during the battle of Stalingrad in January 1943 that the war would be lost. The destruction process was implemented regardless of its costs, not for any material gain and not for any military purpose. Even those Jews that may have been needed by the German war industry in a variety of sectors were killed. It becomes increasingly apparent from the sheer examination of the evidence itself that the destruction of the Jews of Europe was willed for itself and was accomplished for its own sake. That is the quality of the Holocaust that presents us with some of its most profound implications.

A second feature of the process is the circumstance that the Germans, embarking on ever more drastic measures against the Jews, were coming into conflict with fundamental prohibitions in law, mores, and morality. The confrontation with these rules was personal and immediate. Within the bureaucracy, the Holocaust became an increasingly sensitive topic. Rationalizations broke down. Notwithstanding the continuous bombardment of words accompanying the destruction of the Jews, the endless propaganda that was intensified even as more and more of the victims died, those of the perpetrators who were closest to the scene of action could no longer justify their actions—they had to repress them. They knew that they had now taken an unprecedented step that no other bureaucracy, and no other nation, had dared. They had moved beyond the limits; they had crossed the threshold, they were in forbidden territory. Never would they be able to justify what they had done.

We see the long-term consequences of this venture in the nature of relations visible to this very day which Western countries, not only the Jews, have with Germany. Once, before the end of World War II, there were men in the United States and Great Britain for whom the reports of what was transpiring in Axis Europe meant very little, for whom persecution of any kind meant very little, until they underwent the shock of seeing something with their own eyes in 1945. They saw the camps. The questions that were raised then have been perpetuated through the years within the United States and throughout the Western world.

Most intensive, however, are the effects of this massive transgression in Germany itself. I was there in 1976, and I found to my utter astonishment that men in the judiciary, in railroad offices, even in the customs administration, introduced themselves to me somewhat as follows: "My name is Schultze. I am thirty-eight years old." "My name is Krause. I was born in 1939." What a strange introduction. Such is the division in Germany between the generations. In some respects, it is deeper than the political division between East and West. It cuts across both of these entities. Yet, on occasion, a younger hand reaches toward the older perpetrator, a taboo is suddenly broken, and a weird concordance is established with the past.

Take a single example that I witnessed in 1976. I was the guest of the Central Administration of the German Provinces in Ludwigsburg, which investigates remaining war crimes. I was cordially received. I was shown documents that I wanted to see and I was given a very special treat. A forbidden film was being shown, a propaganda film going way back to the Hitlerite period, dealing with the theme of *Jud Süss*, a Jew who takes over Stuttgart in another age, exploits the German people, and is finally put to death. I watched this film, of which only two or three prints were alleged to remain. Very well. The office closed, as usual, at 4:00 or 4:30 p.m. I had nothing to do. I browsed in a bookstore, and I found a book, a paperback published by Suhrkamp, one of the major publishing houses. And here was a new play written by someone born after the war, about a Jew who in the middle of the 1970s takes over the city of Frankfurt and exploits it, while the Germans watch helplessly.* In the text there is a monologue that sounds like so very many that had been written in the past but with one line added: "They forgot to gas him." Thus the play by the German playwright Rainer Werner Fassbinder, since withdrawn from circulation, I understand, because of mounting criticism by the press.

We know, of course, that just as there has been a subtle forbearance by Western countries, and not only by Jews, in their dealings with Germany, there is also a very special relationship of all Western

---

* Rainer Werner Fassbinder, *Der Müll, die Stadt und der Tod. Stücke, Teil 3* (Frankfurt am Main: Suhrkamp, 1976). English Translation: *Garbage, the City and Death*, published in: Rainer Werner Fassbinder, *Plays* (New York: PAJ Publications, 1985).

nations, and not only Germany, with the Jews. It manifests itself in a variety of ways, including the difficult, and continuing existence of Israel, which is a post-Holocaust phenomenon par excellence.

The Holocaust is an irreducible phenomenon. It was a deed that sent shock waves, with long-term consequences, through our society. It was also, at the time of its occurrence, an unexpected event.

The first to be affected by that unexpectedness were the victims themselves. At the moment of extreme danger, they could not perceive impending disaster. They could not envision a Western civilization that would ever be capable of launching a "Final Solution." That is one of the reasons why, in the Jewish Councils all over Europe, nothing was done. Even as rumors of ominous developments began to multiply on the desks of the chairmen of Jewish Councils, they could not believe the country of Beethoven, the home of Goethe, to be capable of deliberate mass destruction. Thus in the summer of 1942, it was the turn of the Jews of Warsaw to be deported. The chairman of the Council of the Warsaw ghetto, Adam Czerniaków, left a diary, a daily series of entries of incomplete sentences from September 1939 to the moment that the deportation began. He recorded all the news, all the reports that reached him actually from Germans he was in contact with, that is, his own persecutors. The rumors multiplied during January, March, and April 1942. Finally, everyone within the ghetto was aware that something was going on, and at this point he went to the Gestapo and asked the crucial question: "Is it true?" "No." "Is there any basis for the rumors?" "No." He was not satisfied. He went to another official. "Is it true?" "I haven't heard anything." "Is it true?" he asked for a third time. "No." "Can I deny the rumors?" "Yes." He went about his business for another day or two. Then he swallowed the poison he had had in his drawer from the beginning. Some months later, the chairman of the Jewish community in Vienna, Dr. Josef Löwenherz, who presided over the deportation of some tens of thousands of people, also had to ask himself the inevitable question. He went to the office of the Gestapo in Vienna where he spoke to the Gestapo man Dr. Karl Ebner. Löwenherz wanted to see the chief of the Vienna Gestapo himself to verify the reports of the Jews being put to death. Ebner thought Löwenherz would have a "bad time" with the chief if he asked about such matters. The Jewish chairman was, however, admitted to the chief's office; then he was asked to wait outside while a phone call was made to the chief of the Gestapo in Berlin. Then the Vienna Gestapo chief denied the reports.

Two incidents; there were more. The leadership of the Jewish people in 1942 and 1943 would not believe the worst. Neither, by the way, did the Allied powers, despite the indications that were coming in, in some profusion, from occupied Europe. They kept checking, and in the final analysis not much was said and less was done during the most lethal hours of European Jewry. Remember, again, that the basic question was whether a Western nation, a civilized nation, could be capable of such a thing. And then, soon after 1945, we see the query turned around totally as one begins to ask: "Is there any Western nation that is *incapable* of it?"

The problem was verbalized by an attorney Edwin Sears in an article that appeared in two issues of the *Jewish Forum* in 1951. More than a decade later, the British writer Frederic Raphael inserted in his novel *Lindmann* a three-page fantasy of Jews being deported by a British bureaucracy from British cities. His depiction of the hypothetical event is particularly startling because the characters are British, their thoughts are British, and the mode in which they speak is—far from any German model—typically and completely British. Finally, I should mention the famous experiment at Yale University by Stanley Milgram who showed that people will, under the influence of authority, push buttons. Once I went to New Haven and, remembering that Milgram had drawn his experimental subjects from the city, asked several of my hosts: "Tell me, are you capable of it? Do you believe it could happen in New Haven?" One woman, who had just moved there from another state, said: "Not in our country, not anywhere in the United States, but perhaps it could happen in New Haven." Another, a Jewish dentist, told me: "Now here is something I want you to know. There was a participant in the experiment who refused to cooperate in it, and that man was a dentist."

In 1941, the Holocaust was not expected and that is the very reason for our subsequent anxieties. We no longer dare to exclude the unimaginable from our thoughts. Yet, our analytical powers to measure the destructive propensities in all of mankind are too meager for adequate prediction. Hence, our current assessments of possible danger are much less the product of systematic probing than a matter of personal disposition and feeling. To put it simply, if you believe that only Germans are capable of such mass destruction as we have seen between 1933 and 1945, you are an optimist. If you think that many nations have that potential, you are pessimistic indeed.

There is one conclusion we may draw from the past. A destruction process is not the work of a few mad minds. It cannot be accomplished by any handful of men. It is far too complex in its organizational build-up and far too pervasive in its administrative implementation to dispense with specialized bureaucrats in every segment of society. The perpetrators who were responsible for "The Final Solution of the Jewish Question in Europe" came from all parts of Germany and all walks of life. One should not assume that a man who may have been an essential individual in these destructive operations is instantaneously recognizable. Let me tell you a short story as a means of giving you a small illustration.

In my quest for railroad documents, I went to the headquarters of the German railways in Frankfurt on Main. After the usual bureaucratic encounters with various offices, I was directed to an annex building in the heart of the section of the city where pornographic materials are sold. That is where the documents center was. A center, incidentally, without documents. By the time I got there it was half-past-eleven in the morning. I stood in the hallway and two gentlemen came by. "What would you be interested in?" they asked. I said, "What I'm interested in is a bit of World War II history." "Ah," they said, "Military trains?" "No, civilian passenger traffic on special schedules." "Ah," said one of them, "Auschwitz! Treblinka!" Somewhat astonished by the quick recognition of what I was asking for from my sheer expression of interest in special trains, I asked him how he could know? And he said, "Oh, railroad people get around." He had seen ghettos. He had been to Katyn. He was the first one there when the grave, with all those Polish officers shot by the Soviets, was opened. I listened for ten minutes. Then the other one, who had been quiet, said, "Look. We're having an early lunch. Why don't you come with us to the commissary? If you eat by yourself it will cost you twelve mark, and with us it will cost you three." "That's very kind."

We came back to the office. He xeroxed cards of books he thought would interest me. He patiently explained to me why German railroad cars had four wheels rather than eight. It has to do with superior German metallurgy. He explained to me technical matters pertaining to how trains were routed through timetable zones. And then I chanced to ask him about a person named Geitmann, whom you would not have heard of even though he was, in the 1960s, a member of the four-man directorate running the *Bundesbahn*, the German railroads.

This man Geitmann was, during the war, a railroad director of Oppeln, which included the death camp of Auschwitz. Like so many of these railroad people, even like the German railroads themselves that never stopped running, he had made a magnificent career after the war. I said, "Well, what can you tell me about Geitmann, perchance?" My host, a rugged, tall man, around the age of sixty, said, "I know Geitmann." Interesting. "How? Where? When?" He said, "I was in the railroad directorate of Oppeln." We went on talking, this way and that. The hour was getting late, but he did not go home. He stayed with me. And then he said, "I have seen Auschwitz." I said to myself: Perhaps this is a German who made a pilgrimage after the war. Aloud I said, "Did you make a pilgrimage?" "Oh, no. I was there, then." "What did you do there?" "I put up the signal equipment." "Are you an engineer?" He said, "Yes." He wanted me to know. He had no need to tell me. I had walked in off the street. He knew who I was and what I was doing, though the word "Jews" was never mentioned. He told me, and I saw the perpetrator. Was he so very different from all the accountants, all the engineers, all the professionals who by reason of something that touched their jurisdiction were drawn into the destructive work? I am speaking not of volunteers but of men who at some point had to deal with the Jews because the matter was at the stage that required their attention, expertise, and efficiency. Amazing to me, after involving myself for thirty years in this research, is still the question: Why were they not inefficient?

When Milgram performed his experiment at Yale, his model comprised an authority figure and men who did as they were told. How accustomed we are to thinking in these terms about the administrative process in totalitarian systems. The reality, however, was much more complex. The bureaucracy that destroyed the European Jews was remarkably decentralized, and its most far-reaching actions were not always initiated at the top. Officials serving in middle or even lower positions of responsibility were producers of major ideas. Every once in a while, a particular set of recommendations would be approved by a superior and become a policy, authorization, or directive. Often enough, such was the genesis of an "order."

Consider a crass but not isolated illustration from the middle of 1941, at a time when the "Final Solution" was in the offing. A letter was dispatched by an SS major in Lodz to his comrade Eichmann about several hundred thousand Jews in the Lodz area. The major thought that during the following winter many Jews would be starving to death in their ghettos. He therefore suggested a quick working device to relieve the unproductive older men as well as women and children of their misery. We cannot determine the exact effect of that communication, but we know that within months "devices" in the form of gas vans were in operation near Lodz and elsewhere. By then, memoranda were hardly even necessary; there was no further need for words. Everyone, in every segment of the bureaucracy, knew what had to be done. Few were the dissenters, fewer the deserters.

You have all heard the saying that a bureaucrat is merely a cog in the wheel—it turns whenever the wheel is turning. As a political scientist, I have a different view: The bureaucrat *drives* the wheel—without him, it would not turn. And who were these drivers? They were, by and large, like the men in the railroads, trained representatives of a society, rather than its aberrants, deviants, or outcasts. Even Heinrich Himmler, Chief of the German SS and Police, may be said to have been typical of a particular class, place, and time. In a biography written by Bradley Smith,* we learn of his upbringing in a reasonably well-to-do family, his formative years with a governess, his childhood illnesses, and his education. Smith possessed a diary kept by the young Himmler from the time he was about twelve to the age of twenty-six. Himmler had his problems and frustrations, but he had not lost his senses or his ability to make calculated judgments. He was not demented. Now, wouldn't you be happier if I had been able to show you that all of these perpetrators were crazy?

They were educated men of their time. That is the crux of the question whenever we ponder the meaning of Western civilization after Auschwitz. Our evolution has outpaced our understanding; we can no longer assume that we have a full grasp of the workings of our social institutions, bureaucratic structures, or technology.

Should we wait for comprehension? Should we suspend our analysis until we have more documents, from more countries, of that period? Should we defer to another generation that may bring to the task its own new perspective? I do not think so. Those of us who have lived during the destruction of the Jews or who have first-hand knowledge of something that transpired at that time will read records with

---

* Bradley F. Smith, *Heinrich Himmler: A Nazi in the Making, 1900–1926* (Stanford, 1971).

a contemporaneous interpretation of their contents. We may identify nuances, allusions, references that may be puzzling to those who come after us. We can therefore make our special contribution to an understanding of this event because we were part of it.

5

INCOMPLETENESS IN HOLOCAUST HISTORIOGRAPHY
(2005)

No EMPIRICAL WORK OF HISTORIOGRAPHY is complete. The condition of incompleteness in such a literature is inherent in the sources themselves. An entire flow of events in all their complexity cannot be carried in the memory of witnesses. It cannot be stored with all of its attributes in remaining artifacts, and it is not replicated in all of its facets in contemporaneous records. All that has gone on in the world, which in theory is the whole of history, can be preserved only in fragments, and these leftovers constitute our material. The attempt to recapitulate anything at all is therefore an exercise that cannot be encompassing, no matter how large or small the subject of investigation may be. The effort will be a compromise between imagined perfection and something that can possibly be accomplished. Empirical historiography is by definition salvage. It cannot be more.

Historians are people who, for whatever reason, decide to pursue a project about the past. They employ resources with which they have to work as best they can. They may be different in their knowledge and intellectual capabilities, but empirical research demands its due. The

---

Originally published in *Gray Zones: Ambiguity and Compromise in the Holocaust and Its Aftermath*, ed. Jonathan Petropolous and John K. Roth (New York: Berghahn Books, 2005), 81–92.

researcher will inevitably traverse three phases. The first is a certain bewilderment as original sources are examined. Who took this photograph? What does it show? Who wrote this letter? To whom? What do the abbreviations mean? What is the content about? After a while—sometimes a long time—connections are seen, meaning is drawn from something that had been incomprehensible, insights are added to insights, and a picture emerges. The work continues in a quest for fulfillment—the elimination of errors, the closing of gaps, the clarification of conclusions. Then the researcher encounters the principle of diminishing returns. More and more searching is required for fewer and fewer results. Resources are exhausted, time limits are reached, inspiration is used up. A compromise is made: the work stops.

These two realities, the one embedded in a preordained impossibility, the other in the limitations of human beings, are well known to practitioners in any field of historical research, and in other disciplines as well. They are reiterated here, because nowadays the words "Holocaust" and "compromise" are usually not found in the same sentence. One should remember, however, that in the early years after the war, the Holocaust had no place in academic life, that it was not even acknowledged as a topic, and that special claims later had to be made for its importance.

The claims are not baseless. It has dawned on the Jewish community that the sudden loss of nearly a third of its numbers in the space of a few years ranked with the expulsions from Spain of 1492 and with the destruction of the Temple in Jerusalem of 70 C.E., that it was a catastrophe that was bound to have consequences in the life of Jewry for many generations. To Germans it gradually became clear that in the midst of all the havoc that the Nazi regime had wrought, the annihilation of European Jewry was a special act that defied understanding and that raised questions about the nature of a society in which such events could occur. This concern surfaced also in countries where governments or volunteers had collaborated with the Germans. And finally, wherever there was a tendency inside or outside postwar Europe to stand by and do little or nothing, the age-old query, "Am I my brother's keeper?" acquired new meaning as new threats arose to the stability of humanity in a shrinking world. Clearly, all these reflections had spawned or catalyzed a growing Holocaust literature, but they did not erase the compromises with which historians must wrestle. Holocaust research still entails the familiar problems of research, and writing about the Holocaust still requires the usual skills of writing.

The evolution of Holocaust historiography had its bare beginnings more than fifty years ago and it is far from finished. What has not been accomplished in the aggregate so far is attributable to two basic factors. One represents the researcher's inability to be more comprehensive, accurate, or descriptive. The other is a form of self-restraint in confrontation with sensitive subject matter. There is an element of insufficiency in the first case and of distancing in the second, but neither is always self-evident.

When an omission is involuntary, the reason may often be found in at least one of several circumstances. An entire segment of the facts may have been bypassed because the researcher could not recognize their relevance. A factual finding may be in disarray because a piece of the puzzle was not at hand. A skeletal picture may have been drawn because a close-up view was blocked. The following are a few illustrations of these difficulties.

Detecting particular aspects of the Holocaust, such as the background of the perpetrators or the connections of the Holocaust with other developments, has been remarkably slow. Even basics that may now be regarded as obvious had to be discovered, and each discovery was a change of a common impression. It is in the nature of things that these accomplishments do not tell us how many revelations are still in the offing. One can only assume that whatever none of us has observed so far, one of us may notice in the future. Here, then, are some advances of the past that serve as a reminder not to conclude at any time that nothing more has to be done.

At the very beginning references to the Holocaust were cloudy. The phenomenon had no name and could not be distinguished from hostility to Jews in prior centuries or from acts of contemporaneous aggression against other groups. The vocabulary generally used in discourse about the Jewish catastrophe was limited to such expressions as "anti-Semitism," "persecution," "atrocities," "Nazis," or "beasts." The words were limited and could not encompass what had happened. They were obsolete, because the German outburst could only be perceived in a fog. Its unprecedented character could not be grasped. Its actuality was unimaginable.

Consequently, many initial attempts at understanding were misguided shortcuts. The SS and the Gestapo were conspicuous, but in one of the Nuremberg trials it came as a surprise that the officers of the *Einsatzgruppen*, who were responsible for the deaths of hundreds of thousands by shooting, were not hooligans but lawyers or other professionals with academic degrees.[1] Again, the leadership of the ministerial bureaucracy in Vichy France, which drafted and signed many anti-Jewish decrees and at first was thought to be a throwback to the nineteenth century, turned out to contain a number of young technocrats who wanted to modernize the country.[2] The Romanian Iron Guard, viewed after the Bucharest revolt of 1941 only as a bunch of street battlers excelling in brutality, had, among others, poets and mystics in their midst.[3]

Nazi Germany as a whole was crudely described as a totalitarian regime, operating under the leadership principle and demanding blind obedience by automatons. Then Uwe Dietrich Adam showed how the system was developing without many new laws and how it was spewing out "implementation decrees" that did not necessarily implement the old laws.[4] Christopher Browning, in turn, found an incident that literally tested the presumption that absolute, uncompromising orders were indispensable. In the Polish town of Józefów, the commander of a newly deployed German police battalion had actually given his men a choice between shooting Jews or stepping aside. A sufficient number were ready to carry out the action.[5]

In the web of decision-making by all sorts of agencies, the Holocaust was a distinct undertaking, but one that was not unseparated from other concurrent operations. The links had to be uncovered, one by one, and that is an ongoing effort. Götz Aly, who is an exceptionally astute practitioner of this art, revealed the strands between the Holocaust and resettlement policies and between the Holocaust and the search for funds to finance the war.[6] Susanne Willems, following on this path, showed how the concentration and deportations of the Jews in Berlin were planned in conjunction with the housing program for the German capital.[7] Walter Manoschek and Ulrich Herbert observed a confluence of goals in military reprisals and the shooting of Jewish men.[8]

In the realm of studies exploring the Jewish communities, Isaiah Trunk's dissection of their reactions was a major step forward. Trunk discovered something that no one had looked for: a Jewish political culture so deeply rooted that it emerged in the closed-off ghettos of Eastern Europe, notwithstanding their geographic isolation from one another and the lack of direct contacts between them. Trunk did not write his massive work as a history of individual ghettos. He cut across all of them to deal with the way they approached problems of housing, labor, health, and other challenges. In that manner he demonstrated that atomized Jewry had a common mode of reacting to restrictions and danger. Trunk did not proclaim his conclusions, but they leap from his chapters. More than thirty years after his book was published, nothing of this scope about the ghetto Jews has yet appeared in print.[9]

Discernment cannot be programmed. One must wait for a researcher who can detect the characteristics of a phenomenon, or explore its environment, or draw its Gestalt. But what if someone is already pursuing a project and something goes wrong? We almost never have all the sources that we might like at our disposal, and sometimes a single missing document may generate a problem. If the historian believes that the item cannot be found or that it no longer exists, what then? Months, years, or decades may be spent in conjectures about its content. Indications may be gathered from other, albeit inconclusive materials, and in a compulsive attempt to complete the picture, something may be said to take the place of the elusive fact. A date may be offered, or the identity of a person—anything that one might wish to know. In lieu of certainty, assumptions will be inserted and extrapolations may be built on them, thereby compounding the author's vulnerability.

The following two cases are examples of what may happen. Both pertain to numbers. This selection is deliberate because the finding of an error in numerical manipulations is unambiguous. The first illustration deals with calculations of the Jewish death toll in Belzec, which was the destination of many transports of Jews from Polish cities and towns and did not receive non-Jewish deportees.

The Israeli historian Yitzhak Arad used a variety of estimates prepared in Poland and Israel to construct a table of deportations to the Belzec camp. The approximate figures pointed to an overall sum of somewhat more than 500,000, including some 280,000 from the Galician district alone. Arad also assumed that German Jews who had been deported first to the Lublin district and only then to Belzec were not counted in his sources. The Jews in small villages, he thought, had not been taken into account, either. Therefore, he believed that at least one hundred thousand people should be added to the list, bringing his total to six hundred thousand.[10] There was, in fact, no such dark area and his upward adjustments were in error. I myself did not make that particular mistake. I made a different one.

Shortly after I began my work in the late 1940s, I examined two documents. One was the report about the results of the "Final Solution," which covered deportations in Poland to the end of 1942, by the SS statistician Richard Korherr.[11] The other was a "Final Solution" report by the SS and police leader in the Galician district of the so-called *Generalgouvernement* of conquered Poland, Fritz Katzmann, dated 30 June 1943, about operations in his territory.[12]

In the Korherr report, I noted two figures:

"Dragged through" the camps of the
Generalgouvernement by 31 December 1942:   1,274,166

Remaining in the Galician district on
31 December 1942:   161,514

In the Katzmann report I noted:

Deported or killed in Galicia by 27 June 1943:   434,329

Remaining in labor camps within Galicia
on 27 June 1943:   21,156

My initial focus was on the number 1,274,166. I knew that three camps were definitely included in this total: Belzec, Sobibor, and Treblinka. I had also found out that gassing had ceased in Belzec on 8 December 1942, but I could not disaggregate the overall figure.[13]

Many years later, when I learned more about the flow of deportees to this camp complex, I surmised that the majority of the Belzec victims must have arrived from Galicia and that virtually all of the Galician deportees must have been sent to Belzec. By 1971, I computed a total of roughly 600,000 dead in the camp,[14] and by 1985, I scaled my estimate down to 550,000.[15] In pursuing the number, I had arranged the three other "Final Solution" figures reported by Korherr and Katzmann in the following manner:

Maximum number of Galician Jews killed in 1943:
    161,514 (alive 31 December 1942) − 21,156 (alive 17 June 1943)
    = 140,358

Maximum of Galician Jews killed in 1942 after the start of deportations:
    434,329 (total killed) − 140,358 (number for 1943) = 293,971

Maximum number of Galician Jews killed in Belzec:
    293,971 the number shot in 1942 = ?

At this point, however, I did not follow the subtractions to their logical conclusion, even though I might have obtained a reasonable approximation. My problem was the 140,348 who vanished between 31 December 1942 and 27 June 1943. Some were undoubtedly in hiding and others had succumbed to typhus and other diseases, but at least 130,000 must have been killed. I could not confirm the sparse witness testimony of Galician deportations to other camps in any German document, and I could not substantiate shootings of such a volume from the fragmentary records at my disposal. Therefore, I set aside Korherr's year-end figure of 161,154. It was not the product of a census, after all, and the local reports from which it must have been constructed were not at hand. Perhaps these reports were rounded, or late, or both. Only after the appearance in 1997 of a highly detailed monograph by Dieter Pohl, who visited archives in Galicia after they had been opened in the 1990s and whose knowledge of their holdings was greater than mine, did I realize that many of the 1943 shootings had escaped my notice. More ghettos than I had suspected were still in existence early in 1943, and several of the larger ones were thinned out more than once.[16]

The actual Belzec toll was revealed in 2001 by Peter Witte and Stephen Tyas. It was 434,508, and the German report containing this number had been unearthed only shortly before among radio intercepts that the British government had kept secret for more than fifty years.[17] I had overshot the mark by more than one hundred thousand.[18] Needless to say, when the breakdown of a sum is incorrect, more than one other constituent number will be wrong. In my case, there were two more: those for Treblinka and Lublin (Majdanek). My suppositions regarding the number of people killed at these facilities were too low. As to Majdanek, I had hesitated to include it as a *Generalgouvernement* (General Government) camp, because it was not under the same jurisdiction as Belzec, Sobibor, and Treblinka. The new document set matters straight also on this point. Majdanek's victims were to be included in part.

A more complicated anatomy of a faulty numerical compilation is exemplified by a table in a book by Israel Gutman about the ghetto of Warsaw.[19] Gutman states that the source of the table, which lists the number of Jews deported daily from the ghetto to Treblinka, is a 1951 issue of a bulletin published by the Jewish Historical Institute in Warsaw.[20] His heading for the table is "German Statistics of the Deportations." The data cover the dates from 22 July to 21 September

1942, and his total is 253,741. For 19 to 24 August, a single entry is a round twenty thousand with the notation "estimate"; for 26 August, a round three thousand (again an "estimate"); and for 11 September, a round five thousand, a third estimate. In addition, two intermissions are indicated as well.

What is unusual about this tabular enumeration is that it conflicts with another number that Gutman must have found in a report made by the SS and police leader of Warsaw, Jürgen Stroop, after the ghetto battle of 1943. There, Stroop states that 310,322 Jews had been deported in the summer of 1942.[21] Could the fact that the table used by Gutman was a detailed accounting, and the number by Stroop only a solitary sum, have been the reason for choosing the former and discarding the latter? His choice, whatever its basis, was fraught with multiple mishaps.

Gutman was evidently not aware that his figures were not German to begin with. They came from the Jewish Council in the ghetto. To the extent that his August numbers were precise, they coincided—except for incorrect copying of a few insignificant digits—with those of the council report for that month. Inasmuch, however, as he did not have that document, he was ignorant of a sentence in its text stating, "We have no statistic of those persons who volunteered to be resettled."[22] The "volunteers" were a large component of the total.

There is a second, partially countervailing complication. Whenever Gutman's table contains an approximation, it is a rounded multiple of the preceding exact figure. Thus, for 19 to 24 August, the twenty thousand are roughly five times the 3,926 for 18 August, and for 26 August, the three thousand are taken from the 3,002 for 25 August, but in the report of the council there are mere dashes beside the dates for which Gutman inserted his estimates. That forcible substitution is negated by entries in a ghetto diary by Abraham Lewin, which Gutman cited repeatedly in other contexts, and includes explicit statements to the effect that no transports left on 19 and 20 August as well as on other specific dates.[23]

Errors, like breakthroughs, are the acts of individual authors. They may be spread when they are copied. It should be stressed, however, that missteps of this sort are not altogether unusual, either in Holocaust historiography or the writing of history generally. They do not invalidate an entire work, unless they are the foundation of everything their creator had to say. When they do arise because a specific item of information was missing, overlooked, or misconstrued, knowledge is not impaired for all time and progress is not foreclosed.

The situation is different when the historian wishes to step closer to the scene of the action, to be inside its space. Most of the sources are essentially dry, not reaching the senses. Generally, they do not have the quality of something that is visible, audible, or palpable. Official correspondence in particular tends to be telescopic, purposeful, and problem-oriented. In such writing, mention may be made in a clinical manner of the psychological burdens carried by shooters, or comments could be added without elaboration to the effect that Jews were literally collapsing in the course of forced labor, but there is seldom more. Witnesses, especially Jewish victims, struggle with language to express what they saw. Consequently, neither Germans nor Jews will convey much about the atmosphere of the time. In this respect, the inadequacy of the sources is a common limitation affecting all historians in all fields, but the problem is more acute in attempts to deal with an event like the Holocaust, which is far removed from ordinary experience.

Although survivors have greater motivations than their tormentors to provide details about the impact of the blows inflicted on the Jewish community, the results are nevertheless meager. A former inmate of the Croatian camp network at Jasenovac, where many Jews, alongside Serbs and others, were held and killed, wrote about his observations at length. His account, however, is filled only with repetitious statements that Jews were "flogged," "killed," "gunned down," "killed behind the kitchen," "clubbed to death," "shot," "bayoneted," "hit," "murdered right then and there," and so on.[24] In the extensive survivor testimony, this kind of rendition is fairly typical.

Less ordinary is the commentary of Stanisław Adler, a lawyer who served as a police officer in the Warsaw ghetto, that is, its Jewish police. In his memoir he relates that toward the end of spring of 1941, when thousands of Warsaw Jews labored in water regulation and other outdoor projects, the returning workers were escorted by Polish police to the "Dulag" (*Durchgangslager*, or transit camp), a spacious school building outside the ghetto boundaries at 109 Leszno Street. Many who were dying or ill with infections rested there, segregated from the others, on bare stone or cement floors. Adler heard their testimony uttered in "monotone." He does not attempt to repeat exactly what they said. We are shown only shadowy figures in tattered clothes. He wonders "when, during their tortures" these people had time to work. He is "unable to explain by what miracle" some of them survived after having been chained and dragged on the ground for several kilometers. In short, we see the men in a mirror. The reflector is Adler, who tells us what he perceived and to what he reacted.[25]

In the testimony of a German policeman who participated in mass shootings, there are denials and hints that raise suspicions but leave little certainty. Yes, he stood *in* the ditch when the victims, lying down, were shot. No, he did *not* stand on bodies. Yes, he shot children but told the mothers to hold a child tightly during the shooting. Yes, he smoked during these actions, but there was no alcohol. And no, he did *not* eat at the site. Eating would have been impossible because of the odor. Then he described what kind of odor it was.[26]

Infrequently, a shimmering sentence in a report evokes presence. "Barley soup with chunks of beef was served," a captain of the Order Police, who had accompanied a transport of Jews from Düsseldorf to Riga with a small detachment, noted in his report. He did not forget to praise the German Red Cross who fed his men when the train had halted after three days in Siaulai, Lithuania, during a wet and cold December night in 1941. The Jews, who had to manage with provisions they had brought with them, were allowed only water en route.[27]

Rare also is the description of food purchased in the Lodz ghetto in February 1944, after the Germans had decreed that during work hours no Jew would be allowed in the streets or an apartment. To obtain their weekly ration of two kilograms of bread, the workers, many of whom had not eaten during the previous day, hurled themselves after 5:00 p.m. at the distribution centers to avoid having to wait at the end of a line outside in the snow and in fear that a "shortfall" would leave them emptyhanded. They banged on the windows, shouted, and pressed against each other tightly, eyeing the loaves. The passage about this scene, which was written in the official Jewish Lodz ghetto chronicle for posterity, has remained unpublished.[28]

Through lengthy searches, it is possible to uncover other scattered images, but such descriptions cannot be manufactured by the historian. It is for this reason that novelists and film directors step in. To fill the gap they promise an imaginative reconstruction, but given the manifest difficulties it is often imaginary.

In sum, when we consider the inabilities of observers to recognize a pattern in a maze, or to steer around a missing link, or to penetrate the blackness surrounding the nucleus of an event, we surmise the existence of an elusiveness—a quality that is unreached and unachieved. Yet there are also questions that are consciously avoided. To this day, one topic that is noticeably underdeveloped touches on an issue of prime importance, and that is the story of how specific groups in the Jewish community, caught in the grip of destruction, reacted daily to restrictions and danger. What did coping look like? In their dilemma, what did lawyers do or illiterates? How were family relations preserved or transformed? What was the significance of age? What role did money play? What might have been the personal budget of working Jews in the Berlin of 1941, or the Saloniki of 1942, or the Theresienstadt ghetto of 1943? Information about such seemingly mundane matters in published essays and books is rather fragmentary or presented in outline form.[29]

One reason for this dearth is plainly the loss, in the course of ghetto clearing operations or the clearing of Jewish apartments, of the great bulk of Jewish records, including private diaries and letters, as well as correspondence and reports of Jewish councils. Another is the failure, especially during the initial postwar years, to question Jewish survivors in detail about conditions and occurrences that were antecedent to climactic moments. Ultimately, however, there is a persistent reluctance to approach the subject of interpersonal relations among the Jewish victims. The "No Trespassing" signs were placed at the boundaries of this topic by the researchers themselves. For some, the markers set up by the British army in Bergen-Belsen in April 1945, "Here Lie Buried 2,000 Bodies," "Here Lie Buried 2,500 Bodies," "Here Lie Buried 5,000 Bodies," were the final word. Nothing more could be said about these people, united and indistinguishable in death. Others, like Primo Levi, called upon everyone to heed the command not to make judgments. Who, after all, could step into the shoes of those victims? No one. For still others, the psychological limit had been reached. There were some things they did not want to know.

Still, when Primo Levi wrote about a "gray zone," he placed the problem on the agenda. Levi, the chemist and Auschwitz survivor, measured freedom of action and gradations of behavior. Moreover, he had to have symmetry between victims and perpetrators in his analytical commentary. Although he would not allow any merging of "prisoners" and "custodians," as he called them, he did not hesitate to attribute weaknesses to the former and to grant saving graces to the latter. He cites the case of two merchants, one who was the Jewish "Elder" of the Lodz ghetto, Chaim Rumkowski, the other the ghetto's German manager, Hans Biebow.[30] Both were ambitious and both had a vested interest in preserving the ghetto from deportations. Rumkowski even sacrificed children to maintain the ghetto as a manufacturing enterprise, and Biebow—with his staff of 198 employees—concerned himself with food rations, production, and ghetto exports until the last moment, that is, just before the transportation of the Lodz Jews to Auschwitz, when he told them in a duplicitous manner that they would be resettled for their safety from Allied bombs. Rumkowski perished in the camp and Biebow was executed after the war. Levi did not know the whole story of the strange symbiosis that paired the two men, but he understood that each played his role consistently. They may have been self-serving, but they pursued the same goal. In the end they failed, and that failure sealed also their personal fate.

Rumkowski has received considerable attention because he is commonly regarded as the most notorious ghetto leader. With few exceptions his counterparts in other places remain indistinct. They are described in the aggregate but seldom as individuals. Noteworthy is the fact that an extensive memoir by the last Slovak Jewish council chairman, Oscar Neumann, written in the spring of 1946 and published ten years later in the original German language, never appeared in English,[31] and that the diary of the French Jewish leader, Raymond-Raoul Lambert, published in France, is also unavailable in English translation.[32] We hardly have to remind ourselves that such firsthand accounts are not abundant.

The inhibition to study the invisible victims is even greater. Information about them is not completely unattainable, since it may be located, at least in the charts and tables of remaining Jewish council reports, as well as in other sources, but its implications have not been seriously addressed. Unanswered are principally those questions that hint at fissures and breakdowns in the Jewish community and that point to differential vulnerabilities of its component groups. These variations emerged during the earliest anti-Jewish constrictions and became more pronounced in the ensuing years. When, for example, only half of the Jewish school-aged children in France or Częstochowa received an education, which ones were selected and which were in the other half? When Jewish men were impressed for labor in Poland or

Romania, who had to work and who was exempt? When the number of calories consumed on average in a ghetto was such and such, which families were near or above that line and which fell to the bottom? Primo Levi raises this question briefly when he alludes to Auschwitz survivors as having eaten more than the usual camp ration.[33]

A handful of authors probed the lives of ordinary people at some depth. One was Stanisław Adler, who wrote his sophisticated memoir at the end of the war in Polish. He committed suicide in 1946 and a friend brought his manuscript to Israel. An English translation was published by Yad Vashem thirty-six years later, but the book was not distributed in the United States.[34] Another was the American sociologist John K. Dickinson, who spent several years in Germany during the 1950s, where he interviewed 172 persons about the life and death of a single unknown Jewish victim. He wrote a biography of this man, giving him a fictional name. The publication of the account in 1967 did not attract much public or academic interest.[35] In 2001, it was still one of a kind. Reissued that year by a small publisher who had edited the book thirty-four years earlier, but this time with an appendix identifying the place of the story and revealing the real names of the victims and witnesses, the monograph was largely ignored again.[36] The relative silence that greeted the insightful work of Adler and Dickinson is symptomatic of an extraordinarily low receptivity to issues at the core of the Jewish catastrophe and of an unmistakable psychological unpreparedness to examine them.

We have always known that the progress of research depends, in the first instance, on accessibility of source materials. What we did not readily admit to ourselves for several decades is that even sizable stockpiles of records in wide-open archives do not guarantee any substantial growth of interest. We have had to learn the hard way that advances of knowledge are not automatic. They become possible when someone steps out of a habitual framework of thought to recognize complications or connections not seen before, or when fortuitously a missing fact is found, or when patient sifting through large collections of records allows glances at life as it was lived. All this is part of a process that may span several generations of researchers. The sheer passage of time governs also the slow disintegration of inhibitions that have blocked questions and answers with respect to the behavior of victims in extreme situations. But the reticence that persists will be overcome, and the ambiguities that it produced will disappear.

Notes

1. See the opening paragraphs, listing the academic and professional qualifications of the accused, in the sentencing portions of the judgment rendered in *United States v. Ohlendorf* (the *Einsatzgruppen* case), in Nuremberg Military Tribunals, *Trials of War Criminals* (Washington, DC: U.S. Government Printing Office, 1946–49), vol. 4, 510–96.
2. See Jean-Pierre Azéma, *From Munich to Liberation, 1938–1944* (New York, 1984), 56.
3. Radu Ioanid, *The Sword of the Archangel: Fascist Ideology in Romania*, trans. Peter Heinegg (Boulder, CO, 1990).
4. Uwe Dietrich Adam, *Judenpolitik im Dritten Reich* (Düsseldorf, 1972).
5. Christopher Browning, *Ordinary Men: Reserve Police Battalion 101 and the Final Solution in Poland* (New York, 1992).
6. Götz Aly, *Endlösung: Völkerverschiebung und der Mord an den Europäischen Juden* (Frankfurt am Main, 1995), [and *Hitler's Beneficiaries: Plunder, Racial War, and the Nazi Welfare State* (New York, 2005).]
7. Susanne Willems, *Der entsiedelte Jude: Albert Speer's Wohnungsmarktpolitik für den Berliner Hauptstadtbau* (Berlin, 2002).
8. Walter Manoschek, *"Serbien ist judenfrei": Militärische Besatzungspolitik und Judenvernichtung in Serbien 1941/42* (Munich, 1993); Ulrich Herbert, "Die deutsche Militärverwaltung in Paris und die Deportation der französische Juden," in *Von der Aufgabe der Freiheit*, ed. Christian Jansen, Lutz Niethammer, and Bernd Weisbrod (Berlin, 1995), 439–40, 447.
9. Isaiah Trunk, *Judenrat: The Jewish Councils in Eastern Europe under Nazi Occupation* (New York, 1972).
10. Yitzhak Arad, *Bełżec, Sobibor, Treblinka: The Operation Reinhard Death Camps* (Bloomington, IN, 1987), 126–27, 383–89. Arad also referred to a German court judgment setting forth six hundred thousand. The number appears in a Polish handbook as well. See Główna Komisja Badania Zbrodni Hitlerowskich w Polsce and Czeslaw Pilichowski, *Obozy hitlerowskie na ziemiach polskich 1939–1945* (Warsaw, 1979), 293–94.
11. Korherr to Himmler [27 March 1943], Nuremberg trials document NO-5194.
12. Katzmann to Higher SS and Police Leader Friedrich Krüger, 30 June 1943, Nuremberg trials document L-18.
13. I listed only "hundreds of thousands" for each camp. Raul Hilberg, *The Destruction of the European Jews* (Chicago, 1961), 572.
14. Raul Hilberg, ed., *Documents of Destruction: Germany and Jewry, 1933–1945* (Chicago, 1971), 206.
15. Hilberg, *The Destruction of the European Jews*, 2nd ed. (New York: Holmes & Meier, 1985), 893, 1219.
16. See Dieter Pohl, *Nationalsozialistische Judenverfolgung in Ostgalizien 1941–1944* (Munich, 1997), 245–65.
17. Peter Witte and Stephen Tyas, "A New Document on the Deportation and Murder of Jews During 'Einsatz Reinhardt' 1942," *Holocaust and Genocide Studies* 15, no. 3 (2001): 468–86. The item was a radiogram by an SS officer,

Hermann Höfle, who was stationed in Lublin, to another SS officer, Franz Heim, in Krakow, 11 January 1943, decoded by the British Code and Cypher School. "Reinhardt" was the German code name for the operation that eventuated in 1,274,166 Jews dead by the end of 1942. The figure in the radiogram was the same as Korherr's.

18. I corrected the error in the third edition of *The Destruction of the European Jews* (New Haven, CT: Yale University Press, 2003), 958, 1320.
19. Israel Gutman, *The Jews of Warsaw, 1939–1943* (Bloomington, IN, 1982), 212–13.
20. Żydowski Instytut Historyczny (Varsovie), *Biuletyn Żydowskiego Instytutu Historycznego* 1 (1951), 81, 86, 90, as cited by Gutman with his table.
21. Stroop to Higher SS and Police Leader Krüger, 16 May 1943, Nuremberg trials document PS-1061.
22. Chairman of the Jewish Council in Warsaw, Marek Lichtenbaum, to the German Kommissar of the ghetto, Heinz Auerswald, 5 September 1943, Zentrale Stelle der Landesjustizverwaltungen in Ludwigsburg, Akten Auerswald, Red Series 365e.
23. For an English-language translation of the diary, see Abraham Lewin, *A Cup of Tears: A Diary of the Warsaw Ghetto* (Oxford, 1989), 160–62. Gutman's error also had reverberations. Thus, his underestimate of the deportations is coupled with his corresponding failure to gauge the actual size of the ghetto population just before their start. That figure must have been over 380,000 rather than his 350,000. See the census count (397,016) for 1 March 1942 in a report by *Regierungsdirektor* Curt Hoffmann (Labor Office, Warsaw District), 12 June 1942, Zentrale Stelle in Ludwigsburg, Red Series 365d. Gutman did not have that statistic, either.
24. Duro Schwarz, "The Jasenovac Death Camps," *Yad Vashem Studies* 25 (1996): 383–430.
25. Stanisław Adler, *In the Warsaw Ghetto, 1940–1943* (Jerusalem: Yad Vashem, 1982), 211–12.
26. Excerpts from the testimony by Adolf Petsch, a member of the Security Police in the area of Pinsk-Stolin who participated in massacres during 1942 at Janov, in the indictment of the prosecutor at the Landgericht Frankfurt am Main, 4 Js 901/62, dated 28 March 1968, 64–66.
27. Report by Captain Paul Salliter, covering 11–17 December 1941, in Hans G. Adler, *Der verwaltete Mensch* (Tübingen, 1975), 462.
28. Typescript of the entry of 26 February 1944, with the initials of Alice de Bunom. Courtesy of Lucjan Dobroszycki.
29. See, for example, the fragmentary description of conditions affecting Parisian Jewry by Renée Poznanski, *Jews in France during World War II* (Hanover, NH, 2001), 327–32.
30. Primo Levi, *The Drowned and the Saved*, trans. Raymond Rosenthal (New York, 1988), 60–69.
31. Oscar Neumann, *Im Schatten des Todes: Vom Schicksalskampf des slowakischen Judentums* (Tel Aviv, 1956). The book has three hundred tightly printed pages.
32. Raymond-Raoul Lambert, *Carnet d'un témoin* (Paris, 1985).

33. Levi, *The Drowned and the Saved*, 41.
34. Adler, *Warsaw Ghetto*.
35. John K. Dickinson, *German & Jew: The Life and Death of Sigmund Stein* (Chicago, 1967). "Stein" is a pseudonym. The publisher, Quadrangle Books, is now extinct.
36. The publisher was Ivan R. Dee, the editor of Quadrangle Books in the 1960s.

Bibliography

Adam, Uwe Dietrich. *Judenpolitik im Dritten Reich*. Düsseldorf: Droste Verlag, 1972.
Adler, Hans G. *Der verwaltete Mensch*. Tübingen: Mohr, 1975.
Aly, Götz. *Endlösung: Völkerverschiebung und der Mord an den Europäischen Juden*. Frankfurt am Main: S. Fischer, 1995.
Arad, Yitzhak. *Belzec, Sobibor, Treblinka: The Operation Reinhard Death Camps*. Bloomington: Indiana University Press, 1987.
Azéma, Jean-Pierre. *From Munich to Liberation, 1938–1944*. New York: Cambridge University Press, 1984.
Browning, Christopher. *Ordinary Men: Reserve Police Battalion 101 and the Final Solution in Poland*. New York: Harper Perennial, 1994.
Dickinson, John K. *German & Jew: The Life and Death of Sigmund Stein*. Chicago: Quadrangle Books, 1967.
Gutman, Israel. *The Jews of Warsaw, 1939–1943*. Bloomington: Indiana University Press, 1982.
Herbert, Ulrich. "Die deutsche Militärverwaltung in Paris und die Deportation der französische Juden." In *Von der Aufgabe der Freiheit*, ed. Christian Jansen, Lutz Niethammer, and Bernd Weisbrod, 427–50. Berlin: Akademie Verlag, 1995.
Hilberg, Raul. *The Destruction of the European Jews*. Chicago: Quadrangle Books, 1961.
———, *The Destruction of the European Jews*. 2nd ed. New York: Holmes & Meier, 1985.
———, ed. *Documents of Destruction: Germany and Jewry, 1933–1945*. Chicago: Quadrangle Books, 1971.
Ioanid, Radu. *The Sword of the Archangel: Fascist Ideology in Romania*, trans. Peter Heinegg. Boulder, CO: East European Monographs, 1990.
Lambert, Raymond-Raoul. *Carnet d'un témoin*. Paris: Fayard, 1985.
Levi, Primo. *The Drowned and the Saved*, trans. Raymond Rosenthal. New York: Vintage International, 1988.
Lewin, Abraham. *A Cup of Tears: Diary of the Warsaw Ghetto*. Oxford: Oxford University Press, 1989.
Manoschek, Walter. *"Serbien ist judenfrei": Militärische Besatzungspolitik und Judenvernichtung in Serbien 1941/42*. Munich: R. Oldenbourg, 1993.

Neumann, Oscar. *Im Schatten des Todes: Vom Schicksalskampf des slowakischen Judentums*. Tel Aviv: Edition Olamenu, 1956.

Pohl, Dieter. *Nationalsozialistische Judenverfolgung in Ostgalizien 1941–1944*. Munich: R. Oldenbourg, 1997.

Polsce, Główna Komisja Badania Zbrodni Hitlerowskich w, and Czeslaw Pilichowski. *Obozy hitlerowskie na ziemiach polskich 1939–1945*. Warsaw: Panst Wydaw Naukowe, 1979.

Poznanski, Renée. *Jews in France during World War II*. Hanover, NH: University Press of New England, 2001.

Schwarz, Duro. "The Jasenovac Death Camps." *Yad Vashem Studies* 25 (1996): 383–430.

Trunk, Isaiah. *Judenrat: The Jewish Councils in Eastern Europe under Nazi Occupation*. New York: Macmillan, 1972.

Willems, Susanne. *Der entsiedelte Jude: Albert Speer's Wohnungsmarktpolitik für den Berliner Hauptstadtbau*. Berlin: Edition Hentrich, 2002.

Witte, Peter, and Stephen Tyas. "A New Document on the Deportation and Murder of Jews During 'Einsatz Reinhardt' 1942." *Holocaust and Genocide Studies* 15, no. 3 (2001): 468–86.

Żydowski Instytut Historyczny (Varsovie). *Biuletyn Zydowskiego Instytutu Historycznego* 1 (1951).

II

CONTROVERSIES AND DEBATES

6

BITBURG AS SYMBOL
(1986)

FOUR DECADES AFTER THE END of World War II, the people of West Germany were thriving with comforts and luxuries, but their lives had no luster. At one time, a German politician looked at the youth of his country and said:

> Our youth, primarily, but also all the others among us, do not have it as good as other peoples. Our country has nothing that glitters. Probably a long time will pass before anything in this state will glitter. That is rooted in the war; it is rooted in the "Thousand Years" and many other things besides, but that is the way it is, and it is very difficult for a people to live satisfied merely with itself and its ordered way of life in the grey of everyday, and that which in the American Declaration of Independence is called "pursuit of happiness." All this is necessary, but it is not enough by itself. One cannot live solely with prosperity and the attainment of an ever-rising standard of living. It is important and necessary that one reaches it, but in addition a human being needs something else, something to look up to. Since that does not happen here, this people is restless.[1]

The Federal Republic has rebuilt its cities and its political parties. Its new architecture lacks the massiveness that was the style before

---

Originally published in *Bitburg in Moral and Political Perspectives*, ed. Geoffrey Hartman (Bloomington: Indiana University Press, 1986), 15–26.

1945. Neither graceful nor imposing, these unostentatious structures have the appearance of pure functionalism. The government of the Federal Republic has been fashioned in the same way. Colorless and undramatic, it veers toward the center of any conceivable political spectrum. Characteristically, a public opinion poll in March 1985 revealed that on a scale of +5 to −5, ten prominent individuals in Germany's political leadership, including men in power as well as those in opposition, were bunched in the middle from +1.2 to -0.3.[2] Germany is no longer a country of political oratory. The German language is filled with English or anglicized expressions, particularly in advertisements. The German armed forces are allocated in their entirety to the overall defense of the North Atlantic Community. Germany has become a "good citizen."

The Federal Republic is [i.e., 1986] densely populated with more than sixty million people inhabiting territory that is almost exactly half the size of Germany's area in 1937. Its economic power is still concentrated in its manufacturing industry, much of it where it always was, in the Rhineland. From its expanding gross national product, West Germany set aside sums of money for reparations to Israel and for indemnification of refugees and survivors. These payments are the material "amends" for the physical annihilation of a third of all the Jews in the world. There is also a diplomatic and commercial relationship with Israel, which was begun with much uneasiness, but which has been continued with sizable exchanges of goods and a considerable annual flow of German tourists to the Holy Land.

Of course, postwar German society has not been totally divorced from the Nazi era. The first chancellor, Konrad Adenauer, for all his stature and authority, could not overshadow the phalanx of former anti-Jewish perpetrators who found employment in high positions of his administration. It has taken many years for all of these people in the ministries, the railroads, the diplomatic corps, and the military to pass from the scene. By 1985, however, a younger generation, headed by Chancellor Helmut Kohl, was definitely at the helm. In Germany, the new regime is sometimes called the government of flak helpers. Flak is the acronym for *Flugabwehrkanonen*, or anti-aircraft guns, and the helpers were adolescents near the end of World War II, too young for frontline service, but old enough to haul ammunition to anti-aircraft crews shooting at Allied bombers. For Kohl, age is an important part of his credentials. As he viewed the date on his birth certificate, he felt that he had been given a special mission. For forty years,

Germany had lived in psychological isolation, and 1985 was the year in which he was going to lead the German people out of the desert.

When Western leaders met in 1984, they celebrated the anniversary of the landings in Normandy without Kohl. Deeply stung, Kohl received small consolation from a ceremony with French President François Mitterrand at a Verdun cemetery of World War I. For the Germans of the 1980s, the resurrection of 1914–18 was not the right commemoration, and the holding of hands by the two men at Verdun lent itself to caricature. Kohl needed a more powerful presence, on German soil, at a place symbolizing the *Second* World War. The man to be invited for this purpose was the genuine head of the Western world, the president of the United States, and the site of his visit was to be a typical German military cemetery near the town of Bitburg. About two thousand fallen soldiers of the Third Reich lay buried there. Interspersed among these graves were those of forty-seven or so SS men.

The forty years since 1945 have been much shorter for the Jews. Benumbed by the unprecedented blow of Nazi Germany, Jewry had been living in a make-believe world of its own. The American Jews in particular were slow to recognize the enormity of the loss in Europe. For several decades they were still preoccupied with the final stages of their emancipation as Americans with full political, social, and economic rights. At the same time, they were galvanized by the creation and wars of Israel. Although they knew that the drive for equality and the rise of Israel had been catalyzed by the catastrophe in Europe, they did not gaze back at this cauldron and they made no organized effort to recapture the memory of the European Jewish community.

Memorialization as a concerted undertaking is a fairly recent phenomenon that began in the mid-1970s and reached its peak only a few years ago. "Holocaust"—the word itself—is relatively new. A pivotal role in this awakening has been played by survivors.

As a group, survivors are not a random sample of prewar European Jewry. The nature of ghettos and camps was such that small children as well as elderly men and women died first, and anyone incapable of labor or prone to disease was eventually doomed. The "luck" of survival, of which so much is said in memoirs, was thus not simply the consequence of sheer accident. The survivor was a person with special occupational skills, or with exceptional physical stamina, or with an ability to make rapid, logical decisions in moments of crisis. More than a few of these individuals were in their teens or early twenties in

1945, and today they are not much older than the former flak helpers in Germany. Not surprisingly, some of them have achieved material success in their new homes, and several of them know how to speak about that which makes them a living link between the extinct communities and the untouched Jews of the United States.

They speak, however, at some cost. Part of the problem is that one cannot effortlessly say everything. It is not easy to recount the full extent of one's helplessness and humiliation in extreme situations. More than that, it is difficult to find the proper wording to convey even the bare essentials of an Auschwitz experience to someone "who was not there." For Jews, words have been the ancient, primeval form of preserving memory. Painting is subsidiary and music is ancillary. But the words of the most articulate survivors are inadequate for *this* reality. The dictum of Theodor W. Adorno that it is "barbaric" to write poetry after Auschwitz may be extended to all forms of expression. It is barbaric to write footnotes, to give lectures, or to make speeches. The words usurp and destroy the event taking its place in memory. That is why the greatest spokesman of the survivors, Elie Wiesel, writes sparingly and espouses silence. That is also why Charlotte Delbo, a poet-prisoner of Auschwitz, is a minimalist. One must be artless in describing this event, discarding adjectives and adverbs. Yet that is the highest art of all. That is *Genesis* itself.

Those who make the attempt pay a price every time. Each explanation, tale, or poem, is a compromise. But the effort has been made despite the cost "to tell it to the world." Then came Bitburg. A US president, standing amid the buried German soldiers and SS men, was to place a wreath to commemorate them all without distinction. Was this to be an act of total redemption of Nazi Germany? Had the survivors' testimony not been heard? Had the captured documents of Adolf Hitler's Reich been overlooked? Had the message failed? Under President Jimmy Carter, Congress had established a United States Holocaust Memorial Council. Elie Wiesel was serving as its chairman. President Ronald Reagan had personally received the council in the White House during his first term. Was he now negating its mission? Was he playing politics with memory?

A key element in the debate was the cluster of SS graves at Bitburg, and everything seemed ultimately to depend on the measure of their significance. The history of US policy toward postwar Germany had been an attempt to whittle down the size of the Nazi problem, to diminish the ranks of those who were to be held accountable for the Nazi regime. The beginning was the rejection of "collective guilt." The next step was a judicial division of organized German society into two segments, one of which was to be left largely undisturbed, while the other was to be pursued further. The first group included the vast majority of the judges, generals, diplomats, civil servants, industrialists, and bankers, only a handful of whom stood trial for an activity deemed contrary to the old laws of war or the new law of aggression. The second group consisted of power centers that were found by the Nuremburg International Military Tribunal to have had a criminal purpose.[3] If a member of such a hierarchy had joined or remained in it voluntarily with knowledge of its character, he had committed a crime. One of these criminal organizations was the leadership corps of the Nazi Party; another was the Gestapo and Security Service; the third comprised all SS men, except draftees who were given no choice and who had committed no crimes. Eventually, the SS in particular remained in the public eye as the hard core of Nazism. Adolf Eichmann was an SS officer, Josef Mengele belonged to the SS, and many others, known and unknown, were part of it. SS men were at the forefront of the shootings of hundreds of thousands of Jews in occupied Eastern Europe, and SS men were implicated in the killing of millions in the camps. As of 1985, there was still a Central Office of the State Justice Administrations for the Investigation of National Socialist Crimes in West Germany, gathering evidence against SS men and party stalwarts for prosecutions in West German courts. At the same time, there was an Office of Special Investigations in the US Department of Justice charged with instituting proceedings for denaturalization and deportation of individuals from the Baltic area, Ukraine, and elsewhere, who had served as willing accomplices of the German SS and Police in lethal operations against Jews, Gypsies, and others. In this manner, the notion of culpability for inexcusable offenses, no matter what the date of their commission, was still being upheld by West Germany and by the United States in tangible legal actions. With the advent of Bitburg, however, a psychological reversal was in the offing. The president's wreath seemed to cover the entire history of the Third Reich with a nebulous collective innocence.

Aggravating the situation were all of the circumstances leading to the decision. President Reagan announced at first that he would not visit a concentration camp, lest he "reawaken the memories and so forth, and the passions of the time."[4] After protests were voiced about Bitburg, he decided to go to a camp after all, but when he announced the additional visit to Bergen-Belsen, he antagonized the protesters even more, for now he was going from the mass graves of Jews to the headstones of SS men, explaining that both were victims.[5]

The survivors, and more generally the Jewish community, were of course not the only complainants. Several veterans' groups and majorities of the US Senate and House of Representatives went on record against Bitburg. Opinion polls revealed that, on the whole, the people were divided on the issue—about half did not agree with the president. But there is no question that the issue was felt most intensely by the Jews.

For President Reagan the prospective visit to the cemetery became an increasingly onerous proposition. It was a classic political situation of confronting seemingly contradictory demands from unyielding friends. The contemporary presidency, for all the power at its command, frequently operates like a brokerage house. The White House staff and other decision-makers of the executive branch are sometimes candid about this method of accomplishing their ends. "They owe us one," they might be heard to say, or "We owe them one." In the case of Bitburg, however, the fine art of the balancing act must have been extraordinarily difficult, because the problem could not be resolved with dollars and cents or with political trade-offs of one sort or another. Weighing the pros and cons, the president's advisers could defend a decision in favor of Germany. They could point to the ideological affinity of Kohl and Reagan. They could refer to the German polls, which indicated that three-quarters of the German population favored the visit, and to an overwhelming vote in the Bundestag against any cancellation.[6] At a time of weakening support of US policies around the world, they could verify the reliability of Germany as a NATO partner, and they could cite, among other things, the deployment of Pershing and cruise missiles on German soil. Could US Jewry muster such "credits"? There were certainly Jewish conservatives who supported the president's goals, but as an electorate, the Jews of the United States were still voting overwhelmingly for Democratic candidates. And Israel, strong friend that it was, depended heavily on US assistance. Given this equation, no one could assert that the president's attitude toward Jewish causes had not been generous in any case.

Moreover, Reagan "had given his word" to Kohl. He may have done so with insufficient preparation or knowledge, but now his "credibility" was involved. Unless there was an overwhelming reason—something the Germans had not told him that he should have known—he would have to walk the walk. In the Jewish community, the search for some incriminating evidence had begun, but the quest was hampered by lack of organization and resources. While the television cameras were trained on the graves of SS Panzer grenadiers, feeble attempts were made to learn something about some of these men. Might someone have served in the *Einsatzgruppen* that killed Jews in the east? Could one have participated in razing a French village? Was there a possibility that one of the SS men helped in the shooting of unarmed US prisoners of war? The Germans were annoyed. The cemetery was not a Nazi institution in appearance. It had no swastikas, and the SS designations on the stones were carved in ordinary script, not the ZZ of Hitler's time. Yet the constant attention lavished on the SS graves at Bitburg was disintegrating the principal point the Kohl regime had been trying to make. How could one de-nazify a cemetery? In the end, an attempt was made to do just that. A great many of the soldiers and SS men in Bitburg had been killed late in 1944 or early in 1945, when German manpower was depleted and many youngsters were appearing at the front. It was consequently not difficult to hand President Reagan the name of one adolescent who had been killed a week before his sixteenth birthday. The president, seizing this fact, repeated it in a speech.[7]

The deepest psychological conflict between the Germans and the Jews had become a contest of public relations in which only simple, visible cues could matter. Few newspapers and fewer television programs could cope with the complexity of the issue. No one approached the question of the German army. Here was a cemetery in which most of the fallen had been soldiers. Was it "contaminated" only because of the relative handful of SS men buried alongside these men? Would the controversy have been prevented altogether if the choice had been a "pure" military burial ground? The Germans had certainly spent years trying to conjure up an image of the Wehrmacht, which was the name of the armed forces during the Third Reich, as a military organization like other armed forces fighting for its homeland. The Wehrmacht, after all, was the successor of the prewar Reichswehr and the precursor of the postwar Bundeswehr. It was a link in a long chain of generations that belong to the same culture and share its traditions. Dismantled in 1945, the German army was reborn in the early 1950s, when the personnel files of World War II German officers, located with captured German document collections in the Federal Records Center at Alexandria, Virginia, were returned to Germany. The new

Bundeswehr remembered its old battles and wore its old decorations. The dead of Bitburg are some of its old comrades. But what can be said to contrast Germany's military veterans of World War II with the SS?

In truth, the separation of the military from the SS in terms of the soldierly professionalism of the one and the ideological fanaticism of the other has always been strained. The German army played a huge role in Adolf Hitler's Germany, and it cannot be detached from the Nazi regime, because it was an integral part of it. The people of the United States have not been well informed and the press has not been explicit about such topics as the fate of Soviet prisoners of war in the transit camps (*Dulags*) and main camps (*Stalags*) of the German military. By the end of the war, well over two million Red Army men in German army custody were dead of starvation and exposure.[8]* By the same token, the general public is not aware of the multiple functions performed by uniformed members of the German armed forces in the destruction of the Jews. The list of these activities is long, as even a brief recapitulation will show:

1. The German army in the east established many Jewish ghettos.
2. The German army gave logistic support to the *Einsatzgruppen* of Heydrich's Reich Security Main Office. Intelligence units helped locate Jews for shooting.
3. Military governments in Belgium, France, Serbia, and Greece issued anti-Jewish regulations in the economic sphere, including "Aryanizations" of Jewish property and taxes in the form of "fines."
4. Armament officers administered contracts with German firms employing Jewish slave labor. The German army itself made use of such labor in its own installations.
5. Transport officers in France, Greece, Italy, and elsewhere were involved in the dispatch of trains to death camps.
6. German troops stood by to deal with Jewish resistance. An artillery unit fought in the Warsaw ghetto battle. A battalion of security troops was alerted for the suppression of the revolt in the Sobibor death camp. The military was available to frustrate any large-scale breakouts from Auschwitz.
7. The German army transferred Soviet prisoners of war who were Jewish to the SS to be shot. It engaged in killings of its own,

---

* Currently the number of estimated deaths of Soviet prisoners of war is 3 million.

shooting the Jewish men in Serbia and wiping out a population of 10,000 Jews in the Głębokie region of Poland.[9]

That the German military could not be regarded as innocent in its entirety was implicitly recognized from the beginning, when Field Marshal Wilhelm Keitel and Colonel General Alfred Jodl were hanged in Nuremberg, and when other German generals stood trial before US military tribunals. The judicial proceedings, however, served also as a purification rite, in that they facilitated the orderly retirement or reemployment of all those professionals who were not indicted. Examples are: General Hans von Grävenitz, in charge of prisoners of war, who lived peacefully in Stuttgart after the war; General Fritz Rossum, commander of the military district of Warsaw during the mass deportations in 1942 and the subsequent Warsaw ghetto battle in 1943, who lived in Konstanz; and General Otto Kohl, transport officer in Paris, where he volunteered his services to the SS for the rapid deportation of the French Jews, who was a postwar resident of Munich. General Max Pemsel, who had been the chief of staff of the military command in Serbia when the Jewish men were shot there by the army, and who was not ready for retirement in 1945, rose to high rank in the new Bundeswehr.[10] If generals could fare this well, what need be said about the much larger numbers of implicated majors and sergeants not listed in any Who's Who?

Hardly anyone in the Federal Republic of Germany had associated the Wehrmacht with the Jewish catastrophe. The emphasis had always been placed on the blamelessness of soldiers, and now this point was reiterated. When Alois Mertes, representative of Bitburg in the Bundestag and minister of state in the Foreign Office, sat next to US Senator Charles Mathias at a conference, he passed him a note in effect saying: "The Senate resolution on Bitburg should not have ignored German soldiers who were not Nazis—Germans such as Richard von Weizsäcker, Helmut Schmidt, Franz Josef Strauss, Walter Scheel, Alois Mertes."[11]

The Germany army was not the only reversible symbol at Bitburg. An effort was made to transform World War II to make it look like World War I. The strategy was a mirror image of the Mitterrand-Kohl meeting at Verdun in 1984, where the French government had substituted World War I for World War II. The French, of course, had good reasons for centering attention on the older battlefield, if only because there they could console not only Kohl but also themselves. France had suffered five times as many casualties in 1914–18 as in 1939–45, and their dead in World War II included Vichy troops who had battled the British in Syria, Alsatians drafted into the German army, and ideological French collaborators in formations fighting on the German side to the bitter end. Bitburg presented more subtle problems. Not only were tripods for television cameras banned, lest an SS grave be glimpsed by viewers, but an air of timelessness was to be introduced, a blending of the wars, a walk across the ages. At the side of a US president in his mid-seventies stood a US general who was even older. During the wordless ceremony, a German bugler played "Ich hatt' einen Kameraden" (I had a comrade), a song that predated the Nazi regime. An American television audience could see nothing wrong in this scene, and Germans could be reminded of an earlier history, the period before 1933, to which no shame was attached, or for which at least no exclusive responsibility had to be taken.[12]

The complexities of history are buried in books and journals. Collective memories are highly selective and often embrace only a partial past in the form of nostalgia. How much time will pass before a future generation in Germany will have difficulty distinguishing between the two wars that occurred twenty years apart in the first half of the century? Did President Reagan already have such a moment of confusion?

At a news conference on 21 March 1985, the president said that "The German people have very few alive that remember even the war, and certainly none that were adults and participating in any way."[13] He himself had been in his thirties during World War II, yet he pushed the whole war back a couple of decades because of another issue with which he had to deal just before his trip: the seventieth anniversary of the Armenian disaster, in the course of which at least 600,000 Armenian men, women, and children are estimated to have died at the hands of the Ottoman Turks behind the lines of the Turkish-Russian front in World War I.[14] Armenians have not forgotten this event and periodically they ask others not to forget it. In 1983, President Reagan's reaction to a reminder at a press conference was that, after all, the Ottomans of 1915 were long dead. When the seventieth anniversary was close at hand in the early spring of 1985, he was under strong pressure from the Armenians for official recognition of the disaster, and from the Turkish government for an abstention from such a step. The harried president was now facing two similar crises simultaneously, and, having been told that the Ottoman Turks were genocidal like the German Nazis, he thought of the same argument for the Germans that he had made for the Turks.[15]

In Bitburg, there were to be no winners. Even before the president's visit, Chancellor Kohl was aware of Jewish sensitivity. He cultivated US Jewish organizations[16] and planned an establishment of a remembrance committee composed of German appointees and members of the US Holocaust Memorial Council.[17] But for the Germans, the lesson of the wilting garland from the United States was not lost. The ceremony had not lifted any burdens, and the past was coming back.[18]

After Bitburg, a number of complaints were heard in the streets of Germany about the power of US Jews who had managed to reduce the visit to eight minutes. The Jews of the United States, however, were perturbed because the president had gone to the cemetery in the first place. Neither abandoned nor victorious, they had to ask themselves once more whether drawing in was to be preferred to reaching out.

President Reagan lost too. Caught in the middle of a situation his staff had not prepared him for, he confronted a dilemma from which he could not extricate himself. He went with anguish and possible doubts, losing his surefootedness and sacrificing his image as a man who acted out of conviction. During a press conference on 18 June 1985, he was asked whether Bitburg and other reverses were signs that his luck was running out. In his answer, Reagan spoke of Bitburg at length, describing a reward he had received in Germany. It was given to him, he said, when he made a speech before "10,000 young teenage Germans and at the end of that heard 10,000 young Germans sing our National Anthem in our language."[19]

Notes

1. Carlo Schmid, "Dieser Staat ist ohne Glanz," *Süddeutsche Zeitung*, 9 May 1968.
2. The poll was reported in *Der Spiegel*, 22 April 1985. Chancellor Kohl's rating was +0.6.
3. A portion of the Nuremberg judgment is printed in *Bitburg in Moral and Political Perspective*, ed. Geoffrey H. Hartmann, Bloomington, 1986, 273 ff.
4. Text of news conference held on 21 March 1985, *New York Times*, 22 March 1985.
5. "Responses of the President to Queries on German Visit," *New York Times*, 19 April 1985.

6. *Newsweek*, 6 May 1985. The vote was 398 to 24.
7. Transcript of the president's speech of 5 May 1985, *New York Times*, 6 May 1985.
8. On the treatment of Soviet prisoners of war, see Christian F. Streit, *Keine Kameraden*, Stuttgart, 1978. In a speech at Bergen-Belsen on 21 April 1985, Chancellor Kohl mentioned the dead Soviet prisoners, but without any reference to the German army. Text of address in German Information Center, *Statements and Speeches* 7, no. 11, 22 April 1985.
9. See Raul Hilberg, *The Destruction of the European Jews*, 2nd ed. (New York, 1985).
10. See the list of World War II German generals, with ranks, commands, and cities of postwar residence, in the loose-leaf edition of Wolf Keilig's *Das Deutsche Heer 1939–1945* (Bad Neuheim, 1956–60).
11. Statement by Senator Charles Mathias, *Congressional Record*, 99th Cong., 1st sess., 20 June 1985, p. S. 8485. Mertes and Mathias were seated alphabetically at the conference. The entry in the *Congressional Record*, made after the death of Mertes, was appended to German Information Center, *Statements and Speeches* 7, no. 21, 1 July 1985.
12. In fact, the legacy of the old days was not devoid of problems. The most controversial book in postwar Germany was not any treatment of the Nazi regime, but a heavy monograph about World War I: Fritz Fischer's *Der Griff nach der Weltmacht* (The grab for world power), translated into English and published in the United States under the more sedate title *Germany's Aims in the First World War* (New York, 1967). Fischer discovered records of the German Foreign Office of 1914, showing some German eagerness for war at that time. The Weimar period is similarly problematic. In 1922, Chancellor Joseph Wirth summarized his "eastern program" in a conversation with Count Brockdorff-Rantzau, saying "Poland has to be finished off." Herbert Helbig, *Die Träger der Rapallo-Politik* (Göttingen, 1958), 118–20. Gordon H. Mueller, "Rappalo Reexamined: A New Look at Germany's Military Collaboration with Russia in 1922," *Military Affairs* 40, no. 3 (1976):109–17. Rapallo was in several respects a precursor of the secret German-Soviet protocol of August 1939.
13. Text of news conference, *New York Times*, 22 March 1985.
14. Arnold Josef Toynbee, ed., *The Treatment of Armenians in the Ottoman Empire 1915–16, Documents Presented to Viscount Grey of Falladou, Secretary of State for Foreign Affairs: by Viscount Bryce* (London, 1916), particularly 664–66.
15. When the president was asked at a news conference with specialized press on 18 October 1983, whether the US government had a stand on the Turkish genocide of Armenians, he said: "I can't help but believe that there's virtually no one alive today who was living in the era of that terrible trouble." The White House/Office of Media Relations and Planning, press release of 18 October 1983. The Armenian Remembrance Day is 24 April, and in April 1985, the US Congress considered a resolution to recognize the Armenian disaster. The resolution was opposed by the executive branch, and the efforts of Republican Governor George Deukmejian of California to change the

president's mind were unsuccessful. William Endicott, "Doukmejian Pleads for Reagan Change of Heart on Armenians," *Los Angeles Times*, 24 April 1985. Richard Paddock, "Ignore Turks' Pressure on Genocide, Doukmejian Asks," *Los Angeles Times*, 28 April 1985. Barry Zorthian of the Armenian Assembly of America declared: "This is another Bitburg." Eduardo Lachica, "Reagan Opposition to Armenian Bill Starts a Second Genocide Controversy," *Wall Street Journal*, 29 April 1985. A diplomat in the Turkish embassy offered the opinion that "This effort to align themselves with American Jewry is sheer opportunism by the Armenians." Megan Rosenfeld, "'The Forgotten Survivors': Armenians Commemorate the 1915 Killings with their First National Gathering," *Washington Post*, 27 April 1985.

16. See the speech by Mertes before the American Jewish Committee, 2 May 1985, *Statements and Speeches* 7, no. 14, 2 May 1985, and the speech by German Ambassador Günther van Well before the Board of Governors, B'nai B'rith International, 21 May 1985, *Statements and Speeches* 7, no. 18, 21 May 1985.
17. See the *New York Times*, 25 June 1985.
18. Domestic speeches were made almost daily, often enough with refined evasions or problematic acknowledgments of the burdensome past. Federal President Richard von Weizsäcker addressed the Bundestag on 8 May 1985, making the following points: The genocide of the Jews was "in the hands of a few people." It was concealed from the public, but no German could have been unsuspecting of Jewish suffering for long. "Whoever opened his eyes and ears and sought information could not fail to notice that Jews were being deported." Too many people, he said, did not ask. Text in *Statements and Speeches* 7, no. 16, 9 May 1985. Richard von Weizsäcker's own father was the second highest official in the Foreign Office when Europe-wide deportations began. After the war, the elder Weizsäcker was tried before a US military tribunal and sentenced to prison for having signed crucial papers paving the way for the transport of Jews from France to Auschwitz. During the trial, Richard found "a good word" to say for his father, and assisted the defense team in the formulation of a legal argument to absolve the old diplomat of guilt in the destruction of the Jews. See Leonidas E. Hill, ed., *Die Weizsäcker-Papiere 1933–1950* (Frankfurt am Main, 1974), 421, 446–69, 452. The *Papiere* are Ernst von Weizsäcker's diary.
19. Text of the president's news conference, *New York Times*, 19 June 1985.

Bibliography

Fischer, Fritz. *Germany's Aims in the First World War*. New York: Norton, 1967.
German Information Center. *Statements and Speeches* 7, no. 11, 14, 16, 21 (1985).
Helbig, Herbert. *Die Träger der Rapallo-Politik*. Göttingen: Vandenhoeck & Ruprecht, 1958.

Hilberg, Raul. *The Destruction of the European Jews*, 2nd ed. New York: Holmes & Meier, 1985.

Hill, Leonidas E., ed. *Die Weizsäcker-Papiere 1933–1950*. Frankfurt am Main: Ullstein, and Vienna: Propyläen, 1974.

Keilig, Wolf. *Das Deutsche Heer 1939–1945*. Bad Nauheim: Podzun, 1956–60.

Mueller, Gordon H. "Rappalo Reexamined: A New Look at Germany's Military Collaboration with Russia in 1922." *Military Affairs* 40, no. 3 (1976): 109–17.

Schmid, Carlo. "Dieser Staat ist ohne Glanz." *Süddeutsche Zeitung*, 9 May 1968.

Streit, Christian F. *Keine Kameraden*. Stuttgart: Deutsche Verlags-Anstalt, 1978.

Toynbee, Arnold Josef, ed. *The Treatment of Armenians in the Ottoman Empire 1915–16, Documents Presented to Viscount Grey of Falladou, Secretary of State for Foreign Affairs: by Viscount Bryce*. London: H.M. Stationary Office, 1916.

7

THE GHETTO AS A FORM OF GOVERNMENT
(1980)

IN 1972, MORE THAN A quarter of a century after the end of the Holocaust, Isaiah Trunk published his pathbreaking *Judenrat*, the first major attempt to portray in systematic terms the institutions and conditions of Jewish life in the ghettos of Nazi Eastern Europe.[1] It is a big volume, some seven hundred pages long, but, despite its size, it is also an understated work, for Trunk is one of those uncommon authors who promises less than he delivers. His preface deals with limits and limitations: an outline of Nazi administration in the East and a recital of sources at his disposal. The introduction, which was written by Jacob Robinson, is partly philosophical, partly polemic, and in no event foreshadows the dimensions of the contents. The substantive account is presented by Trunk in ordinary matter-of-fact language without intensification or climax. As he traverses his terrain, from schools to synagogues, or from labor to deportations, his tone remains constant. In this evenness, Trunk has managed to submerge everything: his range, depth, and findings.

The title of the book is *Judenrat*, "the Jewish Council," or, rather, hundreds of them in various Eastern European ghettos. Trunk wanted to "achieve an objective history of the councils," and thereby "find the key to internal Jewish history under Nazi rule,"[2] but his book is not

Originally published in *The Annals of the American Academy of Political Social Science* 450, no. 1 (1980): 98–112.

merely a depiction of that key; it deals with the whole house, for it is a full-scale political, economic, and social history of the ghetto as such. The various headings of chapters and subchapters indicate the scope of the discussion that comprises a gamut of topics including organizational developments in ghetto bureaucracy, commissions, and police; the problem areas of finances, taxes, production, and purchases; and programs involving bathhouses, kitchens, welfare, or medical aid.

There is a similar richness of documentation. Although Trunk calls special attention in the preface to a survey that netted replies from 927 respondents concerning 740 former council members and 112 ghetto police, this questionnaire material constitutes only about 5 percent of the two thousand citations in the notes, which are filled with references to orders issued by German supervisory agencies, reports of councils to the Germans, minutes of council meetings, newspapers, diaries, memoirs, and memorial books. Text and sources reveal the extent of Trunk's effort, and intricate facts on every page reflect the author's long preoccupation with numerous aspects of ghetto life.[3]

Trunk cautions against overgeneralization. At the outset, he stresses the importance of local conditions and the individuality of leaders in the Jewish communities.[4] Yet he does not present the Warsaw ghetto in one chapter, Lodz in another, and additional ghettos down the line. The fragmentary nature of the source material would not in any case have allowed for an approach of that kind. Instead, he addresses himself to the essence of the ghettos, that is, the mode of their operations in regard to such all-pervasive problems as crowding, hunger, or the demands of the Germans; and he does so implicitly by using almost any item of information about a particular ghetto as illustrative of the situation in all of them. In this manner, he builds a mosaic that is generalization par excellence.

More than that, his whole book is a demonstration rather than a mere assertion that, notwithstanding the different internal structures of the Jewish communities or the diversity of personalities in the councils, the stories of all of these ghettos must be read as one history. This impression is underscored when we consider that Jewish perceptions and reactions were remarkably similar across the occupied territories, despite the relative isolation of the communities and their councils from each other. In the final analysis, the variation among ghettos is not as crucial as their commonality, nor is it primarily the classification of ghettos in terms of demographic or economic factors that counts, but the singularity of meaning in the phrase "Jewish ghetto" compared with everything else that has transpired in recent times throughout the world.

If Trunk had done no more than organize a compendium of facts in subject-matter categories, he would have furnished us with significant additions to our knowledge, but beyond any compilation, he also set forth a series of propositions about the nature of the ghettos and of the councils that governed them. Of course, it would be useless to look for these thoughts in some final chapter—Trunk eschews discoveries, and there is no recapitulation at the end. His summation is confined to five pages and there he considers solely an issue raised by Jacob Robinson in the introduction: the question of the councils' "collaboration" with the Germans. Thus, an entire set of observations and conclusions is left buried in the text, some in lengthy passages, others in single sentences, still others in recurring themes and characterizations. For a review of *Judenrat*, nothing is more important than a consolidation of these points in analytic form. Here they are, under four headings, partly condensed from his account, partly developed from it, but mainly rooted in his evidence.[5]

The Ghetto as a Political Entity

The principal characteristic of the ghetto was the segregation of its inhabitants from the surrounding population. The Jewish ghetto was a closed-off society, its gates permanently shut to free traffic, so much so that Trunk labels as relatively "open" those ghetto communities in smaller cities that dispatched labor columns daily to projects outside the ghetto limits.[6] That is not to imply the total absence of contacts with Germans or Poles. There were telephone, electric, gas, and water connections; removals of human waste; exports of manufactured goods; imports of coal, food, or raw materials; mail and parcel shipments through ghetto post offices; loans from banks, payments of rents, and so forth. In examining these links one must, however, always differentiate between institutional transactions that had to be maintained if the ghetto was to function and private bonds, across the boundaries, that could no longer be tolerated because they were incompatible with the function of the ghetto.

Even the official correspondence of Jewish ghetto authorities with neighboring German or Polish agencies or firms was largely severed, and the flow of orders and reports was confined as much as possible, though never completely, to a channel running from the German supervisors to the Jewish Council. The horizontal relationships built into so much of modern life were consequently replaced by an almost all-encompassing vertical regime, sometimes complex, as in the case of Warsaw and Lodz, often simple, as in outlying localities, but always standardized in a dictatorial manner.[7]

The hierarchical system of German supervision was designed for the purpose of absolutism. German orders were unqualified and council members were required to carry them out promptly and in full. Trunk underscores the fact that the members of the councils were not Nazi sympathizers, that, although some were ambitious and many deluded, they were not, and could not be regarded as, a German institution.[8] They were, in short, Jews, and they could not fail to perceive the fate of Jewry as their fate as well.[9] All the more bitter then was their task of receiving and implementing German decrees. Yet the directives of the Germans were only half of their problem. Less stark but equally burdensome was the necessity of asking for authorization to carry out every function of government, including duties expected of them. The councils had to obtain clearance for a variety of revenue measures; they had to "borrow" Jewish funds previously sequestered or confiscated under occupation ordinances; they even had to request permission to post German orders.

If the councils were rendered totally subordinate and dependent in their relations with the Germans, a corresponding status was fashioned for the Jewish population subjected to council rule. The German sentiment in this matter was expressed unambiguously by one official when he asserted, "It lies in the interest of the difficult administration of the Jewish district that the authority of the Jewish council be upheld and strengthened under all circumstances."[10]

Jewish executives, like the Germans in charge, could make use of coercion and take advantage of helplessness. Compliance and acquiescence were ensured by the Jewish police who had the power to make arrests and guard prisoners.[11] Relief could be dispensed in that the councils controlled food and space: the German shipments of flour, sugar, or coal were doled out under conditions of constantly increasing privation.[12]

Throughout the system, power was exercised in levels of dominance, and each level was fortified in every way. An illustration of such reinforcement was the principle of limiting correspondence and conversations to immediate superiors and inferiors. In conformity with this arrangement, the council could make appeals only to the German supervisory authorities in its locality—it could conceivably urge the city commander or ghetto commissioner to submit a plea to higher officials[13]—but it could not carry messages directly to regional governors or their staffs. The ghetto inhabitants in turn might stand in line to see the Elder of the council, but they had no ordinary access to German agencies. In fact, there is reason to suppose that the councils acquired a stake in establishing themselves as the sole representatives of the Jewish population vis-à-vis German officialdom. They certainly felt themselves empowered to govern the Jews, and, in some ghettos, announced that persons who had failed to pay taxes or report for labor would be handed over to a German office because of their recalcitrance.[14] For Jewish bureaucrats, no less than German, there was no substitute for authority.

The physical and administrative constrictions of Jewry reduced its space and narrowed its horizon but, at the same time, intensified its organizational activity. While the Germans outside became invisible,[15] the Jewish community machinery within evolved into the government of a captive city-state. Trunk explains the transformation as clearly stemming from two causes: one was the necessity of rendering those regular municipal and economic services from which the community was now cut off and without which it could not have survived; the other was the burden thrust upon the council by the Germans who used it as a tool to fulfill German needs.[16] The multiplication of tasks inherent in this dual evolution, coupled with continuing unemployment and periodic fears of disaster, led also to swollen ghetto bureaucracies that were filled with minor functionaries and clerks, both paid and unpaid. In ghettos featuring public enterprise (particularly Lodz and Vilna), the council payrolls at the beginning of 1942 encompassed as much as a fifth of the employable population.[17]

Although ghetto office personnel were often doing very little, some of the officials wielded power—at times almost undisturbed power—in specialized spheres of jurisdiction. One area in particular lent itself to what Trunk calls, albeit between quotation marks, ghetto self-government. This island of Jewish freedom was located in the courts, where disputes between Jewish litigants were settled by Jewish judges without German interference.[18] Consequently, the ghettos were political entities with governmental attributes much larger and fuller than the social, cultural, or religious functions carried out by the prewar communities. Soon, however, councils everywhere came face to face with the basic paradox in their role as preservers of Jewish life in a framework of German destruction. They could not indefinitely serve the Jews while simultaneously obeying the Germans. A good deal of what Trunk calls the strategy and tactics of the councils[19] was in fact their futile attempt to resolve this contradiction. The Jewish leadership was completely nonprovocative. It did not fight the Germans—it seldom fought the orders—but in its distress, it made numerous offerings. From time to time the councils offered words, money, labor, and finally lives.

Appeals were probably the most frequently used device. They were often generated by upheaval, especially at the beginning of the German occupation, during ghetto formation, and at the onset of deportations, but anything could be the content of a plea. The councils asked for permission to turn on the lights after 8:00 p.m. (Lublin), for reductions of confiscations (Bialystok), or for the return of hostages (Warsaw). "Seldom did Jewish petitions have any success," states Trunk, yet one has the feeling from such documents as the Czerniaków diary that an occasional or partial German concession, even if only for the mitigation or postponement of some harsh measure, fueled the pleadings time and again. They remained, throughout, the strategy of first resort.

Trunk devotes considerable space to bribes, which he believes to have been widespread, but which obviously could have been used only under special conditions. They must have been more successful than intercessions, but the objects attained by bribery are likely to have been limited and the effects short-lived. Typical were payments to effect the transfer of a particularly troublesome official or policeman, the ransom of young girls from forced prostitution (a practice that under German "race-pollution" law was in any case prohibited), or the tender of money to avert "resettlement."

Most extensive is Trunk's discussion of the "rescue-through-work" strategy[20] that reflected the consideration that the Germans actually needed the products of Jewish manufacture, not only war material, but also simple things, such as brushes that in labor-hungry Axis Europe could not be turned out in quantity with ease. In Lodz, Vilna, and Częstochowa, this policy led to the construction by the councils of fairly large-scale industries. The factories bought time for tens of thousands, but the Jews were playing a predetermined game in which the outcome was always under German control.[21]

The mass deportations forced the Jews to the extreme ends of the spectrum of alternatives. There was no longer any middle ground between open opposition and total compliance: the Jewish communities were bound to choose the one or the other. Trunk gives some examples of councils with a "positive attitude" toward resistance. However, most of the manifestations of that inclination turn out to have been actions of individual council members in aiding escapes or in establishing contacts with partisans.[22] The predominant pattern was the active implementation of German directives.

The councils themselves organized confiscations and forced labor. In most ghettos, they themselves delivered the victims for the death transports. Of course, the Germans would frequently ask for only a certain number of deportees. It is this request that ignited an internal Jewish argument to the effect that if one thousand Jews were given up, ten thousand would be saved, that if none were sacrificed, all would be lost. In delivering a part of the community, the councils could also choose the less worthy.[23] Trunk quotes Zalman Shazar, a president of Israel, as pointing out in 1964 that the negative selections in the ghettos had been preceded by similar behavior in czarist times when the Jewish community leaders were forced to designate youngsters for twenty-five years of service in the imperial army. Then, too, the councils chose the simpletons.[24]

Because of the compliance strategy, the *Judenrat* could be a dangerous organization precisely when it functioned most smoothly. Impersonality, as in the recruitment of the strong and the weak or the healthy and the sick for heavy labor, could become brutality. Order, as shown in Lodz where smuggling was curbed, could intensify deprivation. Efficiency, in the collection of taxes or furs, could bring about more suffering. Thus many of the virtues of Jewish ghetto government became vices; responsibility was turned into unresponsiveness and salvage into loss.

The Ghetto as a Socioeconomic Organization

The Jewish ghettos mark an interim phase between prewar freedom and wartime annihilation. These last moments of organized existence in the Jewish community were endured in a vise of progressively diminished space and gradually increasing hunger. If social and economic policies in normal societies may have long-range effects on large groups of people seeking comforts, security, or some pleasure in life, the internal measures and practices of ghetto councils were bound to have an immediate, massive impact on a population hovering between survival and death.

We may safely assume that many times the meager resources at the disposal of the councils were strained for the benefit of the community. There were occupational training programs, workshops, rationing systems, housing authorities, hospitals, ambulances, and other services in a large number of ghettos. Their very existence demonstrated what Jewish bureaucrats and technocrats could accomplish even under these conditions. At the same time, Trunk leaves little doubt that the ghettos as a whole were no triumphs of social equality and economic justice. The ghetto was the scene of all forms of corruption, including bribery, favoritism, and nepotism. Moreover, in the critical areas of labor, food, and taxes, the prevailing regulations were particularly harsh for the most destitute families.

Instances of dishonesty are difficult to document, but Trunk cites relevant testimony of survivors from several ghettos. Council members accepted personal bribes for exemptions from labor duty (Zamosc) or deportation (Horodenka and other ghettos).[25] Bribes were said to have been taken for appointments to the ghetto police (Warsaw).[26] Patronage in awarding jobs to inexperienced applicants, sometimes resulting in the employment of entire families, was apparently rampant in Warsaw, Lodz, Bialystok, Lublin, and elsewhere.[27] Friendships were also important in the soup kitchens of Lodz, and the Lodz ghetto chairman, Chaim Rumkowski, is reported to have issued supplementary food ration stamps "at whim," favoring particularly Orthodox groups and rabbis.[28]

While abuses for private ends may be regarded as transgressions of individuals, a regime of exploitation through official routines can only be described as systemic. The difference is important, for the concealed bribes and favors were intrinsically unjustifiable, whereas the open decrees and decisions, which so often took advantage of the most helpless of the population, were defended by councils as being the best they could do under the circumstances. Nowhere is this posture more clearly expressed than in the pronouncements, correspondence, and diary of Adam Czerniaków, chairman of the Jewish Council in the laissez-faire ghetto of Warsaw.

During the early days, Czerniaków excused the well-to-do from forced labor for a fee, in order to finance the compensation of poor families whose men were digging ditches for the Germans.[29] Later, as he struggled with the council's unbalanced budget, he proposed as his principal revenue source a monthly tax on bread.[30] Still later, when the council was threatened with declining German food shipments, cash reserves were created as a precautionary measure by increasing the surcharges on the bread and sugar rations.[31]

One of the effects of ghetto class structure was the emergence of what Trunk calls a "food pyramid." Quite simply, the social ladder became more and more conspicuous by the number of calories consumed. Thus a survey in the Warsaw ghetto in December 1941 revealed that council employees were receiving 1,665 calories; artisans, 1,407; shop-workers, 1,225; and the general population, 1,125.[32] A similar picture of relative starvation may be observed in the Lodz ghetto. There, differential rationing, by type of employment, was official policy.[33] This is how status became instrumental in the prolongation of sheer survival. Czerniaków himself made the point obliquely at the end of 1941 when he observed that the intelligentsia were dying now.[34]

In retrospect, the tiers of privilege in ghetto society should not surprise us. Ghetto life rewarded special talents such as smuggling or wheeling and dealing. It accommodated the more usual skills of the doctors, artisans, or people who could speak German. The ghetto protected its rabbis as well, for the Jews clung to the past and approached even their most extraordinary problems with all traditional means. Finally, the Jewish bureaucrat who ran the ghetto during its formation and who presided at its dissolution was granted his reprieve. In the vast majority of instances, however, the last occurrence of even the most shielded existence was a violent death.

The Ghetto as Mirage

Adam Czerniaków was the sort of man who did not want to draw a salary as long as there was not enough money to pay his staff.[35] In the midst of starvation, he shunned elaborate meals, eating soup for lunch in his office.[36] During a contraction of the ghetto boundaries, he refused a German offer that would have allowed him to keep his apartment on a street from which the Jews were being expelled.[37] In July 1942, when he realized that the Jews were going to be deported en masse, he took his own life. Yet in February 1942, just about six months before that fateful day, Czerniaków had decided to have stained glass windows installed in the council chambers.[38] Czerniaków, as well as most of the other Jewish leaders, acted on the premise that there was a future. From the outset, the councilmen at their desks and the crowds in the streets bore their crushing burdens as temporary inflictions to be suffered until liberation. To the end, Jewish hospitals were trying to heal the sick, schools were continuing to train the young, and kitchens went on feeding the starved. To the ghetto inmates, there was no alternative.

Many ghetto activities, especially in education and culture, bordered illusionary behavior. The Vilna ghetto, for example, established a music school in the summer of 1942.[39] Readers in the Warsaw ghetto fantasized in the pages of Tolstoy's *War and Peace* that a German collapse was imminent.[40] In the upper echelons of ghetto leadership, a kind of unreality surfaced in power struggles in and around the council headquarters.

Jurisdictional questions were a major preoccupation of the ghetto managers. One of these contests was waged between the councils and a centralized Jewish Welfare Service (JSS), which reported to the German Population and Welfare Division of the *Generalgouvernement* in Krakow and maintained local committees in the ghettos.[41] A complex federal structure with built-in frictions evolved in the Warsaw ghetto in which more than a thousand "house committees" began to perform all sorts of voluntary and assigned functions, including the provision of shelter for refugees, the staging of one-act plays, emergency assistance, reports of illnesses, and collections of taxes.[42] In the same ghetto, the council was challenged by an organization known as the Control Office for Combatting the Black Market and Profiteering in the Jewish District under Abraham Gancwajch. Czerniaków won that battle when the Gancwajch apparatus was dissolved with provision for the incorporation of its members into the regular Jewish Order Service (police).[43]

The following story, told by Czerniaków in his diary, illustrates the manner and extent to which administrators in the Warsaw ghetto were absorbed with problems of entitlement. A Provisioning Authority had been formed as a quasi-independent agency in the summer of 1941 to deal with the approaching food crisis. In the council's own labor department, an official wanted the local German labor office to approve applicants for positions in the authority. Incensed, Czerniaków wrote on 15 February 1942: "This clearly amounts to undermining the authority of the council and diminishing its prerogatives. According to the [council's] legal department, there is no basis for this position in law."[44]

Ghetto government at times became a distorted facsimile of a viable political system. The politics in the administrative processes of the ghetto may strike us as a caricature, because so many of the functionaries in this bureaucracy had come to think of life in a German enclosure as a stabilized condition of existence; they claimed not only some of the food, space, or medical services for themselves and their families, but they also fought for a share of power in this "weird, crippled structure." Yes, even in this rundown machine, which could no longer cope with its narrowest tasks, they wanted a piece of the action.

Trunk speaks at some length of "The German Policy of Fraud and Deceit."[45] He says that the Germans kept the Jews in the dark about their intentions. Indeed, the German perpetrators did not install a warning system in the ghetto. They did not practice chivalry toward their victims. On the other hand, the Jewish leaders did not attempt to systematically acquire information about the Germans, and they did not come to grips with disturbing news in time.

At the start, the Polish Jews viewed ghettoization as the culmination of German plans. They failed to think in terms of a further, more drastic stage in the destruction process. The diary of Adam Czerniaków, leader of the largest ghetto in Europe, is the most detailed record of that characteristic train of thought in the face of the imperilment.

Anyone with a deep interest in the Warsaw ghetto might well approach the diary with the direct question, What were Czerniaków's predictions? What were his plans? What did he think the Germans would do eventually, and what did he see as his alternatives? Nothing, almost nothing of this kind will be found in these notes.

Czerniaków does not make forecasts. He does not draw up options. He does not refer to the Germans as a foe. From October 1941 to the spring of 1942 he expresses himself only in subdued tones, very briefly in passing, about ominous reports. As early as 4 October 1941, he quotes an ambiguous and enigmatic statement of a German official: "Bischof disclosed yesterday that Warsaw is merely a temporary haven for the Jews."[46] The entry for 27 October states: "Alarming rumors about the fate of the Jews in Warsaw next spring." On 17 January, he asks whether Lithuanian guards were coming. There are more rumors on 16 February. Disturbing news reached him on 18 March from Lvov (30,000 resettled) and from Mielec and Lublin. As of 1 April, he hears that 90 percent of the Jews of Lublin were to leave their ghetto within the next few days. All this was written in entries of a sentence or two, in the middle of paragraphs containing other sentences on other subjects.

Czerniaków viewed himself as having taken over an impossible task to be pursued from morning to night against increasingly unfavorable odds. He lived through daily nightmares of blocked funds, labor columns, apartment allocations, bricks for the wall, furs for the Germans, and soup for the poor. There was hardly anything that could be put off—everything was urgent. This is why, when the Germans accepted his revenue statute imposing a tax on bread, he felt that he had accomplished something and that he could face the next day. That is also why a modest collection of money for children was entered as a notable success. And this is the reason why in February 1942, when most of the ghetto had not yet starved to death, he could feel a sense of vindication.

Czerniaków and hundreds more on Jewish councils all over Eastern Europe had fallen into a cadence that did not allow for prolonged reflection about the real meaning of the ghetto in the Nazi scheme of things. In fact, any German laxity or inefficiency only served to reinforce the pace and to intensify the activities of the Jewish offices, which worked in tandem with their German supervisors, reporting to them, seeking clarifications, and requesting authorizations. Thus an administrative and economic dependence was increasingly becoming psychological as well. This was the trap into which the Jewish leadership had slipped and from which it could not extricate itself.

On 20 July 1942, the deportations in Warsaw were imminent. Trunk cites an excerpt from the diary describing that day.[47] It was a moment of panic in the ghetto, and Czerniaków went from Gestapo man to Gestapo man in desperation to ask whether the rumors of a "resettlement" were true. The Germans assured him that they did not know anything and that the reports were all nonsense (*Quatsch* and *Unsinn*). The passage is a fairly good example of how crude the Germans could be in their policy of "fraud and deceit." One has the feeling that their simple denials were almost lame. Not so simple are Czerniaków's frantic requests for reassurances. He was not a naïve man. At the beginning of the paragraph, he himself states that he left the office of the Gestapo man Mende "unconvinced," and later in the day he asked for permission to transmit the German denials to the Jewish population. The Germans could see no harm in that, and by evening in *Kommissar* Auerswald's office, they promised an "investigation" of the rumors. Three days after that meeting all the camouflage was gone, and Czerniaków killed himself with poison. We do not know how long he had kept that pill in his drawer.

The Jewish communities were lulled by the continuation of ordinary routines, including the endless rebuilding of walls and fences, the periodic exactions, confiscations, and arrests, and even the desultory firing by German guards into the ghetto. Yet they did not lack indexes of danger. The whole economic system of the ghettos was not geared to long-term survival. There was large-scale, chronic unemployment, and, as Trunk points out in one of his important findings, a finite supply of personal belongings was mobilized to supplement the insufficiency of production in an effort to pay for legally and illegally imported food.[48] The clock was running down, and soon there were signs of massive German violence. As German armies crossed the Bug and San rivers in June 1941 to assault the USSR, mobile units of the SS and Police began to kill Jews by the hundreds of thousands in eastern Poland, the Baltic states, White Russia, and Ukraine. By the spring of 1942, deportations to death camps commenced in the heart of Poland. The deported Jews were not heard from again.

In the remnant ghettos of 1943, the issue of life and death could no longer be avoided. The alternatives were brought forth and discussed: one could plan escapes, prepare resistance, or redouble an effort to produce goods for the Germans. Even in this drastic situation, there was a tendency to veer away from methodical dispersal or organized battle because of the belief that, while it was not feasible for the entire population to participate in acts of defiance, it was possible for everyone to suffer the consequences.[49]

This is how the doctrine of "rescue through work" became paramount from Upper Silesia to Vilna. It was, in more ways than one, the strategy of least resistance. It was founded also on the presumption that if only the Germans were rational, they would not obliterate the work force engaged in so much war production for them. The thought was, of course, a misconception. The Jews had once placed their trust in rules and regulations for protection against the ravages of totalitarianism; now they clung to contracts and deliveries for safety from destruction. Thus the Jews in Częstochowa were bewildered by the report that in the Warsaw ghetto workers had been dragged from their shops.[50] Still, the rationale of work salvation was not dispelled. If the unskilled were lost, it was hoped that the skilled would remain, and when some of those were removed, it was reasoned that the raids would occur only once in a while. In this manner, Jewry sacrificed more and more for less and less until it was annihilated.

The Ghetto as Self-Destructive Machinery

We have seen now that the Jewish ghetto was a provider of administrative services, a social and economic laboratory, and a state of mind. It was also a form of organized self-destruction.

It should be emphasized that the councils were not the willing accomplices of the Germans. Within the German superstructure, however, they were its indispensable operatives. Even when their activities were benign, as in the case of housing refugees or promoting sanitary conditions, they could contribute to the overall purposes and ultimate goals of their German supervisors. The very institution of an orderly ghetto was, after all, an essential link in the chain of destructive steps. In building this order and preserving it, the councils could not help serving their enemy.

We know, of course, that the Germans expected much more than general government of their Jewish deputies. It was German policy to transfer to Jewish middlemen a large part of the physical and psychological burdens of destroying millions of men, women, and children. One aspect of that assignment was financial, another entailed selections, and the third called for enforcement.

The destruction of Jewry generated administrative costs, and, throughout Europe, German agencies attempted to obtain some of the necessary resources from the Jews themselves. As far as possible, the destruction process was to be self-financing. In Poland, too, an effort was made to balance the books without drawing from the budget of the German Reich. Trunk cites the fact that the German administration of the Lodz ghetto (the *Gettoverwaltung*) covered expenses by taxing deliveries to the ghetto.[51] In Warsaw, there was wall building. The Jewish engineer Marek Lichtenbojm and a large crew of Jewish laborers were engaged at the site, and financial responsibility for the wall was passed on to the Jewish community.[52]

Indirectly, the Warsaw Jews may have subsidized Treblinka. From a letter written to the Warsaw Ghetto Commissioner Auerswald by the first Treblinka commander, Dr. Eberl, it appears that the commissioner was to supply various materials to the camp where shortly afterward the ghetto inhabitants were to be gassed.[53] This is not to say that the Jewish leadership was able to decipher the nature of Treblinka while it was under construction.[54] There may also have been remote funding of death transports from Jewish sources. We know, for example, that the German railways in Lodz billed the Gestapo in the city for the one-way fares. The Gestapo passed the bill to the Lodz *Gettoverwaltung* for payment.[55] We can only surmise how this debt was ultimately discharged.

First the Jewish councils handed over money; then they delivered human beings. Let us remember, though, that the process of selecting victims began with the social structuring of the ghetto population. We have seen that from the moment of their incarceration, the Jews were discernably divided according to their advantages and privileges in life. To be sure, few individuals had any inkling then that these stratifications would acquire a special meaning in the "Final Solution." However, growing suspicions and forebodings had the effect of accentuating the differentiations. Everyone was now concerned with his position all the time, and soon the passes and identification cards made out by the councils became more varied and colorful.[56] The papers spelled out a rank order of protection and, by the same token, vulnerability. At last, separation was bound to be a selection per se, since in the course of a roundup, quotas were often filled with readily available old people, hospitalized patients, or children.[57] In the final analysis, the councils only had to save some to doom all the others.

Jewry became a participant in its own undoing at least passively, underwriting German operations through financial mechanisms and involvements and arraying its own people on an axis that defined degrees of safety or danger. Jews were engaged also in a more active and virulent mode of self-destruction when the Jewish police was employed for German designs. Trunk devotes an entire chapter to the order service.[58] Much attention has always been riveted on the Jewish police because of the role that these semi-uniformed auxiliaries of annihilation performed in the pivotal occurrences of 1941 and 1942.

The order service exercised all the expected functions of a regular police department, such as traffic control and the pursuit of petty thieves. Furthermore, it carried out tasks that were normal only in an abnormal society, from the collection of ghetto taxes to the enforcement of compulsory labor and on to the seizure of families for deportation, including penetrating their hiding places. In some of the large ghettos, the organization of the Jewish police revealed distinctly German features, in particular a division into ordinary and security police components, but even more visible was the adoption of German methods, such as the arrest of parents whose sons did not report for labor duty[59] or the sealing of houses in which individual tenants had not paid taxes.[60] The Jewish police arrested people in the middle of the night and beat up smugglers or the reluctant volunteers for death transports. They ate well and frequently filled their pockets with the bribes and ransom payments of frightened fellow Jews. So many were the instances of sheer brutality and corruption that Trunk patiently recites case after case of exceptions.

Yet the composition of personnel for the order service deepens the paradox of Jew acting against Jew. Whereas some of the recruits may well have been drawn from the underworld, and Emmanuel Ringelblum complains that a hundred baptized Jews were serving in ranking positions of the Warsaw ghetto force,[61] some were included for their prior military experience, a large number was fairly well-educated, and many were idealistic.[62] Here there was a concentration of healthy young men, uniquely capable of conducting intelligence operations or psychological warfare against the Germans, or of aiding in escapes, or even engaging in physical resistance. On isolated occasions, Jewish police may have done just that, but most of the time they were the most conspicuous Jewish instrument in the German destructive machine.

Ringelblum wrote in his notes on 19 February 1941 that the Jewish population had an understanding of the difficulties of being a Jewish policeman. It was hard for Jews to take a Jewish policeman seriously, and often, in those days, the order service would refrain from ordering people around and would "discuss" things with them instead. At one point it was therefore said, "You would have minded a Polish policeman, so why don't you mind a Jewish one!"[63] However, this very trust in the Jewish police was to result in one of the greatest moral disappointments of the Holocaust—an experience from which Jewry has not recovered to this day. Irving Louis Horowitz, in reviewing Trunk's *Judenrat*, concludes, "Jewish policemen of Lodz, Vilna, and Warsaw were, after all, still policemen."[64]

The Jewish ghetto has just been opened, and we see it now with all of its institutions and processes. This is Trunk's lasting achievement. On the other hand, the moral questions raised over so many years have not been closed; they have only become more complicated. We know that already the ghetto leaders themselves were fully aware of their dilemma and that for some it was always on their minds. A small, sensitive book by Leonard Tushnet recently illuminated the lives of just three of these figures: Rumkowski of Lodz, Czerniaków of Warsaw, and Gens of Vilna.[65] They were different men by background as well as in their ideas, but in the end, all three declined to save themselves after they had not succeeded in saving their people.

Notes

1. Isaiah Trunk, *Judenrat: The Jewish Councils in Eastern Europe under Nazi Occupation* (New York, 1972).
2. Ibid., xviii.
3. Trunk concentrates his attention on ghettos located within the prewar boundaries of Poland and Lithuania. There are a few details about Riga in Latvia and Minsk in White Russia, but the ghettos farther east as well as the Jewish communities under Romanian administration between the Dniester and the Bug are almost entirely, if understandably, omitted.
4. Trunk, *Judenrat*, xvii–xviii.
5. To allow for deeper treatment of some of the problems, illustrations in this discussion will be drawn mainly from the Warsaw ghetto.
6. Trunk, *Judenrat*, 104.
7. Trunk discusses at some length intra-German rivalries for control of the ghettos, *Judenrat*, 264–76. The police in particular wanted power over the Jews. See letter by the SS and Police Leader in Warsaw (Wigand), 11 November 1941, claiming jurisdiction of his Protective Police (Schupo) over the Warsaw Ghetto "Order Service." YAD VASHEM microfilm JM 1112 (YIVO microfilm MKY 76).
8. Trunk, *Judenrat*, 572–74.
9. In statistical terms, membership in councils was in fact hazardous. Trunk reports on the basis of his questionnaires that the incidence of violent death among councilmen in the period before the deportations was somewhat high; in his group of 720, about one in four was killed in the ghetto, most were deported, and one in nine survived, *Judenrat*, 326–28. However, the ninety-nine councils covered in his survey must have cumulatively contained several times as many members as the number of recollected names. If the forgotten members died in the gas chambers, the ratios would be less striking.
10. Mohns, deputy chief of the Resettlement Division in the office of the governor of the Warsaw District, to Leist, plenipotentiary of the governor for the City of Warsaw, 11 January 1941, YAD VASHEM microfilm JM 1113 (YIVO microfilm MKY 77).
11. Trunk, *Judenrat*, 82–83.
12. Ibid., 99.

13. For an example of such a request, see the diary of Czerniaków, 7 Jan. 1942, in Raul Hilberg, Stanislaw Staron, and Josef Kermisz, eds., *The Warsaw Diary of Adam Czerniakow* (Briarcliff Manor, NY, 1979), 312–13 (hereafter cited as *Diary of Czerniakow*).
14. See Trunk on Lublin, Bedzin, Zamość, Vilna, *Judenrat*, 484.
15. See Trunk, *Judenrat*, 528–29, on the psychological implications of this shift.
16. Trunk, *Judenrat*, 44.
17. Ibid., 50–51; see also Trunk, "The Organizational Structure of the Jewish Councils in Eastern Europe," *Yad Vashem Studies* 7 (1968): 147–64.
18. Trunk, *Judenrat*, 180–81, 185; other areas of autonomy were Saturday as a day of rest and the use of Hebrew or Yiddish in schools, etc., *Judenrat*, 189, 196–215.
19. Trunk, *Judenrat*, 390–95.
20. Ibid., 400–420.
21. Trunk indulges in the thought that if in August 1944 the Red Army had not stopped about seventy-five miles outside Lodz, some 70,000 Jews in the ghetto might have been saved, *Judenrat*, 413. The same speculation is offered by Robinson in the introduction (Trunk, *Judenrat*, xxix) and was reiterated on another occasion by Yehuda Bauer (Holocaust Conference at the Hebrew College, Boston, 1973). The question is counterfactual. Red Army offensives, though broad, were conducted for limited territorial gain to allow for resupply and regrouping. The halting of the Russian drive so many miles from Lodz was in no sense an "accident." The chance event would have been its opposite—a rapid German collapse.
22. In the Minsk ghetto, the entire council appears to have favored a liaison with partisans, Trunk, *Judenrat*, 466. Also of interest are the councils in Bialystok and Vilna that had "ambiguous" attitudes, *Judenrat*, 467–71.
23. See Trunk on the Lodz resettlement commission, *Judenrat*, 52.
24. Trunk, *Judenrat*, 435–36.
25. Ibid., 385–87.
26. Ibid., 385–87.
27. Ibid., 354.
28. Ibid., 385.
29. Czerniaków to plenipotentiary of the Warsaw District for the City of Warsaw, 21 May 1940, YAD VASHEM microfilm JM 1113 (YIVO Institute microfilm MKY 77). The Warsaw district chief was Gouverneur Fischer, his City Plenipotentiary Leist. For examples of similar labor recruitment in other ghettos, see Trunk, *Judenrat*, 379–80.
30. Czerniaków to Warsaw District Chief/Resettlement Division/Exchange, 8 Jan. 1941. JM 1113. (Schön was in charge of the Resettlement Division.) Krakow also instituted a head tax, see Trunk, *Judenrat*, 381. Levies on earnings were considered problematic because in ghettos like Warsaw smuggling accounted for considerable income.
31. Proclamation of the Warsaw Ghetto Provisioning Authority, signed by Czerniaków, 31 August 1941, *Diary of Czerniakow*, 273–74; on 2 February 1942, he noted that the reserve had made possible free distributions of bread and sugar, *Diary of Czerniakow*, 321–22.

32. Trunk, *Judenrat*, 356, 382. For a detailed discussion of the medical aspects of food deprivation in the Warsaw ghetto, see Leonard Tushnet, *The Uses of Adversity* (New York, 1966). See also Trunk, *Judenrat*, 146–48.
33. Trunk, *Judenrat*, 383. In several ghettos (Kutno, Kolomea, Chelm, etc.), the social pyramid was particularly visible in housing, Trunk, *Judenrat*, 374–77.
34. Czerniakow, *Diary of Czerniakow*, 4 December 1941, 305.
35. Ibid., 24 May 1941, 241–42.
36. Ibid., 23 June 1941, 251.
37. Ibid., 6 October 1941, 285–86.
38. Ibid., 4, 10 February 1942, 322, 324.
39. Trunk, *Judenrat*, 227.
40. Emmanuel Ringelblum, *Notes from the Warsaw Ghetto* (New York, 1958), 300.
41. Trunk, *Judenrat*, 332–42.
42. Ibid., 343–45; Czerniakow, *Diary of Czerniakow*, 27 June 1941, 252–53, 3 December 1941, 304–5. Trunk mentions house committees also in Bialystok, Trunk, *Judenrat*, 515–16.
43. Trunk, *Judenrat*, 505, 644. The text of the agreement between the council and the "Control Office," dated 5 August 1941, appears in the *Diary of Czerniakow*, 265–67.
44. Czerniakow, *Diary of Czerniakow*, 325–26.
45. Trunk, *Judenrat*, 413–36.
46. The remark is cited in another connection by Trunk, *Judenrat*, 292.
47. Trunk, *Judenrat*, 414.
48. Ibid., 101–2.
49. Ibid., see 451–74.
50. Ibid., 404.
51. Ibid., 282–83; see also requisitions of furnishings, etc., 66–67, 296; *Diary of Czerniakow*, 22 July 1941, 260, 28 Nov. 1941, 302.
52. Documents in YAD VASHEM microfilm JM 1112 (YIVO film MKY 76); Czerniaków letter of 8 January 1941, JM 1113 in *Diary of Czerniakow*, 5 July 1941, 254–55, 30 December 1941, 310–11. In Warsaw, Lodz, and Kaunas, the councils had to build bridges to connect ghetto sections divided by Aryan streets, Trunk, *Judenrat*, 110.
53. Eberl to Auerswald, 26 June 1942. Facsimile in Jüdisches Historisches Institut Warschau, *Faschismus-Getto-Massenmord*, 2nd ed. (Berlin, 1961), 304.
54. While Czerniaków became aware of "resettlement" and was told about Treblinka, he did not connect the two. On 17 January 1942, he asked whether Lithuanian guards were coming and was assured that the rumor was false, *Diary of Czerniakow*, 316–17. That same day, he talked to Auerswald who informed him of a conversation with Generalgouverneur Frank as a result of which Jewish prisoners held in Warsaw's Pawiak prison would, if fit for labor, be sent to Treblinka to work. Two days after, Czerniakow noted that Auerswald was going to Berlin. In this entry, Czerniaków also expressed fear of mass resettlement. (In fact, a conference of bureaucrats on the Final Solution was held in Berlin on 20 January 1942. Trunk comments on Auerswald's deception, *Judenrat*, 295–96.) On 19 February 1942, Czerniaków complains

that German prosecutors had failed to produce the appropriate papers for the "release" of prisoners to Treblinka, *Diary of Czerniakow*, 323–24. A day later, the prisoners left. On 10 March, he records the departure of five Jewish clerks to the camp, and on 7 April some 160 young German Jews, recently arrived from the Reich, were sent there, *Diary of Czerniakow*, 333, 341.

55. Facsimile, *Getto-Faschismus-Massenmord*, 214; both items of correspondence, dated 19, 27 May 1942, on a single sheet of paper.
56. Trunk, *Judenrat*, 175–77. The crass illustration is Vilna.
57. Ibid., 507–8, 514.
58. Ibid., 475–527; see also passages in other chapters.
59. Bedzin, Sosnowiec, Zawiercie, Bialystok; Trunk, *Judenrat*, 584. In Warsaw, members of house committees were taken hostage, if a tenant did not present himself for labor. Ringelblum, *Notes*, 176.
60. Częstochowa, Radom, etc. Trunk, *Judenrat*, 483.
61. Ringelblum, *Notes*, 138.
62. Trunk, *Judenrat*, 489–998. The finding that Jewish militants (Betar, etc.) were well-represented in the police is interesting.
63. Ringelblum, *Notes*, 125–26.
64. Irving Louis Horowitz, *Israeli Ecstasies/Jewish Agonies* (New York, 1974), 197.
65. Tushnet, *The Pavement of Hell* (New York, 1972).

Bibliography

Hilberg, Raul, Stanislaw Staron, and Josef Kermisz, eds. *The Warsaw Diary of Adam Czerniakow*. Briarcliff Manor, NY: Stein & Day, 1979.
Horowitz, Irving Louis. *Israeli Ecstasies/Jewish Agonies*. New York: Oxford University Press, 1974.
Jüdisches Historisches Institut Warschau. *Faschismus-Getto-Massenmord*. 2nd ed. Berlin: Rütten & Loening, 1961.
Ringelblum, Emmanuel. *Notes from the Warsaw Ghetto*. New York: McGraw-Hill, 1958.
Trunk, Isaiah. "The Organizational Structure of the Jewish Councils in Eastern Europe." *Yad Vashem Studies* 7 (1968): 147–64.
———. *Judenrat: The Jewish Councils in Eastern Europe under Nazi Occupation*. New York: Macmillan, 1972.
Tushnet, Leonard. *The Uses of Adversity*. New York: Thomas Yoseloff, 1966.
———. *The Pavement of Hell*. New York: St. Martin's Press, 1972.

8

THE *JUDENRAT*
CONSCIOUS OR UNCONSCIOUS "TOOL"
(1979)

MORE THAN THIRTY YEARS AFTER the end of the holocaust, the Jewish Councils remain a difficult topic. We have hesitated to approach them as phenomena that must be analyzed, and we have known for some time that our caution is at least partly psychological. How can we talk about the Councils objectively, without accusing them, exonerating them, or praising them? How can we come to an understanding of the manner in which they arose and functioned, particularly as "tools" of the perpetrators? How can we face that history without raising basic questions that have massive implications for traditional views and assessments of the whole of diaspora history?

Nor is sensitivity our only obstacle. There are intrinsic problems stemming from the fact that our information about the Councils is disconnected and unbalanced. We know more about some of them than about others, more about certain surface aspects of their behavior than about some deeper characteristics not so easily retrievable from documents, memoirs, or questionnaires. In a sense, the task is now more burdensome than ever. The investigator may not lightly skip over data that have already been collected, or country studies already completed, or generalizations already formulated, but the moment has

---

Originally published in *Pattern of Jewish Leadership in Nazi Europe 1933–1945*, ed. Israel Gutman and Cynthia J. Haft (Jerusalem: Yad Vashem Publications, 1979), 31–44.

clearly not yet arrived for a grand summation. This quandary is manifest particularly for anyone who must deal with the Councils quite specifically as agencies or implements of the Germans.

A full description of the Councils in that role demands an overview of two separate subject areas: the Jewish communities and the Nazi German state. These were two worlds apart, but in the course of the ghettoization process, the institution of the Judenrat makes its appearance at the interface between them. In a formal sense, the Councils were supposed to monopolize contacts between the Jewish population and the German machinery of destruction. They were organizationally a link in the communication chain. They expressed Jewish needs to the "authorities" and they transmitted orders from above to Jewish families and individuals. To appreciate that function at all, one should therefore keep in mind both the needs and the orders, the degree of Jewish deprivation and suffering, and the nature of German decisions not to speak of actions taken by collaborating non-German ministries, commissariats, and municipalities in occupied and satellite countries.

Noting the administrative placement of the Councils in the larger structure is a key prerequisite for any exploration of their activities, but the sheer depiction of lines and channels will yield only a motionless, static picture, without a sense of the accentuation and intensification of anti-Jewish measures as they occurred from month to month. We must accordingly specify a second requirement for our analytical effort, and that is a visualization of the Councils in the context of an evolving destruction process. The Germans, after all, developed their assault upon Jewry step by step, and to them the Councils were primarily a control mechanism to be employed in an intermediate stage. In German eyes at any rate, the segregation of the Jews was not an end in itself. Hence, our own approach to these events must be made up of two ingredients, one "spatial," the other transformational over time. We must, in short, ask ourselves not simply what the Councils were at the outset, but what they were to become in the end.

The Jewish Councils became a German tool as a consequence of their origin, condition, and strategy. That is a large statement, bridging a variety of Councils in various parts of Europe, and blotting out considerable differences between them. It is a generalization holding that from the beginning, virtually all of the Councils were placed into an irreversible position, regardless of the thoughts or perceptions of their leaders. Of course, local particularities had a great deal to do with the dependence of a Jewish community on its Judenrat and, for that matter, the relations of a Council with German offices and personnel, but geographic variations, great as they were, did not change the substance of its involvement. The inextricable linkage of the Councils with some German or satellite control office was the common feature of all of them.

The sameness in the history of the Councils should not astonish us. They were established in a standard manner, they faced a host of identical problems, and they confronted their overwhelming dilemmas with remarkably similar policies fashioned out of the bedrock of Jewish experience. Crucial is the circumstance that these very factors contained an inescapable contradiction, a fatal paradox. In a word, the problem was that the Councils were serving the German persecutor with their "good" qualities as well as their "bad" ones, and their positive attributes and achievements became functional in the overall German design.

One may observe this phenomenon in the first instance by examining the mode in which the Councils were installed. They derived their authority from German decrees or, in the satellite countries, from ordinances of collaborating governments. A basic rule in every case was the specification that directives had to be carried out promptly and with exactitude, no matter whether they were anticipated or handed down in peremptory fashion, and regardless of whether their contents were beneficial, innocuous, or disastrous. Theoretically, the principle might apply even in a situation where no means were given to carry out an assignment. The Councils could petition for alleviation or postponement, but they were expected to accept denial and not to protest it. Many times, in many places, the Councils were thereupon required to perform acts that were integral steps in the implementation of destructive operations: registrations for housing or ghettoization, statistical and other informational reports, taxation or sequestrations for German uses, wall building, notification of victims to report for labor or "evacuation," even the compiling of transport lists, as well as round-ups conducted by Jewish Police. In this direct sense, the requirements of the perpetrators rendered the Councils implements of the German will almost as soon as there were Councils to which orders could be given.

Yet the symbol of German authority did not divest the Councils of their authentic Jewish roots. On the whole, the Jewish leaders under the Nazis were not personalities newly arrived at the field of action; frequently they were the prewar chairmen of communities, or deputies or stand-ins for those who had "deserted" or fled from their posts. If, in the turmoil of German occupation, they were not exactly volunteers, neither were they hand-picked collaborators. Equally, they do *not* qualify as a group for selection as the best, most heroic, most martyred element of Jewry, or, for that matter, the least prepared, least able, least virtuous segment of the community. They were, if anything, somewhat representative of the political culture of the time, in that many of the Council members had been "prominent" in some of the endeavors that had always been valued in the Jewish community. The vast majority of them maintained tangible ties with Jewry or at least represented it vis-à-vis the outside world. They were merchants symbolizing Jewish success, professionals exemplifying Jewish intellect, rabbis incorporating the Jewish past, or perhaps welfare officials and other bureaucrats whose careers had been identified with some Jewish cause. They were therefore plausible, genuine Jewish leaders even if their stationary stamped them as "elders" in a Judenrat.

It is that authenticity of the Councils that made them all the more lethal. In all of Europe, the Quislings were openly identified with the Germans, but in the Jewish community the Council members were always regarded as a part of Jewry, even if they passed on calamitous German orders or dispatched Jewish Police into Jewish homes to arrest recalcitrant taxpayers or reluctant deportees. That is the meaning of an incident in Vienna, when in June 1942, a member of the Jewish war veterans realized that the Viennese Community chairman, Josef Löwenherz, had extracted information on lists kept by the veterans organization, which were then used for deportation purposes. He spoke as though Löwenherz had betrayed him. The sentiment was shared by several of his colleagues. Everyone could see now that the *Kultusgemeinde* was a "messenger" of the Gestapo.[1]

Not everyone saw a Gestapo messenger in the person of Józef Szeryński, chief of the Warsaw ghetto Jewish Police, who helped round up several hundred thousand Jews for deportation in August and September 1942. Szeryński was completely alienated from the Jewish community—he was a Christian convert and, before the war, had served as a high-ranking Polish police official. From a Jewish contemporary account we learn, however, that two or three weeks after the beginning of the deportations, Szeryński was approached by a group of Jewish porters and cart drivers (experienced in smuggling) with a plan of "resistance." Szeryński told them that he had seen postcards from deportees in Treblinka, attesting to the safety of the Jews in the camp. The porters and drivers believed him with the "naïveté of athletes."[2]

Again and again, Jewish Councils made implicit appeals to Jewish men and women for trust. As late as March 1944, after the entry of German forces in Hungary, the Jewish Council in Budapest addressed the community in paragraphs that included such terms as "open" and "unambiguous." Nothing was being held back. The Jewish population was to carry out all instructions. No one would be arrested simply for being Jewish. The authorities had said so.[3] Barely two months later, the Hungarian transports were on their way to Auschwitz. Once more, a Council had used its image, which was now a tool in itself, serving German interests and blocking Jewish escape.

Government is not merely the issuance of orders or the open application of compulsions; it is also a mechanism for responding to people in need. The Jewish Councils, particularly in Eastern Europe, were governmental entities, and the Jewish communities under their care were highly dependent on assistance and relief. Often the Councils were supplies of these essentials; it is to the Councils that destitute or desperate people turned for a job, an apartment, or a loaf of bread. And as soon as they did so, they could find the Council manipulative and "bureaucratic." The ghetto inmate had to stand in line, his life was filled with identity cards, fees, chicanery—all of the grinding experiences of men and women exposed to procedures, rules, or whim.

Viewed from below, the ghetto offices seemed to be clogged with the rising tide of pleas for favors, privileges, and grants. But dependency did not stop at the door of the Council chairman. He, in turn, had to appeal to "supervisory authorities" for much of what he was expected to deliver. All the way to the top, that was a situation in which inactivity—the opposite of decision—spelled death.

We know from such documents as the diary of Adam Czerniaków that at times the Councils strove to do what they could in a nightmarish environment of uncertainties, shortages, and violence. Their task was all the harder because their "achievements" tended to be short-run. Food was consumed, fuel was burned, even while poverty and crowding continued with unabated effect. Relief was always temporary, whereas the loss of possessions and strength was felt like a cumulative and unending deprivation. Yet the failures of a Council did not necessarily nullify its power; insufficiencies could increase the need of the people. The Councils passed on the appeals, more and more of them for fewer and fewer results.

These implications were not only material; they were psychic as well. For the members of the community receiving handouts from ghetto offices, the Council acquired an ambiguous quality, as a source of life-giving and death-dealing forces simultaneously at work. In the crassest case, during the darkest hours of the Warsaw ghetto, the Council promised bread and marmalade to starving people who would report voluntarily at the railway tracks.[4] They came.

The Councils themselves could easily become psychological captives of the perpetrator. The very setting of their official activities was conducive to a state of institutionalized subservience. They were either waiting for word, or rushing an assignment to completion, or rhythmically preparing monthly reports. On occasion, they wanted to be backed by their German supervisors before imposing a new regulation on the community, and sometimes they might seek an expression of German approval for work they had already done. Consider the linguistic quality of a conversation held on 27 January 1943 in an air of civility between Jakob Edelstein, the "Elder" of Theresienstadt, and two SS captains. Edelstein was told in the course of this meeting that on the very next day a number of prominent Jews would be arriving at Theresienstadt from Berlin and Vienna, and he would no longer be in charge of the Jewish Council. He would have to serve in a triumvirate that would be headed by Dr. Paul Eppstein of Berlin and would also contain a Viennese. Edelstein knew that Eppstein had been involved in deportations. He knew the record of the Vienna *Kultusgemeinde*. What he said to the German was that after fourteen months of "building" the ghetto (*Aufbauarbeit*), he could not receive their announcement with "satisfaction." The two Germans reassured him that they did not intend to slight his accomplishments.[5]

If the Councils appeared two-sided to the Jewish population, a similar image could sometimes be conveyed by the German administration to the Councils. The German supervisor was not always a taskmaster, he could also be a patron. The Germans would ship soap to a ghetto.[6] In Lublin, they saw no "obstacle" to the creation by the Jewish Council of schools or vocational training courses.[7] In several districts, they considered the necessity of allowing Polish municipalities to transfer revenues derived from Jewish payments to a Jewish welfare organization.[8] Such measures might have been perceived as favors in the Jewish community. From the German point of view, however, they were the modicum of effort required to avert uncontrolled epidemics, sudden instability, or premature disaster. Gestures and concessions were thus never bona fide acts of support. Benefits accorded by a German—whether they were imagined, contingent, or real—were always misleading and disorienting. They fostered fantasies, occasionally producing a Jewish leadership that was in a trance at the controls.

The duality that pervaded the Councils in their origin and functions turned out to be a fatal combination. Seemingly contradictory elements were fused: Jewish authenticity aided German authority; bread, soup kitchens, and sewing machines became fasteners in the German destructive machine. The most far-reaching involvement, however, was a consequence of the strategy of the Councils. Isaiah Trunk calls it—with reference to the Eastern ghettos—the policy of salvation through work. In the western and southern regions of Europe, the Jewish communities had very few workshops, but the objective of their Councils was not unlike that of their counterparts in the east. There is a generic name for such decision-making: it is called minimization.

The Jewish Councils, West and East, tried to postpone disaster or, failing in that attempt, to reduce its extent. They cautioned against provoking the Germans and sought ways to create work projects that would make as many Jews as possible indispensable to the war economy. The effort played into German hands. The perpetrators too had a minimization strategy. They wanted to reduce their costs to a minimum, keeping guard forces small, and exploiting scarce Jewish labor until the last moment. The Jewish and German policies, at first glance opposites, were in reality pointed in the same direction.

If we look at the Councils as Nazi Germany saw them, they were clearly tools created for the purpose of maintaining order and mobilizing the Jewish community for German ends. They were all the more effective to the extent that they were authentic, concerned, and compliant. We might add that often enough the Councils were necessary tools, that they relieved a burden on an overtaxed German apparatus, that in supplying information, money, police, and labor, they performed tasks for which the Germans themselves did not have sufficient means. By and large, the Gestapo and the civil administration did not finance ghetto walls, did not keep order in ghetto streets, and did not make up deportation lists. They availed themselves of the intermediary structure of the Jewish Councils and offices. We can see that syndrome now, but was it observable then? In particular, were the Councils themselves conscious of being tools?

To answer that difficult question, we must first ask another: tools for what? The anti-Jewish destruction process fell into two phases.

During the preliminary operations, Jews were defined, expropriated, forced into labor projects, and concentrated under Jewish Councils. In the course of the annihilation phase, the occupied USSR was the scene of periodic "combings" of Jewish communities for mass shootings, while other areas of Europe were organized for deportations to unspecified destinations: the death camps. That is a chronology in which open measures preceded secret ones. The beginnings, at any rate, were unconcealed.

Indeed, there is some evidence that well before the annihilation process began Zionists in Slovakia and the Netherlands believed that a Council could not help being a conduit for orders of the perpetrators, and it would not be able to separate its responsibility to the community from its responsiveness to its supervisors; a tool is a tool, one and indivisible. Whether Council members themselves believed that they were German implements is quite another matter. They had their reasons—or rationalizations—for being and remaining in office; some of them thought that they had a duty to stay at the helm. Occasionally, they fought hard to maintain their jurisdiction against internal challenges, as in the case of Warsaw and Vilna. Sometimes they sought to extend their powers as the Amsterdam Council did when it succeeded in becoming the *Joodse Raad* of all Holland—all of it to help the community.[9]

The second part of the German destruction process, starting on 22 June 1941, with the mass shootings in Russia and going on with the deportations elsewhere thereafter, now looms in our mind as a radical break with two thousand years of anti-Jewish activities. In the ghetto, however, the Final Solution was not proclaimed by the perpetrators; it had to be inferred from events. At this point, the Councils had to ask themselves what was transpiring, and why.

In the territory wrested from the USSR, all of the Councils were established in the wake of massacres. Death surrounded these ghettos from the day of their founding. We know from a detailed report of *Einsatzkommando* 3 in Lithuania that seventy-one Jewish communities there were decimated. Fourteen of them, that is, the larger ones, were struck more than once at intervals averaging a week.[10] Yet even such inundations were not necessarily conclusive. More often than not, we suspect, they were evaluated as single episodes, rather than as a patterned destruction process. If half of a community was destroyed in three successive shootings, perhaps the other half would be left alive. If surrounding ghettos were wiped out, the remaining one might be spared. Never was the past the inevitable future.

These thought processes may be illustrated with discussion at Council meetings in Białystok, a city taken by the Germans during the opening battles with the Soviet Union. In November 1941, the chairman of the Białystok Council, Rabbi Gedaliah Rosenman, spoke with a sense of "hope." The next speaker, the engineer Efraim Barasz, echoed his remarks. The ghetto had endured confiscation, forced labor, and "evacuation," but the Jews had been quartered in a section of the city that was not the worst, they could hand over three pounds of gold instead of twelve, and a demand for a large monetary contribution had been dropped altogether. Later on, in the summer of 1942, Barasz had not lost his confidence. True, he had been given to understand that "too many" Jews were still inhabiting Białystok, but these were the words of newly arrived Germans; the old cadre was still "for the ghetto." The Jews were still needed. In October 1942, Barasz criticized physicians who were excusing tubercular patients from work. These doctors, he said, did not understand that nowadays people were going to die, not from tuberculosis but from not working.[11] Barasz was quite correct. By February 1943, several trainloads of Białystok Jews were on their way to Auschwitz.

In the larger part of the destructive arena, west of the Bug River in Poland and away from the open-air shootings, the view was more opaque. The gas chambers were hidden in camps. When rumors, signals, or reports were received, the Councils often kept such information to themselves. They did not want to share their apprehensions with the population; they could not cope with disclosures. In Paris, on 15 July 1942, the UGIF* (the Jewish Council of France) employed several women to attach pieces of string to squares of cardboard. It occurred to one of the women that she was preparing signs that could be tied to children. The roundup began the next day. Thousands of children were among the victims.[12] Sometimes, the news was discounted or disbelieved. We all know the oft-told story of Carl Bertel Henriques, president of the Copenhagen Community, who in September 1943, replied to a warning from a prominent Dane** with the words: "You're lying."[13]

---

* L'Union générale des israélites de France.
** I.e., Hans Hedtoft, former leader of the Danish Social Democrats (1939–1941) and, after the war, two-time Prime Minister of Denmark (1947–1950 and 1953–1955).

In Warsaw, Adam Czerniaków recorded his suspicions and fears in his diary. He became aware of ominous developments as early as October 1941, and he noted them in several entries during the following months. Finally, when deportations were impending, the Jewish leader asked the Germans themselves whether the rumors were true. The SS men denied everything, but he remained unconvinced. A few days later, Czerniaków killed himself.

In Vienna, there was a similar inquiry. The following is an account of it by Dr. Karl Ebner who was the IV B of the Viennese Gestapo:

> The director of the Israelite Community and later of the Jewish Council of Elders was Dr. Josef Löwenherz. I would come into contact with him several times, one could safely say often. He was the one who first brought to me a rumor that Jews in concentration camps were being gassed and annihilated. He came to me one day after 1942, in other words, presumably in 1943, an utterly broken man, and asked for a meeting with Huber [Chief of the Vienna Gestapo]. I asked him what he wanted and he told me that the Jews were allegedly being put to death, and he wanted to be sure that this was in fact the case. I thought that he was going to have a bad time with the chief and that he might conceivably be charged with spreading enemy radio reports. Löwenherz said that was all the same to him [*es sei ihm alles egal*] and thereupon we went to Huber. When Huber was put into the picture, he then called the chief of office IV in the Reich Security Main Office (Müller) on the direct line, while we waited outside. As we went in again, Huber said to us Müller had dismissed these allegations as evil reports. Löwenherz was visibly relieved.[14]

As we all know, Löwenherz kept his post until Germany's collapse.

Not so Bernard Zundelewicz. As a member of the Warsaw Ghetto Jewish Council, he had survived the massive summer deportations of 1942. Thereafter he headed the Council's Labor Division, an agency in its very nature concerned by then with a substantial percentage of the remaining Jewish population. In January 1943, the Germans conducted another roundup. Papers were to be checked and people were to be screened. Zundelewicz and his family were themselves endangered. His wife and son wanted to hide, but he relied on the word of the Germans promising immunity to Council members and their closest relatives, and he believed himself doubly protected because of the central role in the "productivization" of the ghetto. He reported with his wife and son as ordered and all three were deported to Treblinka.[15]

From one end of Europe to the other, Jews were loaded on trains and not heard from again. Occasionally, as in Slovakia, escapees from Auschwitz brought back the dire news. In Brussels, an attempt was made to discover the fate of the people who had been moved to the East. A Belgian engineer, charged with the task, brought back a description to the Auschwitz camp, complete with smoking chimneys.[16] Polish Jews crossed the frontiers into Hungary and Romania and reported that in the southern part of Eastern Galicia, Jewry had "bled to death."[17]

In the Łódź ghetto, official Jewish chroniclers actually recorded what had been discovered. Deportations from January to mid-April 1942 had resulted in the disappearance of 44,000 Jews, more than a fourth of the entire ghetto population. On 12 April, according to the chroniclers, an SS officer visited the ghetto and said that the deportees had all been brought to a camp near Warthbrücken and that a total of 100,000 Jews were already located there. The SS man indicated that earlier, 30,000 German resettlers from Galicia had stayed there and that they had left behind well-equipped barracks and even furniture. Provisions for the Jews were excellent and deportees fit for work were repairing roads or engaged in agriculture. A further entry in the chronicles, at the end of May, makes note of the perplexing arrival of large shipments of clothes in the ghetto. Heavy trucks were being unloaded at warehouses for days on end. The cargo consisted of personal belongings, many of them wrapped in blankets and bedsheets. Evidently the owners had not been the packers. In the ghetto, the sorters found skirts, pants, underwear, jackets, coats with torn seams, window curtains, prayer shawls. Often letters and identification papers fell out of the garments indicating addresses in Germany, nearby towns, and Łódź itself.[18] From that moment, the ghetto was presented with the inescapable discovery that Chełmno was a death camp.

Even if the members of a *Judenrat* were completely sealed in their ghetto, they had to be conscious of the silence. Therefore, the question is not when they knew, or how much they knew, or who knew what. Rather, it is the more fundamental problem of why these men took any action in the absence of detailed knowledge, why they participated in the delivery of victims to the railroad tracks when they had not found out the route of the trains and were not told the last stop.

We know what happened in several cases when premonitions were confirmed and when doubts vanished. In Slovakia, the Council's deportation expert, who had made up many transport lists, offered Adolf Eichmann's representative $20,000 as a start toward a long series of ransom negotiations.[19] Ghetto Police in Kovno, Riga, and Minsk aided partisans and assisted in escapes.[20] According to a letter by SS Captain Dieter Wisliceny to the German Military Administration in Salonika, Rabbi Zvi Koretz approached the Greek puppet prime minister and, "losing his self control," tearfully asked him to intervene with the Germans so that the two-thousand-year-old Salonika community might not be "liquidated."[21] In most instances the Council chairmen went on, taking one fatal step after another, guided by the thought, not of how many people would be going to their destruction, but how many could be saved. In September 1942, Rumkowski of Łódź thus "cut off the limbs to save the body." The limbs were the children under the age of eleven.[22]

In Berlin, the chief of the city's Jewish community, Moritz Henschel, justifying the participation of Council machinery in the roundups, reasoned: "If *we* do these things, then this will always be carried out in a better and gentler way."[23] Rabbi Leo Baeck, in a statement describing those very events, used the same word: "gentle."[24] In such a manner, the leaders of the Jewish community in Germany evolved their own brand of euthanasia.

We must not conclude, however, that the Jewish Councils were an aberration, alienated from the Jewish community and from its attitudes or beliefs. In the very first article, published in the very first issue of *Yad Vashem Studies*, in 1957, Benzion Dinur wrote:

> The councils cannot be considered in isolation. They constitute an expression basically of what remained of the confidence the Jews had in Germany even under its Nazi regime. The Jews obediently carried out the various regulations enacted even when at a certain risk they could evade them; they registered when they were required to do so. The Jews of the Netherlands hurried with luggage to embark upon the trains carrying them to the East, disbelieving the tales they had been told of death journeys. Even in Warsaw and Vilna, in Bialystok and in Lwow for a long time such reports were discredited...[25]

In the final analysis, the Councils succumbed to an illusion. They followed precedents in unprecedented situations. Believing themselves to be leaders, they were led along most of the way. Above them stood a machine of destruction as relentless as any that had ever existed. Below, a ghetto population, clinging to the past, held them in place by sheer force of gravity, until death overtook them all.

Notes

1. Minutes of conference of invalid war veterans, 9 June 1942, YIVO Archives, OCC E 6a–18.
2. Stefan Ernest, "Trzeci front; O wojnie Wielkich Niemiec z Żydami Warszawy 1939–1943" (The Third Front: The war between great Germany and the Jews of Warsaw), 143–45. Unpublished manuscript in the private collection of Dr. Lucjan Dobroszycki. Ernest wrote his memoirs while in hiding early in 1943.
3. Text in Randolph L. Braham, "The Role of the Jewish Council in Hungary: A Tentative Assessment," *Yad Vashem Studies* 10 (1974): 88–89.
4. Facsimile of the order in Jüdisches Historisches Institut (Warschau), ed. *Faschismus—Getto—Massenmord*, 2nd edition (Berlin: 1961), 309.
5. Memorandum by Zucker and Edelstein on conference with SS *Hauptsturmführer* Seidl and Möhs, 27 January 1943, Israel Police doc. no. 1239. The Viennese was supposed to have been Löwenherz. His deputy in deportation matters, Rabbi Murmelstein, came instead.
6. Report by the *Kreishauptmann* of Radzyn (Lublin *Distrikt*) for February 1941. Signature illegible, possibly Dr. Schmige, Yad Vashem Archives (hereafter: YVA), JM/814.
7. Remarks by *Schulrat* Klünder at Lublin *Distrikt* conference held on 5 December 1940. Text of conference summary in YVA, JM/814.
8. See, for example, report dated 7 March 1941 by the *Kreishauptmann* of Petrikau (Radom *Distrikt*) for February 1941. Signature illegible, YVA, JM/814.
9. Joseph Michman, "The Controversial Stand of the *Joodse Raad* in Holland: Lodewijk E. Visser's Struggle," *Yad Vashem Studies* 10 (1974), 22–34.
10. A copy of the report, dated 1 December 1941 is in the Institut für Zeitgeschichte (Munich), Fb 85/2.
11. Records of the Białystok *Judenrat* in YVA, M-11. English translation from Yiddish in Lucy S. Dawidowicz, *A Holocaust Reader* (New York, 1976), 273–87.
12. Claude Lévy and Paul Tillard, *Betrayal at the Vel' d'Hiv'* (New York: 1969), 66–67.
13. Aage Bertelsen, *October '43* (New York: 1954), 17–19.
14. Statement by Dr. Karl Ebner in Vienna, 20 September 1961, *Strafsachen gegen Novak* 1416/61, *Landesgericht für Strafsachen Wien*, Band VI, 111–16.
15. Ernest, "Trzeci front," 124–27.

16. The report, by Victor Martin, was made after the agent traveled to Upper Silesia in October 1942. Text in YVA, O-2/300.
17. Letter dated 6 January 1942, from Romania to "Relico" (relief organization in Geneva), YVA, M/20.
18. D. Dabrowska and Lucjan Dobroszycki, eds., *Kronika getta Łódzkiego* (The chronicle of the Lodz Ghetto) (Łódź Wydam: 1965), 1:457–58, 1:619–20.
19. Interrogation of Wisliceny in Bratislava, 7 May 1946, YVA, M-5/36 (1).
20. Isaiah Trunk, *Judenrat* (New York, 1972), 521–22.
21. Wisliceny to Merten, 15 April 1943, Federal Records Center at Alexandria, Va., EAP VIII-173-b-16–14/26.
22. Rumkowski's speech in diary of Józef Zelkowicz in YIVO. English translation from the Yiddish in Dawidowicz, *A Holocaust Reader*, 306–9.
23. Statement by Moritz Henschel in Palestine, 1947. Text in English transcript of the Eichmann trial, 11 May 1961, session 37, Nn 1.
24. Leo Baeck, "A People Stands before Its God," in *We Survived*, ed. Eric H. Boehm (New Haven, CT, 1949), 288.
25. Benzio Dinur, "Problems Confronting Yad Vashem in its Work of Research," *Yad Vashem Studies* 1 (1957): 27.

Bibliography

Baeck, Leo. "A People Stands before Its God." In *We Survived*, ed. Eric H. Boehm, 288. New Haven, CT: Yale University Press, 1949.
Bertelsen, Aage. *October '43*. New York: Putnam's Sons, 1954.
Braham, Randolph L. "The Role of the Jewish Council in Hungary: A Tentative Assessment." *Yad Vashem Studies* 10 (1974): 69–109.
Dabrowska, D., and Lucjan Dobroszycki, eds. *Kronika getta Łódzkiego* (The chronicle of the Lodz Ghetto). Łódź Wydam: Łódzkie, 1965.
Dawidowicz, Lucy S. *A Holocaust Reader*. New York: Behram House Inc., 1976.
Dinur, Benzio. "Problems Confronting Yad Vashem in its Work of Research." *Yad Vashem Studies* 1 (1957): 7–30.
Ernest, Stefan. "Trzeci front; O wojnie Wielkich Niemiec z Żydami Warszawy 1939–1943" (The Third Front: The war between great Germany and the Jews of Warsaw), 143–45. Unpublished manuscript in the private collection of Dr. L. Dobroszycki.
Jüdisches Historisches Institut (Warschau), ed. *Faschismus—Getto—Massenmord*. 2nd ed. Berlin: Government Publication, 1961.
Lévy, Claude, and Paul Tillard. *Betrayal at the Vel' d'Hiv'*. New York: Hill and Wang, 1969.
Michman, Joseph. "The Controversial Stand of the *Joodse Raad* in Holland: Lodewijk E. Visser's Struggle." *Yad Vashem Studies* 10 (1974): 22–34.
Trunk, Isaiah. *Judenrat: The Jewish Councils in Eastern Europe under Nazi Occupation*. New York: Macmillan, 1972.

9

I WAS NOT THERE
(1988)

"IF YOU WERE NOT THERE, you cannot imagine what it was like." These words were said to me in Düsseldorf some years ago by a one-legged veteran of the German army who had been trapped in the Demyansk Pocket on the Russian front at the end of 1941. The man had been wounded six times. One cannot deny that he had a valid point.

I recall another occasion when one of the earliest Holocaust conferences was held in San José, California. It was a gathering called on a grand scale with hundreds of guests. One visitor, an elderly person, perhaps nearing eighty years of age, sat there quietly for the three days. I wondered who he was. Since he had a name tag, and since there was also a book display, I could search for a book he might have written. I found one. It was an autobiographical work about the battle of Verdun, which had taken place in World War I, and the book was titled *Holocaust*.* It may not be said that he was not entitled to the use of this word.

Yet among man-made disasters, such as purges, massacres, and wars, the Holocaust is a novel event and a new marker in history. Contrast it for a minute with warfare. When a soldier speaks of chance, he is usually assessing the possibilities of being killed. A Holocaust survivor who refers to chance is talking about the good fortune of having

---

Originally published in *Writing and the Holocaust*, ed. Berel Lang (New York: Holmes & Meier, 1988), 17–25.
* William Hermanns, *The Holocaust: From a Survivor of Verdun* (New York: Harper & Row, 1972).

been left alive. Nor do the comparative casualty rates constitute the only difference. The Holocaust is unique in structure. It is a process, willfully shaped by perpetrators, suffered by victims, and observed by bystanders. Unlike a battle, which is the same or a similar experience for participants on both sides, the encounter with the Holocaust is one story coming from German bureaucrats, quite another from the Jewish victims, and still another, or others, from numerous, distinct onlookers.

Furthermore, there is no commonality in the form of these accounts. The Germans left a mass of records. The United States alone captured 40,000 linear feet of these documents, that is to say, folders in boxes lining that many feet of shelf. Included in this material are a few orders, some letters, and a great many reports, including official war diaries and the like. Voluminous as these reports may be, they are often extraordinarily terse in content. Thus a single line in a report of the local military headquarters in the Black Sea port of Mariupol, dated 29 October 1941 stated: "8,000 Jews were executed by the Security Service."*

In German documents one may discover the Holocaust in all of its bureaucratic complexity, but records of this kind tend to deal with people in the aggregate. They are filled with references to jurisdictions, procedures, regulations, numbers, places, and dates. Yet if we look for personal accounts of the perpetrators, we will find ourselves largely stymied. The Germans left few private diaries, and their memoirs for the most part are heavily self-censored.

The situation is the reverse in the case of Jewish sources. Jewish documents, in the main the correspondence of Jewish Councils, are relatively sparse in number. Conversely, there are multitudinous statements of survivors recording their recollections. Sometime during the second half of the late 1950s, the historian and bibliographer Philip Friedman, a survivor himself, told me that survivors' accounts were getting out of hand, that they were too numerous to list. At last count there were more than 18,000. That was thirty years ago.

A more pointed statement about survivors' testimonies came from Theodore Ziolkowski of Princeton University writing in the fall 1979 issue of the *Sewanee Review*. Ziolkowski said that these accounts all resembled one another. Whereas each survivor may have thought that

---

* Source: Ortskommandatur I/853 in Mariupol an Korück 533, 29.10.1941, National Archives Record Group 242, T 501, Roll 56.

he had a special tale to tell, a reader stepping back to examine the whole lot would conclude that all these people were speaking in unison about virtually identical experiences: what it was like during the last moments of peace, what happened when the Nazis came, how rapidly the Jewish community was engulfed, how family and friends vanished in gas chambers, and how finally the survivor, all alone, was liberated just in time to start a new life.

There is a sameness in these statements, not only in terms of what is written, but also in regard to what is left out. Survivors by and large are special kinds of people who share personality characteristics, an outlook on life, and a way of describing the world. If we want something else from them—for instance, the "before" and "after" enclosing the Holocaust years, or the nature of their crucial relations with parents or others who were very close to them—then we would have to reduce the tens of thousands of their accounts to a handful. Let me tell you about one of these more unusual testimonies.

The story, which I discovered during a late evening hour in March 1987 while watching television in Germany, begins with a "Catholic author" who died several decades ago and who was almost forgotten after her death, Elisabeth Langgässer. I must confess that this opening on the show almost made me change the channel, but soon I learned that although Elisabeth's mother was a Catholic, her father had been a Jew who converted to Catholicism. In other words, this author was "non-Aryan." During her youth, Elisabeth became a school teacher and writer. She had an affair with a Jew whom she could not marry, because he was already married and the father of children. In 1929, Elisabeth had a daughter with this man and she named the girl Cordelia. By 1933, Elisabeth was isolated. Unable to teach school after she had born a child out of wedlock, unable to publish anything because she was non-Aryan, she married a German. Cordelia grew up in this household and long afterward, in 1984, she wrote her own story in Swedish, translated into German two years later, and published in Munich as a novel, *Gebranntes Kind sucht das Feuer* (Burned child seeks the fire). By the time I bought the book, a day after the television broadcast, it had gone through eight printings.

Cordelia is Cordelia Edvardson now, but she does not live in Sweden. Her childhood in Germany was peaceful enough—she remembers having attended an SS wedding as a nine-year-old and having danced with an SS officer who was unaware of her background. Gradually, however, the situation became more ominous. In September

1941, the Jewish star was introduced and before long the first transports moved to the east. Cordelia's mother was protected by virtue of having been half-German, Catholic, and married to a German, but Cordelia herself, three-quarters Jewish by descent, was considered a Jewish person under the Nuremberg law, without regard to her adherence to a Christian religion. The frantic mother attempted to arrange a marriage with a Spanish officer who had volunteered to serve on the Russian front, but Cordelia was too young. She then attempted to place her with an older Spanish couple for adoption, so that the youngster might have the protection of the Spanish flag. The stratagem was discovered by the Gestapo who confronted not the mother but the daughter with the following proposition: first, evading the anti-Jewish decrees was a crime for which the mother might be sent to a concentration camp, but second, if Cordelia signed a piece of paper accepting her status under German law, her mother would be excused. Cordelia recoiled, then signed.

The daughter had protected her mother and now she was unprotected herself. She was dropped from her Catholic club, the motto of which was "one for all and all for one." Adopted by a Jew who was deported, she was lodged in Berlin's Jewish hospital for a while. Then she was sent to Theresienstadt, a ghetto in Czechoslovakia, from which most inmates were deported to Auschwitz. Cordelia herself was sent on to this camp. She was number A 3709 there. Since she was young and alert, she had a chance to survive. At the end of the war, the emaciated girl was brought to Sweden for recovery. Her mother wanted to know all about Auschwitz so she could write a novel about it. Cordelia stayed in Sweden, married there, and had a Christian family of her own. During the October War of 1973, she rebelled. Drawn to Israel, she dropped her Catholicism and stayed in Jerusalem, while her daughter, in Germany, went on to edit Elisabeth's manuscripts.

The survivor knows isolation. Survival is a solitary experience in any case, but Cordelia was doubly alone because she had suffered a Jewish fate as a Christian. She did not know her Jewish father and she could not go back to her half-Jewish Catholic mother. She was becoming middle-aged before she liberated herself to settle in Israel. At long last, she stands before us, not with a fragment of her life, but with her entire exceptional existence and that of her mother.

These then are our primary sources. There is incompleteness in them, and taking them as a whole, there are imbalances within imbalances. Nor can this state of affairs be corrected. Even if we keep searching for more documents in archives—and we will—or generate more testimony in oral history projects—and we do—the resulting picture will surely be more detailed, but it will not contain a sharply new perspective.

And that is only half of the problem, because the question is not confined to what we should describe; it is also a matter of how we should write. Are there any rules? Friends of mine who write novels tell me that there are no commandments to the creator of imaginative literature, that the imagination cannot be hemmed in, that the page facing the writer is as blank as the canvas of the artist. Yet one hears about rules governing the exploration of this subject almost all the time. We may label them political or even religious, but these concerns are secondary or subsidiary when the main issue is art. Once we speak of writing as an art form, we raise the question of if Holocaust writing is fraught with risks not encountered in the treatment of other topics. To be sure, the Holocaust has caught us unprepared. Its unprecedentedness and, above all, unexpectedness, necessitates the use of words or materials that were never designed for depictions of what happened here. This is a problem that affects everyone, including those who had seen these occurrences firsthand.

Let me cite two examples from the plastic arts. I recall visiting Auschwitz and Treblinka in 1979. The trip was organized by President Jimmy Carter's Commission on the Holocaust and our purpose in traveling to these sites was the hope of finding some guidance in the planning of our own Holocaust museum in Washington, DC. Treblinka, the death camp, does not exist anymore. It was torn down by the Germans, and after the war, Polish sculptors created a stark symbolic camp of stone in its place. When we went on to Israel, our chairman, Elie Wiesel, said something startling. Everywhere we had gone, he said, the places we had seen were beautiful. Indeed, Treblinka, where bodies were once lying around unburied and clothes were heaped high, is now a serene memorial.

Another story, told by the late poet and survivor, Abba Kovner of Israel, also refers to Treblinka. In a kibbutz near Haifa there is a scale model of the camp, built by one of the few Treblinka survivors who happened to have been a carpenter. When the model was finished, its maker called Kovner in for an opinion. Something was missing, said Kovner. But what, asked the survivor. After all, the fence was in place, and so were the reception barracks, the S-shaped curve to the gas chambers, and the gas building itself. What could have been missing? And Kovner replied: the horror was missing.

I am told that when the memorial authority Yad Vashem was founded in Israel during the early 1950s, it was imbued with a philosophy that there should not be analytical writing about the Holocaust. The activities of Yad Vashem staff were to be concentrated on collecting the data: the ingathering of the documents. Soon enough this self-confining impulse vanished, but that it should have existed in the first place is not without significance.

Among the early researchers were the editors and compilers, notably H. G. Adler, who worked on Theresienstadt, and Lucjan Dobroszycki, the elegantly sophisticated specialist on Lodz. Both Adler and Dobroszycki made extensive use of texts, replicating documents with brief explanations that did not obliterate the records in their pristine form.

The step beyond compilation is reportage, a kind of writing that hews close to the primary sources to portray an event, but which submerges these sources in the story that is told. Some of these works are biographical. John K. Dickerson interviewed 172 persons to write a pathbreaking book about an obscure Jewish victim, *German and Jew* (Chicago, 1967). Gitta Sereny talked to witnesses on three continents for her study of Treblinka commander Franz Stangl, *Into That Darkness* (New York, 1974). Reportage are also those books, based partially or significantly on comments solicited by the author from participants, describing what happened to an entire community, such as Robert Katz's work on the first transport from Rome, *Black Sabbath* (New York, 1969).

The authors of such works espouse actuality, but that is not to say that they have replicated it. They may have dipped into document collections that, despite their size, are incomplete, and they may have seen something relevant in the material, overlooking or discarding the rest. If they were going to rely on oral testimony, they could not—to borrow a phrase from Pablo Boder—interview the dead.* Even among the living, they may have engaged in—if one may use the term—a selection. Claude Lanzmann's massive film *Shoah* (Paris, 1985) encompasses the testimony of perpetrators, victims, and bystanders. It includes Germany, Corfu, Auschwitz, Treblinka, Sobibór, Chełmno,

---

* David Pablo Boder, *I Did Not Interview the Dead* (Urbana: University of Illinois Press, 1949).

and it is nine and a half hours long. Yet in its raw, unedited state, questions and answers take up something like 350 hours.

How much more removed from the actuality of reportage are those works whose authors have introduced a theory or theme or just a visible thought to which the evidence has been subordinated? These recreators of the Holocaust, be they historians, sculptors, architects, designers, novelists, playwrights, or poets, are molding something new. They may be shrewd, insightful, or masterful, but they take a larger risk, and all the more so, if they take poetic license to subtract something from crude reality for the sake of a heightened effect.

It is at this point that we must become specific about rules. One of them is, paradoxically, silence. Of course, there cannot be silence without speech. Silence can only be introduced between words, sometimes with words. We become aware of silence in Lanzmann's *Shoah*. There is a long painful lapse when Lanzmann interviews the barber Abraham Bomba who is admonished to speak of the days when he had to practice his craft in Treblinka on Jewish women about to be gassed. There is a scene with the Polish station master Jan Piwonski at Sobibor who explains that after the first trainload was delivered to the death camp, it was the silence that alerted him to something ominous. And at the end of the film, a veteran of the Warsaw ghetto battle, Simha Rottem, tells Lanzmann how he returned to the rubble immediately after the fighting. In the dark night, Rottem heard the voice of a woman but could not find her. He was all alone then and thought of himself as the last Jew.

Another rule is aimed at a kind of minimalism. Elie Wiesel once said about the museum to be built in Washington, DC, that it must be spare like a cathedral. Minimalism is not to be confused with length or size. It is the art of using a minimum of words to say the maximum. Wiesel himself is a practiced minimalist. Few readers are familiar with his first book in its first version, published in Yiddish in Argentina under the accusatory title *And the World was Silent*. Everyone knows the condensation of this work in French, or in the English translation from the French with the brief title *Night* (New York, 1960). Wiesel made his work spare. Sometimes he speaks elliptically in order to voice ultimate thoughts. A half-crazed woman spots a flame as the cattle car enters Auschwitz, but no one else can see the fire. Describing what had happened in the camp, he draws his famous apotheosis of a young boy being hanged, next to or flanked by two hanging adults. Where is God? asks one voice. It is the boy, answers another.

If it is a novel, it is not about Auschwitz, says Wiesel, and if it is about Auschwitz, it is not a novel. The statement is not an observation, but a law. It prohibits trivialization, above all, the deliberate bending of known facts to cajole the reader. In regard to Holocaust literature, we often hear the word "genuine." Perhaps we should add the obvious conclusion that the opposite of genuine is "forgery."

Examples of counterfactuality in Holocaust novels and plays are legion. It may, therefore, suffice to cite the most extreme illustration, Rolf Hochhuth's play, *The Deputy* (New York, 1963). Hochhuth, a Protestant German writer, condemns a pope and praises a Protestant SS officer, Kurt Gerstein. The names in the play are real, but many invented words are put into their mouths, and situations are created that did not occur and could not have occurred. Not mentioned by Hochhuth is the sheer fact that as late as 1944 Gerstein delivered gas to Auschwitz.

The rules, whatever their contents, have evolved with the literature, sometimes after offending literary works appeared, but forty years ago, when I began my work, I was not aware of any restrictions save those that I imposed on myself. As far as I knew, I was the only one addressing this subject analytically, at least the only one dealing with it as a whole. In my quest, I also felt alone, a reaction faintly similar to that of survivors whose preoccupation with their experiences was not welcomed or understood. I worked at first on the dimly lit fourteenth floor of the Columbia University Library, where I read the transcript of a trial, *U.S. v. Altstötter*. It was one of the so-called subsequent Nuremberg trials, and the defendants, just below the uppermost tier, had been officials in the German Justice Ministry or they had been judges themselves. As I paged through this material day after day, I hardly grasped what I was reading. At one point, I saw references to a mysterious "Night and Fog" decree, and it took me some time to discover that this measure, imposed on the occupied Western countries in December 1941, provided for the arrest of suspected members of the Resistance, who were to disappear in a concentration camp as if in night and fog. Some of the defendants were tried for a trial they had held in which the crime of the Jewish victim had been "race pollution" and in which the Jew, an older man who had been a leader of the Jewish Community of Nuremberg, had been condemned to death for allegedly touching a young German woman who had been his ward.

I sat there all by myself with this eerie transcript. One day, a young friend of mine who specialized in political theory and German affairs, dropped in. I said to him that the case I was reading was so different from anything I had ever come across, so much was reflected there from the Nazi depths that I should really write a play about the Altstötter trial. Of course, I dismissed the thought as soon as I had uttered it. Many years later, I watched the first few reels of a certain film; it was immediately evident to me that someone had examined the case and written a screenplay based on the testimony. The writer's name was Abby Mann and the film, made by Stanley Kramer, was *Judgment at Nuremberg* (1961).

You all remember Theodor W. Adorno's dictum that it is barbaric to write poetry after Auschwitz. I am no poet, but the thought occurred to me that if the statement is true, then is it not equally barbaric to write footnotes after Auschwitz? I have had to reconstruct the process of destruction in my mind, combining the documents into paragraphs, the paragraphs into chapters, the chapters into a book. I always considered that I stood on solid ground; I had no anxieties about artistic failure. Now I have been told that I have indeed succeeded. And that is a cause for some worry, for we historians usurp history precisely when we are successful in our work, and that is to say that nowadays some people might read what I have written in the mistaken belief that here, on my printed pages, they will find the true ultimate Holocaust as it really happened.

III

Memories and Memoirs

10

THE HOLOCAUST MISSION
29 JULY TO 12 AUGUST 1979
(1982)

AT THE END OF 1978, US President Jimmy Carter established a Commission on the Holocaust. It was charged with the task of proposing an appropriate memorial to the Jewish victims of the Nazi regime. There was an element of retroactivity in the president's decision, a reaching out for the five million dead* whose very identity as Jews was not readily recognized by the United States at a time when they were being subjected to a systematic process of destruction. Now they were to have a monument under official US auspices to recall the days when they died alone.

The drafting of such a recommendation is quite an undertaking and the work was to be carried out by (1) a small staff consisting of a part-time director, full-time deputy director, and full-time assistant; (2) the "President's Commission" itself—a large body of twenty-four members chosen from the public, plus five from the Senate and five from the House of Representatives; and (3) an advisory board almost as big as the commission. To finance the half year or so of deliberations and planning, a modest budget was allocated to the commission by the Department of the Interior. Commissioners and advisory board

---
Originally published in *St. Johns Review* 34, no. 1 (1982–83): 105–12.
* The estimated number of six-million murdered Jews is more common. Hilberg himself calculated "the Jewish death toll ... slightly above five million" (see chapter 1).

members accepted no fees and their official travel outside the United States was to be billed to them personally.

Most members of the commission as well as the board were Jews, a number of them survivors. The most conspicuous profession in the group was the clergy (Jewish, Protestant, and Catholic), albeit one that was drawn mainly from academic life. There was an obvious tilt to the northeast, although several members had come from Georgia. A number of commissioners could be described as prominent in public or cultural life. Few—very few—were young.

I had little inkling or knowledge of the consultations that led to the creation of the commission and the selection of its membership. No doubt I was approached because I had devoted about three decades of research and writing to the Holocaust, but I have long been accustomed to working in solitude. No wonder that in one of the first telephone calls informing me of the commission's existence I was admonished not to turn down an appointment if I should be requested to serve. I would be needed because the memorial was to be more than mute stone; it was to contain records, books, films, and it was to be a depository of such materials in order that one might progress beyond remembering the imperfectly known to know what was imperfectly remembered.

This was the offer I could not refuse. To my surprise, virtually all of the commissioners espoused the idea of a "living" memorial, a building in which one could meet, learn, and think. More than that, there was to be an endowment to aid researchers with fellowships and grants. Of course, most of the funds for this program would have to be private. We would not only have to recommend a broad framework, but we would also have to think about the means.

During an early meeting, mention was made by the director of a journey abroad, to visit some of the principal sites in Poland and the USSR where the Jews had been killed and to survey hitherto unavailable documentary holdings in the archives of these countries. This mission preoccupied me from that very moment; it filled my mind long after it was over.

I had never been in Poland or the USSR; I had never visited Auschwitz, Treblinka, or Babi Yar. Something—not only lack of money—had kept me from traveling to these places. I had "seen" them, of course, in German documents. It is in those files, thousands and tens of thousands of them, that I had wandered and it is there that I had encountered "planet Auschwitz" and the "concentration camp universe."

Eventually I had become familiar with these phenomena, their terrain, logistics, and operational characteristics. Yet in essence they remained mysterious to me and inexplicable.

"No one who has not been there can imagine what it was like." How often had I heard this phrase from survivors. Its implications could hardly be overlooked: those who had not lived through the experience would not be able to recreate it, even if they studied the original records or examined the old barbed wires. There is no way one can be in Auschwitz anymore; it is not a concentration camp today, but a museum. Nor can one be in Treblinka; it is a sculpture. One cannot be in Babi Yar either, it is a monument in a park. What then could one recapture in those surroundings? What could we do there now?

The survivors on the commission were to be our guides. The Holocaust mission was in the first instance their journey. At the opening meeting of the commission in Washington, DC, a procedural point had been raised by a Christian member. He said that survivors should always speak first. He was gently overruled by the survivors themselves who preferred to follow a proper US alphabetical order, but here, on the grounds where they had been the outcasts of mankind, orphaned or widowed in a single night, they were to be at the head of the procession.

The undisputed spiritual leader was Elie Wiesel, once an inmate of Auschwitz, now the chairman of the commission, "prophet-like," mesmerizing, saying at every occasion not merely that which must be said to a host, but also those things that for most of us would have been unutterable, and saying them in the morning, the afternoon, or the night. Fluent in French, English, Hebrew, Yiddish (not to mention Hungarian), the gaunt figure moved among us, sleeping little and eating almost nothing.

We almost did not go. The Soviet Union issued visas to us on the Saturday prior to our scheduled Sunday departure, and it denied entry to the part-time director of the commission as well as to a member of the advisory board. (Both had visited the USSR before and had apparently been in contact with dissidents.) The detailed itinerary was a series of last-minute arrangements that must have been put together with the assistance of extraordinarily diligent officials of the Department of State and embassies abroad. The group was large. Though it included fewer than half of the commissioners and advisory board members (none at all from the legislative branch), there were wives, reporters, and invited guests, some of them financial supporters of remembrance projects. At the many ceremonies at graves and monuments, the cameras would sweep across this crowd numbering between fifty and sixty.

Only after we had left the United States did I understand the multiple purposes of the mission. We would not only have to absorb much that we would encounter during our hurried visits and meetings; we would also have to impart information to others. Our foreign hosts in Eastern Europe would ask us what we meant when we said the word "Holocaust," and we would devote more time than we had anticipated to answering that one question above all.

Poland

Today [i.e., 1982] Poland is a homogeneous society. Unlike the Polish state of 1939, the present republic has no substantial minorities. The territories inhabited by Ukrainians and Lithuanians were yielded to the USSR, and from the western provinces acquired after the war, the Germans were expelled. The Jewish community, once 3.3 million dispersed in the large cities and smaller towns, now numbers six thousand. Ninety percent of the prewar Jewish population were killed in the Holocaust; most of the remainder survived as soldiers, refugees, or forced laborers outside or inside the destructive arena, and these people have since moved to other countries, mainly to Israel and the United States.

The three million Polish Jews who succumbed to German destruction represent nearly three-fifths of all the Jewish dead. Moreover, Poland (as defined by the boundaries of 1939) is the graveyard not only of those three million, but also of a million more transported there in special trains from several countries of German-dominated Europe.

Before their final destruction, the Jews of Poland were incarcerated in hundreds of ghettos, large and small. Death camps appeared near some of these ghettos. From these ghettos, Jews were moved to the gas chambers where they were killed along with the other Jewish deportees from the northern, western, and southern portions of the continent.

Few traces remain of Jewry in the physical panorama of contemporary Warsaw. As we stood in front of the monument—cast in heroic proportions—of the Warsaw ghetto fighters, I glanced at the ordinary apartment buildings erected by the Polish government on the former ghetto site. They were already showing signs of wear. I knew that the old quarter was no more. For several years, I had been one of the editors of the diary kept by the man who was Chairman of the Jewish Council of the Warsaw Ghetto, Adam Czerniaków.* Again and again, I had consulted a map of the T-shaped walled ghetto, some ten full blocks at its widest and twenty blocks long, which housed well over 400,000 people in three- or four-story buildings. After the deportations and the battle ignited by the armed resistance of the last ghetto inhabitants, the SS razed the Jewish quarter lest Warsaw regain its prewar population size. Now that there are Polish houses where the ghetto stood, it is difficult to visualize its former boundary even at the *Umschlagplatz* through which the official ghetto exports and imports passed and from which more than 300,000 Jews were taken to Treblinka.

On the first day we visited a Polish monument commemorating the Polish struggle against the Germans. At that ceremony, specially chosen Polish troops stood by and the US ambassador was present as we placed flowers at the foot of the memorial. The Polish People's Republic does not deny the Holocaust, it does not obscure the fact that Jews died as Jews, but it will remind the world of the Poles who died as Poles, and it will present the two fates in a formula suggesting parity. Repeatedly we heard a statistic indicating that three million Polish Jews and three million non-Jewish Poles had died as a consequence of the German occupation. The Polish toll—casualties in battle, deaths in camps, and fatalities in epidemics—was calculated a long time ago and may well be reexamined by experts, but when Polish Justice Minister Jerzy Bafia referred to this "Golgotha" as a trauma that after thirty-five years was still being felt in every walk of life, I believed him without need for any substantiation.

For Czesław Pilichowski, Director of the Main Commission for Investigation of Nazi Crimes in Poland, the double disaster inflicted on Jews and Poles by the same implacable foe was more than a matter of juxtaposition. He cited a poem, "To the Polish Jews," by Władysław Broniewski, which contains the verse "Our common home has been wrecked and the blood shed makes us brothers, we have been united by execution walls, by Dachau, Auschwitz, by every unmarked grave,

---

* I.e., *The Warsaw Diary of Adam Czerniaków: Prelude to Doom*, ed. Raul Hilberg, Stanislaw Staron, and Josef Kermisz (New York: Stein and Day, 1979).

every prison bar." I took down these words and almost memorized them; they rang in my ears longer than any others expressed in these official meetings.

Yet I knew that during our century, Jews had endured misery in Polish society. It is hardly an unknown story and in the US Jewish community it has shaped sentiments much less mellow than my own. I could imagine a reaction in the United States to what we were hearing in Warsaw that day. It would be said in our country that Poland is embracing its Jews, now that they are gone, as much as it was rejecting them when they were still alive. In the extreme form of this view, Poland has been the anti-semitic nation par excellence, discriminating against the Jewish population before the war, welcoming German actions against Jewry during the conflict, and all but expelling the remnant thereafter. I myself have always attempted to assess evidence of Polish hostility toward the Jews in the broadest possible context. Long before the Holocaust, there was little tranquility for Jewry in several countries of Europe. After the German invasion of Poland, the ghettoization process instituted by the occupation authorities resulted in a reallocation of Jewish housing and Jewish trading to the Polish sector. The Poles profited, if that is the word, from a Jewish misfortune. The Germans set up their death camps on Polish soil, not, however, to take advantage of any Polish hospitality, but to reduce costs, particularly of transportation. There was no central Polish authority under German rule and it is not Poland that destroyed the Jews—this deed was performed by Nazi Germany.

Still, I could not ignore the circumstance that for the remaining handful of Jews, life in Poland had become difficult and even oppressive. Only a few days after our stay in Eastern Europe, I was to meet a middle-aged Jew in Denmark who had emigrated from Poland nearly a decade ago. I asked him what his profession had been before his emigration. He was a major in the Polish army. Had he retired? No, he had been dismissed abruptly in 1967, one week after the outbreak of the Six-Day War between Israel and the Arab states. No doubt the reasons for the action against him were linked to foreign policy issues, but I could not help being troubled by his experience and the similar dilemma faced by other Jews in the Soviet Union. The problem is the age-old lesson so ingrained in the mind of the Eastern European Jew that eventually he will suffer, not for a religion he does not practice or a Zionist cause he does not espouse, but for the fact that in the eyes of all those around him he remains unalterably a Jew.

Our hosts placed stress on the Polish agony during the war, and they implied that since those trying days Jews and Poles have had much in common. They also reminded us of the help that ordinary Poles had given to endangered Jews in the course of the German occupation. This chapter in the history of Polish-Jewish relations was emphasized in speeches, books, and exhibits. I had occasion to look at some of the evidence—it was documentary. In German parlance, Poles who had extended shelter or sustenance to Jews were guilty of *Judenbeherbergung*, a crime for which the penalty was a swift death. The Germans had the habit of posting the names of Polish men and women who lost their lives for such activities.

We had a great many meetings. Addresses were given, points made, themes stressed. At the end of a long day, I would walk alone in Warsaw. Once, before midnight, I saw a Polish family placing flowers on a plaque at the entrance of a park.

We have moved from cemetery to cemetery, said Elie Wiesel later in Jerusalem, and everywhere we went we found a strange beauty. This observation about localities in which masses of people were killed expressed in quintessence a thought I had during our visit to Treblinka.

We had traveled to the site of the death camp in the stifling heat of a Hungarian bus. On the way, a survivor pointed out to us the small Jewish towns that had once existed nearby. We passed old wooden houses, rode over a narrow bridge, and saw old freight cars at a railway siding—a deportation train preserved there by the Polish government. I wish we could have approached the camp by rail, as the deportees of 1942 had done, but we were arriving on a very warm day at the end of July, at a time of year when the first of the Warsaw ghetto transports were being hauled into this killing center. Though the distance is not long, the Jewish victims had been moved much more slowly than we, and they must have jumped out of the cars with forebodings and partly in shock, but also with some sense of physical relief. Did they notice the sky and the trees? It took but two hours for the deportees to be deprived of all their personal belongings and to be walked the incredibly short distance to the chambers where they were gassed.

A small German guard force, augmented by Ukrainian auxiliaries, killed three-quarters of a million Jews in Treblinka on a virtual assembly line. Several hundred Jewish inmates employed in maintenance and facing certain death rebelled in August 1943. Few were the survivors of the break, but those Jews who did not escape from Treblinka did not outlive the camp. In the end, the bodies in the mass graves were exhumed. All the installations were razed, and a Ukrainian farm was established on the site to restore its pastoral appearance. Only a cobblestone path, built by prisoners, was left where Treblinka had existed. After the war, the Polish government laid down concrete ties, arranged as a symbolic railway track, and set up hundreds of jagged stones, each representing a Jewish community, around the stone memorial. For this construction, the entire terrain was used on a scale of 1:1 in the place where it had all happened. A guide pointed out that after every heavy rain, tiny bone fragments are disgorged by the earth and mix with pebbles on the ground. Involuntarily, one or two visitors bent down to pick up what might have been such relics, only to drop them quickly. I was still gazing at the woods and I thought I heard the whine of heavy trucks in the distance. Where is the highway, I asked? Where are the trucks going? There is no highway and there are no trucks, I was told. I was hearing the famous Treblinka wind moving through the trees.

Much farther from Warsaw, to the southwest, was Auschwitz, the most lethal place in Nazi Europe. One million Jews died there, as well as several hundred thousand Poles, Russians, Frenchmen—all the nationalities in the orbit of the German army and the German Security Police. Auschwitz was a complex of three camps: the main one, or Auschwitz I, which housed the administration as well as a large number of inmates; the killing center of Birkenau, designated Auschwitz II; and the industrial camp, Monowitz, or Auschwitz III. The entire cluster was photographed repeatedly by allied reconnaissance aircraft in 1944.

Auschwitz I is still intact. Its barracks stand where they were, a reconstructed gas chamber may be viewed, and the crematory is in working order. The death camp of Birkenau is almost bare; the tall smoke stacks of the crematories are gone, but near the railway track one may climb over the ruins of the largest gas chambers ever built.

Adjacent to Auschwitz I is the city of Auschwitz with its large railway yard. Houses now filled with children are ranged along the edge of the former camp. Every day the inhabitants of these buildings may look out of their windows and see the roofs of barracks.

We stepped in, wearing our tags with the emblem of the United States and the legend "President's Commission on the Holocaust." The main entrance crowned with iron grill work still proclaims the slogan *Arbeit macht frei* (work sets you free) and a smaller sign at the side says *HALT Ausweise vorzeigen* (Halt—show identification). The walkways and buildings were those of a permanent military fort, but that appearance was deceptive. On iron bars still flanking the street on which we were walking, men had been hanged. Individual buildings, which the Germans called blocks, were put to unique concentration camp uses: in one, surgical experiments were performed, in another, prisoners were pushed into a cage and starved to death. Between two of the barracks there was an alley used for shootings. The windows of the building to the left had been filled so that prisoners housed there could not see the executions. To the right, however, no such precautions had been taken, since the only inmates kept there were the condemned, waiting their turn.

Each of the buildings is part of the Auschwitz museum. I went to see the exhibits of old shoes, eyeglasses, prosthetic devices, utensils, and luggage left behind by the Germans because of their unsuitability for shipment to the Reich. I saw a hallway filled with photographs of Polish prisoners, young men and women, who were brought here in 1942 and 1943. Each of them looked healthy since their pictures had been taken on the day of arrival. For each the SS had noted also the date of birth and the date of death. Most had lived only a few months in Auschwitz. I peered at these photographs, one or the other adorned with fresh flowers left by Polish friends or family. I wanted to find some young man who had been as old as I was at that time. The search did not take long. My contemporary, born a few days before me, was dead as a teenager in Auschwitz even before my schooling in New York was interrupted by the war.

In Birkenau, standing on earth, sand, and what may have been ashes, I attached myself to a Polish young lady of noble beauty and refined features who explained the history of the camp. She was obviously a professional historian and I admired her grasp of complex information. She was preparing an album of German SS photographs of Auschwitz and I promised her aerial photographs from our own archives.

Our group was about to be divided, some to visit an old synagogue in nearby Krakow, the others to stay in Auschwitz. Just at that moment I began to feel an unmistakable pain, a cramp brought on by a kidney stone I must have formed. I am prone to this malady when there is too much heat and not enough water to drink. The pain always worsens and then I need morphine for relief. Obviously, I should have left immediately to see a physician in Krakow, but instead I raised my hand to join those who chose to remain in the camp. I returned to the barracks, the old shoes, to the photographs of the dead Poles, to the alley, to the cells. I wanted to stand where the present pontiff [i.e., Pope John Paul II] had knelt in prayer. My pain subsided, my muscles relaxed, and at the end of the day, I knew that I would have no need of drugs.

There was to be one more visit to a cemetery in Poland, a real one in Warsaw. By now, I had run out of time—time to look at documents in the Jewish historical institute, and time to survey the land behind the tombstones where 80,000 Jews, dead of emaciation and disease, had been buried during the ghetto days. I wanted to see only one grave, a regular large slab half hidden in the growing thicket of weeks. It is the resting place of Adam Czerniaków, the chairman of the Warsaw Jewish Council, who took his life upon the outbreak of deportations after he had failed to save his people.

The Soviet Union

I was startled when Elie Wiesel, the chairman of our commission, called a meeting of the group in the open environment of a dining room of our Warsaw hotel to discuss the advisability of proceeding to the Soviet Union in the light of the refusal of visas to the director of the commission and to a member of the advisory board. So far as I was concerned, that issue had been settled before we left our homes in the United States—we would go. Much to Wiesel's dismay, several of us spoke up to reiterate the earlier decision. Exhausted by a full day, we reassured him in a sluggish manner that at some appropriate time in the future we would express our outrage to protest the Soviet action. Only one member of our group, Bayard Rustin, understood immediately that Wiesel was attempting to elicit our outrage on the spot in order that he might use it for yet another attempt to obtain the visas. I was too concerned with the possibility that he might actually abandon our original plans to be of help to him. For me, the visit to the Soviet Union was essential, if only because we *had* been admitted as members of an official Holocaust commission. Already my head was filled with burning curiosity. *How* would we be received? *What* would be said to us?

The director of the commission, Irving Greenberg, was not in Europe. Perhaps he had expected an immediate statement of solidarity from the membership. The advisory board member whose visa was also denied, had come with us as far as Warsaw. He had, in fact, been instrumental in arranging the entire journey. It was his miserable travel bureau we all had to use. Now he conceded defeat: he wanted us to continue without him. He only asked that we would say one prayer for him at Babi Yar and another in the Moscow synagogue. His voice breaking, he sat down, but then rose again to apologize for having displayed his feelings so openly. Now he wanted to give us a reason for leaving him behind. He had been a member of a partisan unit in Eastern Europe during the war. There was an iron rule in the unit that a wounded man would be shot by his comrades lest their mission be jeopardized. I liked Miles Lerman. This former partisan and current oil distributor personifies the character traits I have come to associate with survivors. They are men and women with fast reactions, high intelligence, great endurance, and an extraordinary capacity for regenerating their lives from the impact of shattering experiences. When I saw Lerman again in Copenhagen, barely a week after our meeting in the Warsaw hotel, he was talking to all of us, full of inquiries and plans.

I was not prepared for the Soviet Union. As a political scientist, I should not have been surprised by anything, not the standard of living as exemplified by the merchandise in a department store, nor the restrictions so evident in the mere absence of foreign non-communist newspapers in the lobbies of our hotels. I knew of the Soviet belief that distant goals require constant sacrifices: for capital formation and industrialization, many consumer goods are not produced; for the stability of the regime, intellectual and physical mobility is curtailed; and for the sake of unity in the Soviet Union, the separate memories of constituent nationalities, including the Holocaust that befell the Soviet Jews, must be submerged. What I had not quite expected was backwardness in so much art, architecture, and historiography, that stale conforming manner in which Soviet designers and writers are casting the aesthetic qualities of life. Hence I was taken aback also by the counterpart of this stylistic retardation in the formula-ridden answers of bureaucrats to central questions about World War II and the Holocaust that had transpired in its course. The approach of Soviet officialdom to the meaning of history is fixed and rigid; the encounter of these men with us could be no different.

In Poland, we had not only been warmly received; we were given assurances that the Polish archives would be open to US researchers interested in the German occupation. Poland holds a large quantity of German documents, particularly records portraying the destructive scene at a local level. Much that occurred in the final hours of Polish

Jewry and of other Jews deported to Poland is reflected in these files. The USSR also possesses documents of German occupation authorities, not to speak of contemporaneous Soviet correspondence dealing directly with the German onslaught and its effects on the civilian population. I was interested in these materials, though I realized that access to them would be a major problem. Not only would a segmentation of occupation history into Jewish and other subject matter be unwelcome in principle, but such sorting requires an examination of all the German records in detail. We know enough about these documents to expect any report, whether by German SS offices, civilian overseers, military government, railroad directorates, or economic agencies, to contain information about a variety of events—the production of wooden carts and the shooting of Jews might be described on a single page. Moreover, the researcher might be particularly interested in comparisons and contexts; he might wish to investigate the German "racial ladder" and the placement of various groups in this scheme, or the role of native auxiliaries in German service, or the psychological repercussions of shootings on White Russian or Ukrainian communities. It would be inherently impossible for Soviet authorities to permit foreigners the pursuit of information about any aspect of the Jewish catastrophe without allowing them some insight into the entire fabric of Soviet society at a time when it was undergoing its greatest stress.

Tactically, there was yet another problem, one which affects all attempts to effect exchanges of knowledge with the Soviet Union. The United States is an open society, our libraries and archives are accessible to all visitors without any stipulation of reciprocity. What Soviet or East German researchers want to know is given to them without restrictions; for what we attempt to find out, we have no more to give. In Kiev, on our first night, walking with Bayard Rustin, I voiced the thought that one argument—the only argument—might be the point that it would be in the interest of the USSR to open its shelves to us, that in the United States there was little appreciation of the Soviet agony or the Soviet contribution in World War II, that findings made by US researchers in the Soviet Union would carry more weight in our country than the selection and presentation of topics by Soviet historians and journalists. Rustin was without question the most astute and experienced member of our mission, and what he said to me that evening in Kiev was somewhat as follows: "I hope you do not mind, my friend, my telling you that you are naive."

Kiev has the appearance of a new city. Before the war, its population was nine hundred thousand; now the number is 2.15 million. From 19 September 1941 to 6 November 1943, Kiev was in German hands. As soon as the city had been captured, a unit of the SS and Police, *Einsatzkommando* 4a, ordered the Jewish inhabitants by means of wall posters to assemble for "resettlement." They were taken to a ravine at the city boundary where the *Kommando*, a small company-size unit augmented by detachments of German Order Police, massacred them in a three-day shooting operation. The count was 33,771 Jewish dead. When, in the spring of 1942, the commander of *Kommando* 4a, Paul Blobel, received a visitor from Berlin (Albert Hartl), he pointed to the mass grave, explaining that the Jews were buried there. Now, more than three and a half decades later, the Chairman of the Executive Committee of the Kiev City Soviet of Peoples' Deputies welcomed the Holocaust commission to the city, and Soviet guides showed the recently built memorial to the visitors from the United States.

I do not know what route the bus was following from our hotel, but the ride seemed very short and when we arrived at the ravine called Babi Yar I immediately asked how far we were from the center of the city. Barely two miles was the answer. I could not help wondering then how many people, including the victims themselves, must have heard the rifle shots and machine gun fire. Babi Yar is a moon shaped depression in the earth, covered with grass and surrounded by trees. Raised on a ridge that is jutting into the center of the dish is a Janus-like monument. Facing the street are heroic figures, while on the far side one may see the tormented faces and contorted bodies of Soviet citizens, including women and children. I talked to the designer of the memorial who explained that the Germans had shot captured partisans here and helpless civilians there; the sculptor had kept that geography in mind when he shaped the monument. I knew that, unlike Blobel, the Soviet planners of the memorial made no mention of Jews. Our commission had brought a wreath of flowers with streamers commemorating Babi Yar as a Jewish tragedy and laid it down at the foot of the pedestal on which stood the partisans of stone. The cantor sang, and I disengaged myself from the coil of people around him, stepped back twenty feet and looked up at the crown of the monument. Two Soviet photographers rushed towards me and took pictures of me at close range.

We were leaving Kiev for Moscow on a Friday afternoon and I did not think that we would have meetings until Monday. No sooner, however, had we arrived when several of us were asked to go to the headquarters of the Moscow Writers Union, a building which in furnishings and atmosphere reminded me of a typical student center at an American university. It was old and nondescript; on several of its floors people were sitting, reading, eating. Our delegation was headed by Wiesel and included the theologian Robert McAfee Brown, as well as *Time* magazine book review editor Stefan Kanfer, not in his capacity as a correspondent covering our mission, but as a novelist pressed into service at the spur of the moment to match the formidable array of literary talent assembled on the Soviet side. To our surprise, the Soviet chairman introduced the members of his group by citing their military records. Two had evidently received high decorations and another had risen from private to major. "When you introduce us," I whispered to Wiesel, "you may say that I was a soldier." "An officer perhaps?" Wiesel asked quickly. "No, just a soldier." Kanfer did not stir. He is a veteran of the Korean conflict. Wrong war.

The Soviet delegation consisted of eight people; half of them were Jews. Were so many Jews assembled as a courtesy to us? The idea was unsettling. As if to read my mind, one of the Soviet writers referred to himself as a member of a minority—he was a Russian. Later, the Soviet chairman showed us two large tablets listing the names of Moscow writers killed in action. Half were Jewish names, he explained.

We were eating a full meal, the best I was to be served in the Soviet Union, and we were assured that we could have every course without concern—the food was completely kosher. While we were dining, each of us spoke, not as one would in an official meeting with formal agenda, but to say something personal. One of the Soviet writers (the one who had risen from private to major) was Anatoly Rybakov. This is what he told us.

He had grown up with Jewish parents but wholly assimilated into Russian culture. He did not attend religious services and he knew no Yiddish or Hebrew. His eighteen novels had no Jewish content. One day, however, he wanted to write a short story in which the two protagonists, a man and a woman, were Jews. He wanted his story to be about love, not merely the romantic love of young people who had just met, but also the mature love of a husband and wife after they had lived with each other for many years. He decided that his young man should have migrated to Russia from Switzerland in 1910, that he should have met a young woman, married her, and stayed on through World War I and the Revolution. To show them growing older, he had to continue the story to 1941 and the German assault. He had spent three years in research to construct a locality in which his couple might have lived. By then his story was becoming a novel.* He had to place them into a ghetto and inevitably he had to construct the ultimate scene of a German shooting operation. It troubled him greatly that the Jews went to their deaths with apparent docility, but he was convinced that they had no recourse and that they died with dignity. After the publication of his novel he had received hundreds of letters assuring him that he had been right in this portrayal.

Wiesel spoke of his concern about Babi Yar. Having been there only that morning, still agitated by the experience, he had to point out that it was painful to see the monument without an inscription identifying the victims as Jews.

There are monuments and there are monuments, the Russian chairman replied. When, for example, his friend, Yevgeny Yevtushenko, wrote a poem "Babi Yar" explicitly dwelling on the Jewish fate, that verse was a monument. Who could tell which of the two monuments, the one of rock or the other on paper, would last longer?

The Saturday morning was devoted to an appearance by the commission and its guests at the Moscow synagogue. I declined to join the group. Religious observances make me uncomfortable and the political overtones of that particular visit disturbed me. We had come to the Soviet Union as a commission of the president and our mandate was the Holocaust. For me there was no other purpose, but I realized that many of my colleagues did not share my single-mindedness. Our very presence in Moscow on a weekend was no accident; the Saturday in the synagogue had been planned to show support for Soviet Jewry. Later I was to learn that Elie Wiesel had asked for a private moment after a meeting with Procurator General Roman Rudenko to present a list of four incarcerated dissidents to the Soviet official. Wiesel is a deeply sensitive man and he could not bring himself to remember the dead by forgetting the living. I myself was thinking about unknown, Russified, and atheistic people whose lives in the Soviet Union are increasingly filled with questions and quandaries.

In Red Square, of all places, I was to have an unexpected encounter with one nameless individual. It was evening and four of us, still wearing our tags, were standing there. He came up to us and in halting but intelligible English said that he knew about our arrival from broad-

---

* Anatoly Rybakov, *Heavy Sand* (New York: Penguin, 1982).

casts on the Voice of America. His age was about twenty-nine and he was born in a small town far from Moscow of a Jewish father, long dead, and a Russian mother, still living. Some time ago he had moved to the Soviet capital with his Russian wife. By profession he was an engineer and he was working in his field, but lately he was contemplating emigration. "Why?" I asked. "Because I want freedom." Did he have access to military secrets in his job? Yes, he said, and that is why he was seeking employment in a position not requiring knowledge of such information. Once he had made the change he would stay for a period of three years. Two of my companions immediately handed him their cards, but he would not give us his name. Who was he? Why did he approach us? Was I becoming paranoid for asking what his purpose may have been?

Before the commission had left the United States, I had insisted on an opportunity to meet with a representative of the Soviet archival administration. I had familiarized myself as well as I could with the organization and holdings of the Soviet archives by reading the standard work on that subject by the American Sovietologist Patricia Grimsted. In her substantial volume, there is no mention of captured German documents. I would have to inquire about their location and availability in the course of our discussions in Moscow.

The chief of the Soviet team of archivists was the deputy director of the Main Archival Administration, F.[jedor] M.[ichailowitsch] Vaganov. I pressed the attack for the US group, supported at every turn by my friends who were eager to widen any opening and exploit any breach. The Main Archival Administration, said Vaganov, had no German documents. It had no documents at all dated after 1940. Furthermore, there was no "fond" or collection identified as German documents as such. Where were they then? I asked. Did the Defense Ministry retain possession of them? Documents dated after 1940, said Vaganov, were being kept by whatever ministry was the appropriate custodian in accordance with their subject matter. In that case, I asked, when would documents dated 1941 or 1942 be transferred by ministries currently keeping them to the Main Archival Administration? There was a key, said Vaganov, according to which transfers were being made; the schedules varied on the basis of different criteria. The Main Archival Administration did not know when documents would be handed over by the Ministry of Defense. Was he saying, I asked, that he had no German documents? The Soviet Archival Administration, said Vaganov, may have documents needed for investigation of war crimes. One or another document may be found in the files of an Archive in Byelorussia or Ukraine. We should consult the volumes of the Soviet history of World War II for sources. We should avail ourselves of the existing system of cooperation between the Academy of Sciences of the USSR and US academic bodies if we wished to utilize a Soviet Archive.

Even before our queries to the archivists were over, a larger group of our commission had begun a meeting with Soviet historians. We joined our colleagues to talk with members of the World War II Section of the Institute of the History of the USSR in the Soviet Academy of Sciences. The Soviet chairman was V. A. Kumanyov, but the most active discussant at the Russian end of the table was the military historian of World War II Alexander Samsonov. It is Samsonov who challenged our mission and everything we stood for. In pursuing a study of the Jewish disaster, he said, with World War II as a background, we were reversing reality and standing history on its head. As a Marxist he had to conclude that the Fascist assault on the USSR was an attempt to conquer the world. In the wake of this aggression, Jews were killed, Russians were killed, Ukrainians were killed. The Fascist plan was to wipe out entire peoples, including all of the Slavic nations. He himself was a Byelorussian and more than thirty years ago he had seen with his own eyes the devastation visited upon the area that was his home.

Several of us replied to this argument. We said that the Jews had been the victims of German actions from 1933 to 1945. The ghettos were established on Polish soil in 1940 and when German armies suddenly struck at the Soviet Union on 22 June 1941, the Jews were facing mass death. We were not unmindful of the fact that in German plans the Slavic populations of Eastern Europe were destined for rapid enslavement and ultimate extinction. Yet as Soviet forces turned the tide of war in the titanic battle of Stalingrad, the invader's vision of the obliteration of the Slavs was dissipated in the retreat. The Jews, however, were being killed until the end; their annihilation became reality, and European Jewry, as we once knew it, is no more.

Kumanyov now joined the debate. There were differences of opinion, he said, particularly about Nazi policy vis-à-vis the Jews in the total constellation of German planning. To Kumanyov the destruction of the Jews was just an experiment that led to the annihilation of others. Thus he agreed in part with Samsonov, in part with us, but he had to add that if we were to look at the Holocaust in an isolated manner, we would weaken our common struggle against Fascism.

We left the Soviet Union that afternoon. The first of our two last stops was in Copenhagen, where we paid tribute to the Danish people for their singular rescue effort of October 1943 that resulted in the clandestine transport in small boats of almost the entire Jewish population of Denmark to safety in Sweden. Our journey ended with a depleted group in Jerusalem where our Israeli friends were worried that the Holocaust Commission would not succeed in isolating itself from the urgings of nationalities with martyrological claims of their own. At Yad Vashem, Israel's Remembrance Authority, a display had been prepared of original documents. One was the last notebook of Adam Czerniaków (the chairman of the Warsaw Jewish Council) opened to the last entry. My colleague, S. J. Staron, and I had worked with typewritten transcriptions and a facsimile edition of the diary; only now did I notice that at the moment of Czerniaków's suicide, shortly after his final entry, the notebook was just about full.

On 27 September 1979, the commission assembled in the Rose Garden of the White House for a presentation of its report to the president. Elie Wiesel spoke in front of the microphone, as President Carter stood at his side, erect and motionless, looking off into the distance. Was he listening to the words? Was he thinking about one of the many crises with which he had to deal?

Wiesel, still thinking of Babi Yar, remarked that this massacre had occurred just thirty-eight years before. The world had looked on then and in the following years, as the Holocaust swept across the European Jewish communities. The president responded, commending us for our work and the journey that in itself was an act of memorialization. Then he recalled the omissions of the time when the world had looked the other way.

It was in the middle of the afternoon, and for the president, not yet the middle of his working day. He is like a prisoner, I thought, always under guard, pressured by every summons. That day he had given us an hour. Could it be that he had already devoted more time and thought to the Holocaust than his predecessor during the war, Franklin Roosevelt, had managed while the Jews were dying?

It is natural, I said to myself as I was walking in the streets of Washington, DC, that night, for me to feel slightly depressed. Not because of those who would deny the Holocaust, or those who would dilute it, or the others who would forget it—I understand them all. If I did not feel all that well, I was merely experiencing the reaction I always had after some concluding ceremony. What I had to do now was to plan my research. There were documents I had to read, particularly the records in the Polish archives, and I would have to travel again soon. Next year, in Auschwitz.

11

In Search of the Special Trains
(1979)

For several decades I have been preoccupied with the annihilation of the Jews under the Nazi regime. That has been the subject of my life. I have asked myself a number of questions about this event, all of them specific. Quite simply I wanted to find out *how* the Jews were destroyed. I wanted to discover the facts and I tried to understand them. That was my aim.

It occurred to me at the very outset that the destruction of Jewry was a process with a beginning and an end. The Jews of Europe had to be uprooted, their property seized, their social ties with Gentiles severed. They had to be collected and deported to the ramps of the gas chambers. Then they could be killed. All these were complex operations that involved every segment of organized German society, its associations, institutions, offices, and formations. The destruction process was a series of integrated administrative steps. One of them was taken by the German railroads: the transportation of the Jewish victims in special trains to secluded killing centers. It was a crucial contribution to the Holocaust.

My information about the Germans came mainly from German documents captured by the victorious Allies at the end of the war. The documentation that interested me was produced by functionar-

---

Originally published in *Midstream: A Quarterly Jewish Review* 25, no. 8 (1979): 32–38.

ies in the bureaucratic apparatus. The correspondence of these officials consisted of three kinds of communications: (1) orders, which were transmitted from superiors to subordinates; (2) initiatives and reports, which moved in the reverse direction; and (3) letters, sent to equals and often containing enclosed material such as minutes of conferences and texts of agreements. I was to learn that the first rule in reading a message is to note the signer and the addressee. It is because of a sender and a recipient that the contents became action.

Generally, archivists think of a "collection" as a sequence of records that was kept in a particular office: copies of the mail that went out and all the paper that came in. The technical term for the place of origin is "provenance." Over the years, I have examined German documents by the tens of thousands. I saw the files of the SS, the war diaries of the military, the folders of the ministries and banks. The inner workings of the German destructive machines emerged clearly from these pages, but the longer I worked with those sources, the more I became aware of a major gap in the unfolding panorama: there was a dearth of railway documents dealing with Jewish transports. I was missing the packets of railway provenance.

Eventually, two or three railway folders were turned up in Poland and the Soviet Union. In 1968, I visited archives in Jerusalem, Munich, and Koblenz where I found some of this material. I studied it with an organization chart of the Transport Ministry in front of me. In the end, I was utterly frustrated. I knew that special trains for Jewish deportees were procured by the SS, but which railway office was processing these requests? I was aware that the SS was being billed for the one-way fare of the Jews, but by whom? I realized that there was a chain of communications from central offices in Berlin through regional directorates to local levels, but I could not draw a diagram of the decision flow.

To solve these mysteries, I had to go to Germany again. I had to find out where the railway documents were. Even if I were going to spend a relatively large sum of money for fragmentary data, I had to make the attempt. In the back of my mind, I also thought that in the course of the trip I would have a casual look at Germany, and that I would be there longer than at any time since the spring of 1945.

One of the places I wanted to visit was an archive in East Germany. Some time ago, I had actually been invited by a ranking official of the German Democratic Republic to testify at a trial of an absent West German bureaucrat who had drafted many anti-Jewish decrees during the Nazi regime. The letter of invitation had somehow touched me deeply, not because the writer was an important man, but for the way he introduced himself. He had been an inmate of a concentration camp throughout the Hitler years; these were his credentials. As an inducement, he mentioned the archive in Potsdam that, he said, contained many undiscovered items. I did not go to East Berlin at that time, but now I hoped to make up for my earlier omission—I had visions of railway files in that archive. With some anticipation I wrote to the new East German ambassador in Washington, DC, whose answer was quick and cordial. I could have my visa as soon as permission was granted in East Berlin. My application was refused.

I would now have to rely on West Germany and Austria. In particular, I would have to concentrate on offices of prosecutors where depositions and documents had been collected for trials of railway men. The trials were never held, but I might take advantage of all that preparatory work. One organization was of special importance to me: it was the Central Office of the Provincial Administrations of Justice for the Investigation of National Socialist Crimes,* which was located as far as I knew in the town of Ludwigsburg.

Ludwigsburg

I had trouble obtaining the exact address; not even the West German consulate in Boston knew its whereabouts. Apparently, the Central Office was not a federal agency, but an institution of provincial governments that staffed it with prosecutors recruited from various cities. It did not draw up indictments, for it was limited to passing on its preliminary findings to chief prosecutors in the major urban centers. That is where the decisions were made to go ahead or to do nothing.

When I arrived in Ludwigsburg on 9 March 1976, I found the Central Office in a converted prison. The location was ideal for security, the director, Dr. Adalbert Rückerl, explained. The building had once been used for women prisoners who were washing the laundry of men prisoners next door. The advance of women's liberation no longer per-

---

* Another English translation is *Central Office of the State Justice Administrations for the Investigation of National Socialist Crimes*. The German name is *Zentrale Stelle der Landesjustizverwaltungen zur Aufklärung nationalsozialistischer Verbrechen*.

mitted such sexist employment even in a detention facility, and then the prosecutors moved in instead.

Dr. Rückerl, a heavyset jovial man, and his deputy, a scholarly looking one, were among the oldest of several dozen professionals in the agency. Another old-timer was an archivist who shared with Dr. Rückerl the distinction of having escaped from Russian captivity twice. The director was my host, the archivist my daily confidential informant. The fact was, said the archival specialist, that Poland was identifying prospective defendants at this late date solely for the purpose of embarrassing the West German government. The witnesses were scattered and tired of testifying. He did not add that many of the accused, ailing if not feeble, were already enjoying a kind of biological amnesty. For the moment, he was still filing away documents and still making out cards for a vast index of persons I was not allowed to see. Occasionally, he interrupted his work to tell me stories. He had been in the Brown Shirts once, but had resigned from that formation very fast. During the war, he was an ordinary soldier uninvolved with politics. His hearing was affected—one could not very well come out of that experience completely unscathed. His memory, however, was unimpaired; he recalled distinctly the German counteroffensive of 1945 in Hungary and the bodies of Hungarian civilians mutilated by the Russian conquerors. His sight was also good. Every morning, he read the Polish newspaper *Tribuna Ludu* to find out if there were new Polish allegations of German laxity in the matter of Nazi war crimes.

A police sergeant who admitted me to the building each day was also talkative, but his conversation was largely limited to the weather, about which he knew very much. Only at the end did he hand me a petition to sign—it was a plea to the West German government *not* to concede vis-à-vis Czechoslovakia that the Munich agreement of 1938 was void. I pointed out that I was an American and that I could not place my signature on a petition in a foreign country. Oh, but that did not matter, he argued, my support would be welcomed in any case.

One afternoon, Dr. Rückerl invited me to a rare treat. The Central Office possessed a roll of the Nazi feature film *Jud Süss*. Had I ever seen it? No, of course not. In conformity with legal requirements, the motion picture, now banned to the public, was introduced to the specialized audience of prosecutors after an elaborate historical lecture delivered by one of the attorneys who was also a doctoral student in history. The film's theme was the takeover of the German city of Stuttgart by a rich Jew at the time when Württemberg was ruled by a *Herzog*. The Jew charges Germans for walking on their own streets and drives a pure German maiden to suicide. The picture had special meaning in Ludwigsburg, because part of the action took place in the Baroque castle less than a mile from the present Central Office.

When the building was closed after 4:00 p.m., I was usually alone, studying my notes, having my supper, washing my socks, and going to bed. The local newspaper had little to offer, and therefore I would buy the Frankfurt daily [i.e., *Frankfurter Allgemeine Zeitung, FAZ*], the nearest approximation to a national German paper. The news even in that organ was somewhat parochial. There were sterile columns about sterile elections and only rarely would there be a report of a small scandal of the kind caused by a Belgian brigadier general with NATO who had written a doctoral dissertation in political science suggesting that the Soviet Union could cross into Germany with conventional forces, hold a bridgehead at the Elbe, and blackmail West Germany to surrender. It was on the literary page that I found something truly interesting. A prolific German playwright, Rainer Werner Fassbinder, had just published a new drama in which the chief villain was yet another "rich Jew."[*] I rushed to the bookstore, bought the paperbound volume, and read how a Jew took over the city of Frankfurt in the 1970s and how, incidentally, he drove a German prostitute to suicide. In the tenth scene there is a monologue spoken by a German nobleman:

> The parasite Jew. Drinks our blood and makes us the wrongdoer, because he is a Jew and we the guilty ones ... Guilty is the Jew, because he makes us guilty with his presence. Had he remained where he came from, or had they gassed him, I could sleep better today. They forgot to gas him. That is no joke, it seems to me. And I am rubbing my hands when I imagine him choking in the gas chamber.

I went on with my work, trying to decipher the meaning of transport designations, and placing two timetables next to each other to understand the manner in which the special trains were routed to the death camps. Once or twice I looked up at a beautiful young woman in the Central Office. Every day, without fail, she wore the Star of David. Later, I was to see more of these stars on the streets of Stuttgart and elsewhere, always, I thought, a conspicuous decoration of slender girls, gracefully walking with their friends. Surely, even if not all of the

---

[*] I.e., *Garbage, the City and Death*, published in: Rainer Werner Fassbinder, *Plays* (New York: PAJ Publications, 1985).

Jews were gassed, these women could not all be Jewish. They were not. The beautiful employee of the Central Office (she was actually called "*die Schöne*") was purely German. To this day, I am trying to figure out whether in some dimly conscious way these young female Germans were engaging in a protest.

Occasionally, I questioned some of the prosecutors about some puzzling problem in my research, but they were lawyers whose thinking was structured toward a proceeding against an individual rather than a coherent grasp of an entire administrative machine. One afternoon, I asked a senior man what he thought about Hitler's involvement in the destruction of the Jews. Did Hitler order the annihilation of Jewry or was that process begun within the bureaucracy itself? The prosecutor laughed. "We have always played a game here, fantasizing that Hitler was a defendant in the docket charged with the "Final Solution," and wondering what we could do if he demanded a shred of proof!"

After I had been coming to the Central Office for about a week, a few of the younger men invited me to their coffee hour. They were dissatisfied with the caution of their director, the snail's pace of the investigations, the frustrations in their jobs. One or two of them also confided in me their anxiety that employment in the Central Office was not likely to further their careers.

"I would gladly have become a judge," a thirty-eight-year-old prosecutor told me. He was the only one to suggest that I join him for supper at his home, a modest apartment (without built-in closets) that he shared with his wife. Dr. W. was a North German and he thought that Ludwigsburgers had verve. He was concerned with his future—eight years in Ludwigsburg had shunted him from a normal path of advancement—but he was also troubled about the subject he was investigating. The awesome mystery of the genesis of the "Final Solution" weighed heavily on his mind. He was a German. I asked him the forbidden question: What about your father? Dr. W. answered that he was the child of a broken home. His father had been remote to him and in any case sons of middle-class families never asked fathers about money, sex, or politics. In his youth, Dr. W. was in fact raised by a governess. During the war, his father—a lawyer—had served on the staff of the German military government in Athens. Dr. W. had never asked him what he had done there. Some years after the war, when he wanted to go to law school, he wrote his father for financial help. He accepted monthly checks from him, not realizing that after 1945 his father was forced to work with his bare hands.

Dr. W. probed also my mind. I brought up the play I had just read. "What can I do?" Dr. W. asked me, "Tell me, what can I do?"

Frankfurt

There was simply not enough information in Ludwigsburg to give me more than a few clues. To be sure, these materials had greatly reduced my ignorance, which was almost total at the start. At least, I was beginning to visualize the chain of communications in the railways. I dared think that I was coming to grips with the meaning of a timetable, although in this area my confidence was premature. What perturbed me most was my failure to find out what sort of priority Jewish transports had. I did not yet know that the lack of a priority rating did *not* signify the impossibility of dispatching a train. Like a novice, I made the fundamental mistake of assuming that a "priority" (even as a "decision" or "plan") would have to be spelled out in some order; I could not see that in this bureaucracy a sense of what was critically important was not always reduced to writing.

In the meantime, however, I looked for some answers in the headquarters of the German Federal Railways in Frankfurt. I had nothing to lose. The place I had to visit turned out not to be in the new massive office building along one of the main roads, but in a smaller satellite structure reserved for miscellaneous functions. It was situated in the very middle of a pornographic section. There, flanked by sex shows and sex shops, was the railroad library. By the time I found it, the morning was almost gone, and when I stood in front of a locked door in the corridor, two gentlemen with their coats on pointed out that the lunch hour had arrived. I offered to come back, but the taller of the two men, a Dr. K., suggested that I join them in the railroad cafeteria; I would save myself almost ten Mark. Impressed by such thoughtfulness, I accepted the invitation, explaining briefly along the way that I was interested in civilian special trains operated during the war. "Aha!" the heavyset shorter companion of Dr. K. blurted out. "Aha! Auschwitz and Treblinka!" I looked at him startled. He was in his mid or upper fifties, and he explained himself without prompting. During the war, he had seen many ghettos in Poland—railroaders got around—but he also had the rare distinction of having been one of the first to have stood at the edge of a grave near Katyn where Polish officers shot by the Russians were being exhumed under the supervision of German occupying forces.

Dr. K. was not so voluble. He took me back to his office, showed me books and the freight car catalog, and helpfully made photocopies of cards with titles that I might later need. One of the volumes was important to me. Written by a former railroad bureaucrat, Eugen Kreidler and published only in 1975, it had a long title that in English might be rendered The Railroads in the Power Sphere of the Axis States during World War II. The book was carefully confined to transport of troops and munitions, but its wealth of background information was invaluable. The author had drawn on much more than his extensive experience; on page 400, listing his sources, he included documents in his private possession. Significant collections I had been looking for all this time, such as the weekly reports of the General Directorate East (which decided on the car allocations for Jewish transports moving to the gas chambers on occupied Polish territory) were in his hands.

I questioned Dr. K. about small points, for example, the sizes of freight cars, and then asked also about people. He was an old-timer after all, having joined the railroads in 1938, and I wondered if he had heard of a man called Geitmann who was a member of the four-man top directorate of the West German railways in the 1960s, but who had been in charge of the railroad directorate in Oppeln during the war. Oppeln was significant, for the area of that directorate included the giant Auschwitz death camp.

Dr. K. was not fooled by the question. Yes, he knew Geitmann personally. Personally? Oh yes. We talked some more and then Dr. K. said he was familiar also with Auschwitz. Had he been there? Yes. Momentarily, in the pleasant surroundings of his spacious office, I wondered if he had made a pilgrimage to the site of the camp after the War. No, he had been there during the War. He had worked for Geitmann in the railroad directorate of Oppeln putting up signal equipment in the vicinity of Auschwitz itself.

It was late afternoon, and I could muster no reaction. There he was, the enemy: sensitive, honest, even gentle, highly intelligent and very efficient, a technocrat who had been involved in a lethal enterprise. He must now have been sixty, I was some ten years younger. He knew instantaneously who I was and he had to let me know also what he had been. I thought he looked rugged, still strong, still in his prime.

I left late that afternoon. It was after working hours and the railroad building was empty.

Vienna

By now, I already knew that I would strike no gold mines of information. I could go to Vienna and examine the trial records of an SS captain who was sentenced for his activities as Eichmann's transport officer. The transcripts might give me a clearer view of train procurement. Eventually, I would also have to visit the criminal court in Düsseldorf that had the documents prepared for a stalled proceeding against Albert Ganzenmüller, second in command of the German railroads during the war. Because of the central position of this man, I would learn at least something about the railroad structure as a whole. In both Vienna and Düsseldorf my discoveries would certainly be limited. There was but one more document center to which I would have to go, perhaps in the hope of finding the unexpected; that was the railroad archive in Nuremberg. But I did not know if it contained anything at all. The logistics of the situation did not make it imperative that I should be in any one of these places first. I resolved to start with Vienna.

The eleven days of my stop in the city were a longer time than any period I had spent there since my early youth. I was born and I was a child in Vienna, and I stayed on under the swastika for over a year until I was almost thirteen. Now, I spent the late afternoons and weekends literally retracing the steps of my childhood. I was all alone as I took these walks, crossing the Danube canal on the Augarten bridge, and heading along the shore to the house where I had lived. It was an apartment house that I knew had been bombed. The front wall was sheered away, two passersby were killed, but the building remained standing, its interior unchanged. I gazed up at the living room window of our apartment. Two ladies, one in late middle age, the other very old, leaned over the window sill, engaging in the old Viennese pastime of watching the traffic go by. I wondered if the younger of the two women was Mrs. A.G.* whose husband had forced us out of the

---

* I.e., Anna Gruber. Hilberg provided her full name a decade later in his autobiography: *The Politics of Memory: The Journey of a Holocaust Historian* (Chicago 1996), 201–202.

apartment at gunpoint in November 1938. Very slowly, I walked into the building and climbed the spiral stone staircase, stopping halfway up and looking at the courtyard. This was the very place where as an eight-year-old I had pondered the existence of God, and deciding that there was none had almost jumped out of the window into the courtyard just below. I touched the rough walls and made my way up to the next floor. As in my childhood, there was a spigot for cold water in the hallway; I was sure that there was still no running water in the apartments. I wanted to ring the bell, not to confront Mrs. A.G., but to look at the rooms again; I wanted to look out of the window where, as a twelve year old, listening to the drums of the Hitler Youth march by one night, I had rashly decided to become a historian of the Nazi regime, even before it had burst out of these regions to engulf all Europe. It was here, I knew, that my thinking was cast. But I did not ring the bell.

I walked back to the inner city, deliberately taking a circuitous route. How short the distances were that in my early youth had seemed so large. I looked for the Jewish school where I was a student; it was now devoted to other purposes without a sign to mark its former character. I looked for the synagogue that I had been forced to attend in the theocratic Austrian state of the 1930s. An apartment building stood there now; it was built as part of the postwar Viennese housing program. In the Second District, I looked for two nondescript old houses where I knew Jews had been concentrated prior to their deportation to Poland. I was struck by the small size of those apartment buildings and tried to imagine them jammed with the victims. One house was now the headquarters of various Austrian "resistance" groups. Again, there was no sign to note its use during the last hours of Viennese Jewry.

Finally, I stopped on the shore of the Danube canal. I was on the side that I had never liked as a child, but that had been favored by my late father. I could not help thinking of him then. He was an Austrian soldier in World War I; he was buffeted by the great Depression, and at the age of forty-nine, he was expelled from this city to become a refugee. I was precisely as old now as my father had been when he left behind all the foundations of his life. I had been an US soldier in World War II (albeit with much less combat experience than my father had seen), I had been an unemployed PhD at the age of twenty-nine (though I have slowly worked myself up the ladder in a northern New England university), and finally I became a divorced man who had the company of his two small children on weekends and who was a recluse for the remainder of his time.

Nuremberg

I had completed my work in a dungeon of the criminal court building in Vienna and went on to Nuremberg. Since I arrived there on a Sunday, I used the time to orient myself and to pinpoint the railroad archive; it was located in the basement of the traffic museum. Nuremberg was full of toy trains. They were in the museum, in the windows of stores, even in a restaurant for the transport of beer to the tables of patrons.

The man in charge of the archive was young—thirty-eight years old. I had now become familiar with a formula that several younger bureaucrats adopted when they introduced themselves to me. "My name is Schmidt and I am thirty-six," or "Knauer is my name and I was born in 1939." Mr. L. said that he could not give me permission to use the archive without clearance from Frankfurt, but if I would list the topics I was interested in, he would telephone his superior in the main office. I wrote down World War II—civilian traffic—special trains, and specified such railroad directorates as Oppeln. Mr. L. cited the specifications over the telephone without mentioning the special trains or the Oppeln directorate. The Frankfurt chief, apparently suspicious, wanted to talk to me. I was a professor, I said, managing a slight American accent, interested in the manner in which the German railroads managed to transport civilians in the middle of a war. Inasmuch as Herr Ministerialrat Kreidler had already studied military traffic, my effort would be much more modest, but complementary. Yes, that would make some sense, the Frankfurt bureaucrat growled.

Mr. L., I realized, had committed treason, but soon I determined that his gesture was doing me little good. The archive possessed recollections of railroad men, and some of these memoirs were obviously based on material kept in their homes (fairly precise figures were cited of construction projects at Auschwitz), but the documents themselves were unavailable.

"Where are the documents?" I asked L.

"They burned the people," he said, looking me straight in the eye, "why not the documents?"

"Because," I answered, "it is my belief that Germans are not capable of such a thing as burning documents."

I was now somewhat depressed. Düsseldorf was not far and I should have travelled there right away, but I needed an interruption (or so I reasoned) and I might as well use my Eurailpass to spend a few days in Italy. Once, in 1939, after I got off a train that had carried me from Kehl, Germany, across the Rhine to Strasbourg, France, I had felt the momentary sensation of breathing free air. Now, in Milan, Italy, I had that same feeling. For the next few days, I would board express trains to nearby Italian cities, such as Mantua, Pavia, Venice, and Florence, as if slightly drunk. The fact was that I had spent very little money in Germany and Austria, and although it was my own savings account that I used to finance the trip, I was plainly overbudgeted. That knowledge made me a little reckless and in a single day I bought a brand new Expressionist painting of a Venetian scene and an equally new small mosaic of a Florentine street for a bare living room wall back home. Then, I had to return to Germany. Why, oh why, had I not left Italy for last?

Freiburg

The train, at any rate, was direct. I would see the majestic Swiss alps during the day and be in Düsseldorf by early evening. In Basel, the car was pushed back and forth. Idle customs men were lingering on the platform. Why does Europe still bother with them? When the train passed through the freight yards, I would once again peer at the four-wheeled boxcars, trying to decipher their painted lettering that indicated size and capacity. I was about to settle down in my empty compartment when two middle-aged German customs men walked in. At this point I was not listening much and could have been hearing less. The train had come down from the heights, my ears were partially plugged, and I was lost in thought. One of the customs men wanted to examine my luggage. When he saw the package containing the mosaic and the letter certifying it as art, he said that he wished to see the other valise. There he spotted my painting rolled up in a tube. After more questions he said that he could not make a decision respecting an object more than 250 Mark in value. Who would make the decision then? His superior in Freiburg. Was the superior going to board the train in that city? No, I would have to get off.

Somewhat displeased with the prospect of an interruption but reassured by the politeness of the customs agents who insisted on carrying my luggage, I left the train and was told to wait at the office of the railway police. A half hour passed and I was becoming increasingly impatient. Finally, a civilian appeared and addressed me with the words: "You are under suspicion." I cut him off immediately and sharply—I would hold every word he said against him. He answered that he had no business to discuss with me; his colleague in the city would handle my case.

For many years I had had a recurring dream in which I was a deportee to Auschwitz. Why such a dream? Why a deportation train? Didn't I know in my waking state what Auschwitz was? And if I knew, why was I not dreaming of jumping out of the train or of shooting at the guards? Could I, even in a dream, have listened to the false assurances and deceitful statements of German officials?

They were still very polite. One of the customs men actually attempted to be a tourist guide, explaining to me that Freiburg was a famous university town. He made me think of 1933, when its rector was the philosopher Martin Heidegger. He had signed an order denying stipends to non-Aryan students. The denial was based on an analogy principle that provided that if non-Aryan civil servants could be removed from the official payroll, then non-Aryan students could be struck from the roster of scholarship holders.

The customs office was on the third floor of a converted residential home. I was made to carry my luggage, now filled with notes and photostats of documents, up the stairs. The customs official in charge, a somewhat younger man, invited me to show him my art treasures. The gentlemen of the customs service on the train, he explained, had made an official report alleging that, upon demand, I had failed to volunteer information about my Italian purchases. Based on the value of the two objects, he would demand payment of about sixty dollars as deposit for a fine. If I wished, I could avail myself of the services of a German attorney. I replied, my blood boiling, that I would not spend a Pfennig for a German lawyer and that I had no confidence in the German customs administration. I had no confidence in any German office. "I have had my experiences with you."

That was an insult, the young customs official said, he could not tolerate. Were I to repeat my words, he would have to institute "other" proceedings against me. "Go ahead," I said, "and don't forget the foreign press when you do. I will repeat it for you loud and clear. I have no confidence in your law, and I have no confidence in you."

If I were to repeat that sentiment one more time, the customs official said, he would have to institute proceedings against me.

I called a US consul who advised me to pay the sixty dollars in order that I might go about my business. My consular protector was a sane American. Perhaps he was no economist, but he understood the theorem of minimizing one's losses. That, too, is an idea that has made our country great.

When I handed the sixty dollars to the customs official, he offered to take me back to the station, explaining that he could not have acted otherwise, lest it be thought that the customs administration was not strictly neutral. Any deviation in favor or against any man on grounds of his presumed background was inadmissible. Germany was a state of laws.

"I have no confidence in your laws so far as they apply to me," I replied.

"There you go again. If you say this one more time, I will have to act."

"I have experience with you."

"That was another generation."

Some weeks later, at my home in Vermont, I was to receive the official customs decision. The art objects were duty free. If sold in Germany, however, they would have been subject to a turnover tax. In view of my failure to declare them, the customs administration collected an amount that would have been due if I had been liable to pay the tax upon the conclusion of a sale.

Düsseldorf

When I arrived in Düsseldorf late in the evening, I sought out a faded hotel near the railroad station, resolved to spend a minimum of money while I had to remain on German soil. The Freiburg incident kept me awake until the early morning hours, and the next day I staggered about in the streets looking for the court building in which I would have to work. The prosecutor in charge of the Ganzenmüller case would not give me immediate access to the records. The rules forbade it, he said, in the case of an ailing defendant who might recover sufficiently to stand trial. Germany was a state of laws now, he explained, and could not try a man to death; yet every year a new finding of Ganzenmüller's health was being obtained to determine if there might not be a belated improvement. Hence, the case, though dormant, was still active, and I would have to see the judge. To expedite my application, he would give me his own handwritten positive recommendation.

I was in the streets again, waiting for my appointment. It was a large new city with a small old core. I passed through an opulent boulevard and came to the vicinity of the university where a student with a street sign branded the US Army in Germany as an "occupation force." Turning to him, I identified myself as an American and told him that the sign was offensive. US troops were not occupying Germany. "Oh yes, they are," he insisted. "Why?" "Because you never made a peace treaty with us." "With the Germany of Auschwitz one does not make peace treaties." "You are a neurotic," he replied.

The old part of the city gave me an unexpected sense of peace. Cars were barred from the area and Italian restaurants lined the streets. I stopped to watch two young men with Japanese motorcycles gunning the machines to take them up two steps into the hallway of a small house. A shop selling coffee by the kilo was downstairs; an architect's office was situated one flight up. I glanced at an emblem above the ground floor window. This was the house in which the great Jewish poet Heinrich Heine had been born at the end of the eighteenth century.

The judge signed the paper quickly and the archivist in the political division of the criminal court gave me his undivided attention. He found the records forthwith and saved me from the loss of yet another day. I noticed that he hobbled on one leg and asked him when and where he had been crippled. During the first Russian winter, he answered, in the Demyansk Pocket. Russia cannot be imagined, he explained, by those who were not there. His unit had pushed deeply into Soviet territory between Leningrad and Moscow. The fall season was beautiful until November, when suddenly a mist and a drizzle covered the German troops for a period of three days. On the fourth day, the snow and the cold assaulted the invaders who dug themselves into the snowbanks in a vain attempt to keep warm. From all sides, Russian fire poured in as the Germans were encircled. He was hit several times, but the doctor in the first aid station laughed at the blood trickling down the young soldier's face. Finally, his leg was shattered and he was flown out by a good old transport plane. The leg could not be saved and he was out of the war. Nothing, said the archivist, but nothing is as bad as war and now he was determined that his two sons would never fight in one. The eleven-year-old was still young, the other had a safe haven in the police.

I worked without interruption. A young assistant of the archivist brought me a giant soda bottle for lunch. I took notes frantically on depositions of railway veterans who had been promised immunity in exchange for truth. Their truth was partial, sometimes vague, and often misleading, but it told me something nevertheless. I was interested in the system of the wartime Transport Ministry and gradually, painfully, as I learned the railway vocabulary, I began to see the pattern of railway operations. I could see the decentralization of effort in the drafting of timetables and formation of trains at each of the territorial railway directorates. At last I realized how intricate the dispatch of even a single transport must have been as it moved across the timetable zones, shunted aside by armed forces trains, and spliced into flows of trains rolling at a predetermined "tempo" ahead and to the rear. I pondered the difference (how obvious it was when I saw it) between bills of lading accompanying the human cargo and papers made out for the cars. The German railroad men had to keep track of both the Jews and the rolling stock, delivering the people, and recovering the equipment.

As I buried myself in the documents, an older white-haired man walked in. He was exceptionally informal with the two archivists. Sitting down at a nearby table, he addressed me in English: Was I a member of the tribe? Jarred and annoyed by the incredible crudity of the question, I said without elaboration: Yes. "I thought so," my questioner continued, explaining that he had Jewish friends. I gave him no reply. Then he went on, saying that the reason he was speaking English to me was that he did not trust the one-legged archivist and that he thought the young assistant was a moron. He wanted to tell me a story. A few years back, he had prosecuted the members of a police battalion that was stationed in a city of northeastern Poland. They had set fire to a synagogue in which 6,000 victims were incarcerated. "We knew it was 6,000, but charged them with only 1,000 to be on the safe side." He had convinced some of the policemen to testify against the others, but in open court the witnesses forgot the facts and the accused went free. Not satisfied with such a demonstration of memory failure, the acquitted policemen shouted in the corridors at their comrades: "You swine! You were shooting too! I saw you! You were shooting too!"

He wanted me to know what this case meant to him. During the war, he had been a German lieutenant on the Eastern front. In the middle of battle, he was pulled out and deprived of his rank and uniform because he had a Jewish mother. She was transported, apparently as a privileged prisoner, to Auschwitz, and though she survived the death camp, his German father died of a broken heart. In 1948, the young man wanted to fight in the Jewish army for Israel, but his mother would not let him. Later he married. Often he thought of adopting the Jewish religion, but for the sake of the religious unity of his family, he remained a Catholic. His half-Jewish parentage had come to the attention of a superior in the court of another city and in the course of that assignment a promotion was denied to him. In Düsseldorf, however, no one knew his personal history. At Christmas time, or on other holidays, he would refuse to make contributions to Caritas or other welfare organizations. "I said to my wife that all of my charitable donations go directly to the Israel army."

I took my last train to Frankfurt and, forgetting that I could still have another train ride from there to the airport, rode out in a cab instead. What had I accomplished? I had started with a large gap in my knowledge and I was returning with a skeletal collection of texts and notes. The trip had netted very few documents and I would have some problems reading those few and being sure who had written to whom. There was a vast disproportion between what I had found and what was still missing in those archives. But I knew that I was leaving Germany for good. No necessity I could imagine would bring me back. That principle, I thought, should apply analogously to my non-Aryan children.

12

Working on the Holocaust
(1986)

BOB LIFTON ASKED ME TO talk today about my journey with my book *The Destruction of the European Jews* and thereby perhaps give you my conception of the way in which people remember the Holocaust. It's a professional journey but at the same time quite obviously a personal one as well. In general, I perceive three periods in the last forty years when the subject of the Holocaust, although that was not always its name, excited a certain amount of attention in this country and abroad. The first period was immediately after the war and extended through the Nuremberg trials. The purpose then was to write and publish testimony of the Holocaust, to put the matter on record, and then to put it behind us. Even those who came out of the Holocaust as its victims were going to live a new life. To describe their experiences was one way they could perhaps forget. But there was no word for the phenomenon. If you just look at the book titles and the rest of the literature that came out at the time, one talked about excesses; one talked about persecution; one talked about antisemitism. The vocabulary was certainly lacking.

Originally published in *The Psychohistory Review* 14, no. 3 (1986): 7–20.
This is the published transcript of a conversation that took place between Raul Hilberg and several different personalities, mainly psychologists, in October 1985 in Wellfleet, Cape Cod, Massachusetts. See the list of participants on page 223.

It was in this first period that I began my work. I had no special background or interest in the subject. I had been born in Vienna and had lived there under the Nazis for approximately a year from the time of the "Anschluss" in March 1938 to the time my parents and I departed in March of 1939. I went to Cuba, then came to the United States. I had been on German soil again in the spring of 1945. I was in an US army unit that captured Dachau. Although I myself was not there, I distinctly recall the reaction to Dachau in that Oklahoma National Guard Division that I served in. On 30 April, the division attacked Munich. The day is fixed in my mind, because of the odd circumstance that I had been so tired that I fell asleep and my unit had left me behind. My attempt to catch up led me to be one of the first people to be in the middle of the city, in fact in a part of the city we had not yet captured. I recall seeing an older woman who had attempted suicide the day after the capture of the city; she wanted to know whether the Jewish commissars had already arrived. She did not want to live. She wanted to follow the example of Adolf Hitler. I walked around the Nazi party headquarters we occupied without much awareness of what had happened there. I rummaged through the Nazi party library and, I remember, came upon an edition of Luther's book about the Jews and their lies, *Juden und Ihre Lügen*, published by Franz Eher Verlag, the Nazi party publisher. I looked inside and I saw that language I had not yet, in those days, familiarized myself with. After, I put it back on the shelf and I said to myself: "Now what do these people invent?"

After the war, I went back to civilian life and found myself in Brooklyn College. I had been a chemistry major before I went into the army. The army liberated me from chemistry and I drifted into political science. There was one course given at Brooklyn by a professor, Hans Rosenberg. It was called "The Rise of the National State." I felt that that was something I might be interested in. However, the course turned out to be on the development of bureaucracy in Germany, France, and England from 1660 to 1930. Typically, the date when discussion closed, as always in the literature dealing with Germany, was 1930; there was no history after that. The class was full of veterans, slightly older people, and Rosenberg was a brilliant lecturer who did one thing for which I will always be grateful. He called to my attention the enormous importance of institutions. But one day, in the middle of a lecture he made an aside; he noted that the atrocities committed in the Napoleonic period were the worst in modern history. If I may describe myself, I would say I am a protesting sort of person, a nonconformist, even a misfit. And so I raised my hand and asked: "What do you call six million Jews, six million dead Jews?" And he said: "But that is a very complicated question." Now the incident took no longer than this minute that I have just used to describe it. I have a recollection of it as a calm exchange, but thirty years later in Los Angeles, a grey-haired woman came up to me and said "Don't you remember me?" I said I was sorry but I didn't. She said she was in that class. She recalled the incident but quite differently. She said: "We all looked at you, and we thought that you would have a stroke or a heart attack that very moment." I can't say there's any one thing that triggers work worth a life process, but if anything in my life led me to the study of what is now called the Holocaust, it was this incident in 1947 in an undergraduate class on "The Rise of the National State" in Brooklyn College.

I went to graduate school at Columbia in 1948. I had to choose then between the study of international law or that of the Nazi system. I loved international law, because I loved law generally. At Columbia I encountered a man, Franz Neumann, who taught a course called "The Government of Germany." There were no fewer than about a hundred graduate students sitting in on that course. As a text he used his book: *Behemoth: The Structure and Practice of National Socialism*. It is an audacious work that he produced during the war without any documents at his disposal, though he learned much in the Office of Strategic Services and the Department of State, where he was head of the section dealing with Germany in research and intelligence. Neumann's theory was that Germany was not a state at all but a non-state. It had had only one leader with four independent hierarchies under him. Each hierarchy moved alone, without a legislature to define jurisdiction or appropriations. He identified these four hierarchies as the civil service, the army, industry, and the party. The emphasis he put on industry was, I think, in large part due to his slightly Marxist outlook. He had been a student of Lasky's in London, which had followed a juridical degree in Frankfurt. I approached Franz Neumann and said: "I want to write a term paper." He was very hard of hearing so conversations were brief. Everybody made appointments to see him for five or ten minutes; that was it. I asked if I could write about the role of the German civil service in the destruction of the Jews. That was going to be my answer to Rosenberg in Brooklyn College. "All right," he said. "I have a friend, Robert Kempner, who is prosecutor in Nuremberg and the documents are coming in." He meant the Nuremberg documents.

Now there were several Nuremberg trials. The first one, dealing with Göring and his associates, was based on a relatively slight but important documentary source file. But then there were several subsequent trials, in which documents were, interestingly enough, designated NG, NO, NI and NOKW. And they happened to be in the exact same piles as represented in Neumann's theory of government. NG were always ministerial or civil service items; NI were industry; NO were the Nazi Party and its organizations, including the SS; and NOKW simply stood for Nazi OKW, *Oberkommando der Wehrmacht*, or the military documents. I first went to the NG file, and then I asked myself: "What has Neumann really taught me?" I would have to look at all of the collections, because I felt that each was necessarily involved in the destruction of the Jews. This was a bureaucratic state and the process had been bureaucratic. None of the items in the series were indexed, so I had an initial investment of a couple of years just to look at 40,000 unindexed documents; and these were only the prosecution documents. After that, Neumann decided, wisely, that I should go to Washington, DC, to the War Documentation project where at the time we had 28,000 linear feet of shelves of captured German documents. Now you have to understand what is meant by a linear foot of shelf of documents, with due apologies to those of you who know all about archives. A document is a piece of paper, an item of correspondence, an order, a report, a letter, a proposal, conference minutes, or whatever. Documents were bound by the issuing and recipient agencies, respectively, in folders with the most recent correspondence on top. The folders are usually fifty pages thick, but sometimes they're more, and several folders are put into a box. The box stands about 2.5 or 3 inches. You can put four boxes on a shelf occupying a foot. You multiply that by 28,000, and you have a picture of what we had in Alexandria, Virginia, in the Federal Records Center.

I stepped into this building and got a conception of government that absolutely no course, no instructor, no university could ever have imparted. I figured out quickly that even if I were to stay in that archive for a lifetime, I couldn't possibly look at all those documents. But I am a brute force man, rather like Mr. Spock on the starship Enterprise at the moment when the starship is so many miles away from its destination that it couldn't get there in a hundred million years. Spock says: "In that case, we'd better get started." This was my philosophy. It was simply brute force, because I didn't know what else to do.

Of course, I soon developed a sense of where to sniff out important things, where to find them, and how fast to turn the pages. I became a human scanner, but of course I missed a lot.

I began to write in 1952 and spent two years at it. Then I had to go to work. I ended up in Vermont, where I continued writing without a lot of encouragement. I recall going to a publisher, in the latter 1950s, who was an old man and very paternal. He said, "Now, young man, I want to give you some advice." "What is it?" I asked. "Do not complete your work. The whole subject is dead." Nevertheless, I pushed on. When the book was done, I had three experiences with publishers I will relate to you, though that is usually something one keeps as a sacred secret. The first publisher that I negotiated with was Columbia University Press. The Press was obligated, by virtue of an award I had received, to publish my dissertation. With others in the past they had usually printed 850 copies of the book to discharge that obligation. My dissertation was only 450 typewritten pages long, which was 22 percent of the finished manuscript. I had shortened it because Franz Neumann had died in the middle of my typing the work. But I wanted the press to publish the complete, 1,800-page manuscript. That led to protracted and negative evaluations. One reader, in this country, felt I was like a polemical prosecutor and that prosecution had no place in a scholarly study; the other reviewers, in Israel, thought that I was unfair to the Jews. My next attempt, in 1959, was Princeton University Press, which kept my manuscript for two weeks. I received a postcard, not a letter, which read somewhat as follows: "We're returning the manuscript because the subject has been exhausted."

By that time I had an unexpected backer, who was not an academic person but a businessman. He had a daughter at Harvard who had a conversation with a political science professor, Dr. Friedrich, who had actually read my dissertation. He had forgotten the title of the dissertation and, needless to say, the author's name. But he said to this young lady: "Your name appears in it." She related this story to her father, who was totally perplexed. His name was Frank Petschek. The Petscheks had been a major industrial family, one of the richest Jewish families in Europe. He and his brother went to Columbia University and found my dissertation after a three-day search. He called me into his modest ten-room Park Avenue apartment, where he had a few Dutch masterpieces left, which was all that remained of his fortune. He said: "It is important for this work to be published. I read it line by line." A businessman read it, not Princeton University Press. He read the dissertation portion and then he read the remaining portions, and he wanted the manuscript published.

At that point a colleague suggested I publish with Oklahoma Press, because their printing was superb. So I sent the manuscript to Oklahoma. It sat there for sixteen months. Then Oklahoma Press said: "Wait a minute. We're not just a University Press. We are a State University Press, and we will not publish anything about religion. You've got to take out anything you have about Luther, rabbis, and priests." That's how I came to a very small publisher, who was hungry for money. I had not mentioned to my university presses that I had the stupendous amount of $15,000 in backing, because out of vanity I wanted the book to be accepted, not bought. "If it's going to be sold," I had promised myself, "it'll be sold to a private publisher who wants to publish it and who wants to make money." That was Quadrangle in Chicago. It turned out to be a superb publisher (though later it was bought by the *New York Times* and ruined totally).

My book came out in the exact middle of the Eichmann trial in 1961. And that was the second phase of interest in the Holocaust. It was occasioned by the Eichmann trial, and it threw out to the world a new vision of the Holocaust, one that was different from the first because controversy was now entering the picture and of all things the controversy was focused on the victims. I went through the entire transcript of the trial and noticed what had happened. Eichmann had been abducted and was tried in Israel so that the young generation in Israel would not forget the history of the Jewish people.

The new generation had little recollection of World War II. They knew about the War of Independence and of course the Sinai campaign of 1956, but their first question about the Holocaust was, "What is going on here? Why didn't these Jews resist? Are you telling us that they just laid down in the grave and were shot?" At the Eichmann trial, the resistors of course testified, because they were the heroes. But as they testified, the documents in support of their testimony were introduced. And what did these documents say? They told a more complete, that is to say, a different story, which led some survivors to be queried rather brutally. "Why didn't you resist?" was asked repeatedly.

In my own research, I had perused the incidence of resistance wherever I could find it; the word "resistance" is in the index. After I had found all these acts, however, I had concluded that basically there had been no meaningful resistance to the Holocaust. Resistance had been episodic, late, and uneventful. If you divide the Holocaust into a chronological development, you find that the most lethal year was 1942. By the end of 1942, most of the Jews who were going to die had died. Resistance, to the extent that one can notice it, came in 1943 with the Warsaw Ghetto Battle, the uprisings in Treblinka and Sobibor, and the 1944 crematorium uprising in Auschwitz. All of these things were late developments by people who had been left alive because the Germans, reversing chivalry, had killed women and children first and saved the workers and young men, who were then relieved of the necessity of worrying about their families. Hannah Arendt, who covered the trial, saw that there had been no resistance, but she blamed the Jewish councils. Of course she was attacked fiercely, and so was I and so was Bruno Bettelheim. A few months earlier, Bettelheim had published a book called *The Informed Heart* in which he created a psychoanalytic explanation of Jewish nonresistance, to wit, that the victim identified with the SS. This was sacrilegious and aroused a lot of protest. The protestors, I might add, never looked at another book published several years earlier by an Auschwitz survivor, Elie Cohen, a psychiatrist no less, who wrote a work called *Human Behavior in the Concentration Camp*. The first part of Cohen's book is entirely medical and describes what happens when people are deprived of food. He argued, among other things, that psychosomatic illness disappeared in the concentration camp. In the second half of the book, however, Cohen wrote a psychoanalytic treatise arguing that the victims identified with the perpetrators, making exactly the same point as Bettelheim. But Cohen was immune. That made me the third person in this trio of devils. I think I am the only survivor of the three. Arendt was never forgiven, and Bettelheim is still in the dog house. I'm the only one who somehow, though not entirely, has been accepted.

During the later 1960s, I believed that interest in the Holocaust was gone permanently. I really thought this. I recall distinctly giving a lecture once at McGill in 1970, saying: "This is probably the last lecture I will give on this subject." But in 1975 or so, the picture changed entirely. I've been asked more often than I can count: "Why this sudden interest in the Holocaust during the last ten years?" Usually the question is connected with the television play by Gerald Green, "Holocaust." Now we know that's no explanation because Green could not sell his idea to any network years earlier. It isn't Green and it isn't the networks; it is something that is very hard to define. It happened in the United States before it happened anywhere else. Interest in the Holocaust is only now developing in France and to some extent in

Germany. I have the feeling that what happened was connected with the Vietnam war. I have found veterans of that conflict to be disowned, so to speak. Their war was unpopular in more than one sense. It was a war that had not been clearly defined; its goals were not pristine. Vietnam was, in that regard, worse than Korea, and Korea was worse than World War II. World War II was the last war about which there was, in any sense, unanimity. It was the last war fought by the good guys against the bad guys. And the worst thing that was done by the adversary in World War II was the Holocaust. I now have Holocaust classes at the University of Vermont that must be closed because of the number of people interested; nor are all of these students Jews. The Holocaust has become something of a reference point, not only for Jews but for the population at large.

Today, in the third period, I find the Holocaust is internationalized. A few years ago a major congress took place in Paris dealing with the Holocaust. There was another during 1984 in Stuttgart. These were, of course, unusual occurrences. At the Paris conference of 1982, the Germans appeared for the first time. Eberhard Jäckel was there and he organized the Stuttgart conference two years later. After that conference everything was translated in a fantastic burst of German efficiency and was published within a year of the meeting.*

My basic idea all along has been that which was imparted to me by Franz Neumann, namely to look at the Holocaust as a bureaucratic phenomenon. It fed on all the resources of society and touched every aspect of life. The investigator of this system cannot leave out anything because everything was involved. This is what led me to research topics like the German railways and the transport system. Sometimes I came to dead ends, as with my work on the role of the life insurance industry. (There were simply no documents because they were never collected.) Consider all the relations a person has with fellow human beings, the contracts, marriages, friendships, mortgages, pensions, insurance, and you begin to see that everything had to be attended to so that there would be no harm to the German people as a result of the destruction of the Jews. That minimization of harm to the German population was an extremely important element in the process, and that was precisely what led to the widespread involvement of every-

---

* Eberhard Jäckel and Jürgen Rohwer, eds. *Der Mord an den Juden im Zweiten Weltkrieg. Entschlußbildung und Verwirklichung* (Stuttgart: Deutsche Verlagsanstalt, 1985).

body, even the churches, in the Holocaust. I expected that this particular notion of mine would be challenged, particularly in Germany, because what, after all, comes closer to a doctrine of complicity and collective guilt? I'm not saying that all the German people, every man, woman, and child, were involved. I'm not even saying that the bureaucracy was a random sample of the German population. But I am saying that if there are significant tendencies to resist a particular course of action, these propensities will manifest themselves within the bureaucracy. They will result in dilatory tactics, as in Italy; in perpetual postponements, as in Bulgaria; in compromises, as in France. Only in Nazi Germany will you find total efficiency.

I thought some response would come from postwar Germany to this idea. All the talk about the Jewish resistance, its existence or nonexistence, was really secondary. I was making quite a different central point that no one seemed to pick up one way or the other. Then my book came out in German three years ago. There had been an earlier attempt to publish it, in 1964, when a major German publisher, Droemer-Knaur, made a contract with Quadrangle, paid a small advance, and translated one-third of the book. However, they then stopped production and broke the contract. They had discovered what was in the book: The notion that the Jews did not resist. That at least was their given reason. They said it would create anti-Semitism in German, and they were against anti-Semitism. They did not exactly mention Hannah Arendt, but her book had just come out in German. The Germans live with multiple taboos. When my book did come out in German translation eighteen years later, I was interested enough to go to Berlin in order to meet Mr. Ulf Wolter, the head of the publishing firm, Olle &Wolter, who brought it. This young man, who is in his thirties, is a *Nachkriegskind*, someone born after the war. I asked him why he published the book. "Oh," he said, "I took a big chance. But if you look at my list very carefully, you'll see that there's one theme here." I said, "What is your theme?" And he said: "It is injustice." He publishes books about nuclear war, needless to say from the German point of view. He publishes books by the Greens, he publishes Petra Kelly, he publishes some socialists, because that's where his sympathies lie. He said he read my book while still a student of political science at the Free University of Berlin. He had said then that when he started a publishing firm, he was going to approach me. In Germany, of course, the book is almost dead. It's hard to find in bookstores. Sales are modest and it is really accessible only in libraries.

Germany's memory of the Holocaust, like the Jewish memory of it, is very partial. Last May 1984, for example, Jäckel, the historian of Adolf Hitler, came to my house in Burlington and asked me to give a public lecture in Germany. I said, "Well, conference papers are one thing, but a public lecture may be something else." He said it was important. I said, "Look, it's not a simple thing for me to just step off a plane and start talking in German." But we discussed it. He said, "If you had a lecture that was printed..." "Well," I said, "Such things I do have. I have a lecture that was recorded, printed and edited." He said that he would translate it. It was on an innocuous topic, "The Anatomy of the Holocaust." I gave the lecture under the auspices of the Württemberg Historical Society. About three or four hundred people attended. I was introduced by the mayor, Manfred Rommel. Prior to my delivery of the speech, I found myself with him alone in the cafeteria. I learned a lot in those fifteen minutes, as well as in that whole conference. I learned that there is no oratory in Germany. Oratory itself is associated with Nazis. I also learned that there is no small talk in Germany, though one may say, "Did you have a nice trip?" And "What did you eat for breakfast?" But above all I learned of the very sharp division of generations in Germany. I had first noticed this in 1976, when people came up to me and said "Oh, by the way, my name is Kunze and I was born in 1939." How's that? What kind of an introduction is that? Or take a question asked from the floor in the Stuttgart conference by a young lady who was manifestly in her twenties. She said, "Ich bin Nachkriegskind." Why does this young lady have to say this? And what about the mayor of Stuttgart, now in his fifties? During the war, he had been a flak helper because at fifteen or sixteen he was one of those who carried ammunition to the anti-aircraft crews that were shooting at our bombers. This man sought me out in an empty room and said: "My father told me about the gas chambers." In Germany that's a major statement. His father, by the way, was Field Marshal [Erwin] Rommel.

Anyway, I gave this lecture, one of the most innocuous I've ever given in my life. When I was done, the entire audience was totally stunned, as though they were hearing about the Holocaust for the first time in their lives. Nor were these necessarily young people.

Wherever I go in Germany, I first head for the bookstores. Over the years I have found something quite remarkable. In our stores, the public issues books are out front. If Bettelheim writes a book, it will be out in the window. In Germany, the novels are out front and the public issues books are in the back. The nation lives in a kind of novelistic fantasy. Nobody wants to know. In such a country memory can cease altogether.

And what about our country? What particularly about the Jewish community? I find that there's an argument among some Jews, and that it runs somewhat as follows: Holocaust studies are all right, but by now we have too many of them. The fact is, though, that we're not training people at all in the history of the Holocaust at the graduate level. When there are survivors who want to establish a chair in Holocaust Studies, as at UCLA or one of the universities in St. Louis, these chairs simply cannot be filled. The Holocaust is not taught (and never was) at a place like Yeshiva University. It's not taught at Jewish Theological Seminary. Brandeis University has also fought off Holocaust Studies. There is a new association of Jewish Studies that publishes a journal. It first came out in yearbooks and now it is a regular journal. I think eight yearbooks have appeared and two issues of *The Journal of the Association for Jewish Studies*. But not one article is devoted to the Holocaust. In other words, Holocaust studies is a specialty and a very odd one. Far more people study medieval Jewish history than Holocaust history. How can you have historical memory of something that is not studied?

Now the truth is that the literature on the Holocaust is enormous, but very little of it is the product of trained people. I, for one, have never said, "You've got to have a PhD before you can put pen to paper for print." Maybe I'm getting older, but I have a feeling that too much is written with too little knowledge of the prerequisites, whatever they may be. That's because the Holocaust was disowned, because it was taboo, because it was discouraged. Of course now anybody who writes anything that is halfway literate about the subject can find a publisher. There are fewer and fewer people here who have mastered the German language sufficiently to work with German documents. The students working at the Hebrew University or at Tel Aviv are monolingual in Hebrew, or at best they read some English. Their work on the Holocaust consists of topics like the reactions of the Jewish Agency, the governing body of Palestine for the Jewish community during the war. No one has an overview. The obvious things are not put together, or the wheel is reinvented.

Because I see people at this table who are inclined toward psychology, there's one last thing I want to say here to this group. There are several taboos I have noticed in Holocaust studies governing research.

Jews have the prerogative to write about the perpetrators or the bystanders or the victims. An American non-Jew, a Gentile, may write about the perpetrators or the bystanders. Germans may write only about Germany and its collaborators. The sources also develop in the same direction. There are many German documents but there is very little German testimony. We have very few Jewish documents, such as ghetto records, but much Jewish testimony. For the bystanders, there is extremely limited testimony and not too much documentation. So what we remember will also be highly selective, based upon what sources are left to us. Thus we have too many oral history projects of survivors. Why interview a survivor for the third time, forty years after the fact? There is a large community of Slovaks, Lithuanians, and others, who have never been asked what they remember. When I tell that to people, they look at me as though I had just recommended that they take a trip to the moon. I have been a member of the Holocaust Memorial Council since its founding. Eventually, when the museum opens in 1991,* there will be an archive in the library. But in the meantime, no dollars are being expended whatsoever for any attempt to just collect material or to sponsor work. In 1985, curiously, it is like it was in 1945; the work of individuals swimming against the stream.

Bob Lifton: You've raised a lot of issues for us very palpably, very courageously. I want to get at one point I think is central to all of our concerns and very central to my work with Nazi doctors. To put it in a phrase, it's the relationship between the fundamental bureaucratization of killing in order to make it work and the responsibility of individuals within that bureaucracy for the killing. I notice that you struggle in your work, as I do in mine, never to forget the issue of individual responsibility, even while recognizing the extraordinary influence of bureaucratization in the killing process. Let me suggest a model, much of which I learned from you and developed in my own way with Nazi doctors. I sense that many individual Nazi doctors, some of whom I talked to and some of whom I heard about from others, were caught up in a bureaucracy. Once they made a decision to stay in the bureaucracy, for example in Auschwitz as a Nazi doctor, a decision they didn't have to make for they could have left (though that would have meant going to the front), they developed adaptive mechanisms for staying. But they had a lot of conflicts. In other words, the bureaucratization's main purpose, as you said, is to protect the

---

* The United States Holocaust Memorial Museum finally opened in 1993.

German people from the pain, we might even say the realization, that they were killers, that they were killing, and doing it on a large scale. It didn't work fully, so they indeed had conflicts. But mostly they could get over them supported by their peers and by ideology, get over the conflicts and get the work done, the killing. I say that and I want your comments on the larger question of the relationship between the kind of impersonal bureaucracy, on one hand, and the actual actors who felt and had conflicts, on the other.

Hilberg: A lot of people in the bureaucracy had advanced education and a lot of them were very sophisticated. I don't want to suggest thereby that sophistication is limited to people with university degrees. That would be a very bad mistake. In my later research I looked at guards at the death camp Sobibor. I found that the fundamental process and the fundamental truth of the killing was not hidden from them. They knew it and saw through all the ruses. They never lost sight of it. For example, there was a guard along with his brother at Sobibor. All the guards in this camp had come up from euthanasia stations where they were killing mentally defective people, as defined by the psychiatrists there at the time. Sobibor is one of the places of Jewish uprising organized by a man who happened to have been a Soviet officer. The conspirators waited until the guard personnel was at a minimum. At the time of the revolt there were only seventeen guards there. The leader, who was the Red Army lieutenant, knew, however, how hopelessly outgunned they were. Still, they made this desperate break in which most of the escapees were killed. But they in turn killed eleven Germans. They killed one of the two brothers and they put an axe through the skull of the other. The wounded man later became a defendant and testified in a trial in the 1960s. He wanted truthfulness after going around with a headache all his life. In a peculiar way, he must have been close to the victims because he also was a victim, albeit with a difference. He said something like this: "As it happens, I came to Sobibor without any realization of what it really was. I assure you I never pushed people into a gas chamber because that was not my job. I had a different task (whatever it was, collecting clothes or something like that). But at the same time I will say that I was a link in the chain, that I was needed just as much as the guy who pushed them into the gas chamber, that I was just as indispensable in this killing operation, and that therefore we are all murderers." Now this was said by a man without any education. The best lawyer could not improve upon what he succinctly states. Obviously, we see in all of the remarks by perpetrators after the war (and sometimes during the war) the complete realization of what they were doing. The rationalizations were very elaborate. They all had one objective and that was simply to maintain one's stability. I myself can't imagine it because I can't know what it is like to be shooting all day long at defenseless people. I don't know what this is like.

Lifton: On that score, let me mention a psychiatrist I interviewed who was a German neuropsychiatrist of the Wehrmacht. He had SS *Einsatzgruppen* patients who were shooting all day at defenseless people. We talked some about just this point. I was, of course, curious about what happened to them. He thought as high as 20 percent of those who did the actual shooting had breakdowns that were like combat neuroses. It is very hard to gauge the sense of guilt. It wasn't necessarily predominant in them, but there was a sense of an onerous job that was difficult to do and some suggestion of guilt, perhaps in their images or their dreams, that the psychiatrist could detect. To me, of course, it is just as interesting that he cured them and returned them to duty.

Norman Birnbaum: Like Bob, and I think like everybody else, I am immensely grateful for this marvelous and very personal statement that makes the whole process of dealing with this subject come alive in a way a footnoted piece sometimes does not. I am struck by the interesting phenomenon of the conflict of generations you mentioned. It is interesting how a segment, at least, of the younger generation, that generation we associate with the dreams, the peace movement, the engaged Protestants, sometimes engaged younger Catholics, refer to the Holocaust, albeit somewhat stereotypically, as an example of the kind of thing that can happen if the citizenry doesn't activate itself. I also wonder, in terms of the US Jewish community, whether one of the underlying reasons for the drop in memory you discussed is in part because the memory is too painful. Thus we see the rise of so-called neo-conservatism among Jewish intellectuals. I am reminded of a Jesuit colleague of mine at Georgetown who asked me the other day: "I can't see why you didn't become a neo-conservative." I said, "Why?" He said: "You were a Jewish Trotskyite." This phenomenon, in fact, is a result of the end of the belief in progress in the Jewish community, the Jewish community's implicit renunciation of the messianic idea, in favor of a curious vicarious identification with Israel and with a form of self-congratulation about the American experience which exceeds even the illusions of the German Jews.

Hilberg: I am a distant observer of the German scene, because I don't stay there longer than my business requires. I look at East Germany and West Germany and all the indices in terms of GNP per capita, physical quality of life, birth rates, death rates. If you cross from West Berlin to East Berlin and forget for a minute the slogans, you'll see the same society, you'll see the same people. I suppose the same must be true in Korea and in other divided nations. But the generational conflict is something else. It is very subtle and all I notice are the personal examples that come to my attention. I think that the younger generation in Germany is protesting that the older one left it with such a legacy. What had they done to deserve that? I was astonished at something in 1976 in Stuttgart. It must have been a fad because I didn't see it ten years later. Nevertheless, as a trivial fad it interested me. I saw women wearing the Star of David. These weren't Jewish women. What is this demonstration all about? And it was—a demonstration. It was just as much a demonstration as if you picketed some nuclear facility. I also see examples in private conversations. Once in San José I had two people come up to me separately after a talk I gave. One was a very nice young lady about thirty. She was a teacher of English in a Catholic institution in Santa Clara county. Elegantly dressed. Her name was Seidl. She said: "I want to ask you about a man who was the last commander of the Theresienstadt ghetto, whose name was Seidl, S-E-I-D-L. What happened?" "I heard he was condemned to death." "But where is his body? We just want to bury him." At that same conference a young man came up to me and said, "May I see you in private?" There was quite a crowd, so I said "Come up to the hotel room." It turned out he taught in a Catholic college on the East Coast, and he had a noticeable German accent. "What are you teaching?" He said, "I'm teaching Hebrew." I said, "That's a bit strange, but what do you want to tell me?" He came from Recklinghausen in the Rheinland and he was a loner. As a boy he would take his bicycle out and when other kids went on their outings, he went to Bergen-Belsen. He discovered that he was interested in these victims and he wanted to learn Hebrew but there wasn't any place in Germany where he could learn it. So he went to Vienna, where he could. He migrated to the United States, becoming, as it were, an expert in Jewish history and in the Hebrew language, teaching it in a Catholic college. "What else? Are you going back? Do you visit your family at all?" He said: "Once I went back. But I went back with a tape recorder and I placed the tape recorder in front of my father. I said 'I want to ask you some questions and I want you to talk into the recorder. What did *you* do when the Jews were deported from our town?'" The father was momentarily numbed. The father was a psychiatrist, of all things an Adlerian, who during the war was engaged in general practice. Because the town was so small there were no Jewish doctors, and he had also Jewish patients. They disappeared all at once, or course. His father was a bystander par excellence. He saw the people had disappeared in much the way the president of Germany pointed out in his recent speech when he said: "We all knew that they disappeared but we did not ask." And so the son shoved the tape recorder in front of the father with the question: "Did you ask?" They both knew the answer and the son has never since returned to Germany to see his father. This is an extreme incident, but take all the gradations of less extremity with people living in the same town and I think you get the drift.

Lifton: I interviewed the daughter of the chief doctor at Auschwitz [i.e., Eduard Wirth]. I found her very sympathetic. She was a forty-year-old woman with children, a housewife, and without going through all the details, she discovered at a certain point something that her mother had tried to keep from her, namely that her father didn't just die in the war, but that he had been the chief doctor at Auschwitz and had killed himself at the end of the war. He had bounced her on his knee, he was a loving father, he was known as a very decent man in his intimate relationships, even the prisoners liked him. But he also set up the whole system at Auschwitz and had lots of conflicts of the kind that we described. Her struggle was, in effect, what to do with that love that she felt for him and he felt for her, when she learned that he was one of the murderers. The question she asked of me was, "Can a good man do evil things?" I said, "Yes, but then he's no longer a good man."

Robert Holt (to Hilberg): Why did you think the man you just described wanted to talk to you?

Hilberg: I think that all these people walk around with a tremendous burden and they come to me as the footnote writer. I have credentials of sorts. I understand, but at the same time I'll be gone. I'll be in San José one day and then I'm off. I'm not the psychiatrist they'll come to see every week.

John Mack: I had some sense in Hamburg talking to young German analysts that they are playing an important role in the inquiry about what happened, not just with their parents but with their patients and with their own analysts, some of whom they feel incompletely able to ask certain questions. They know their analysts can't handle certain things because they have too much feeling about it. This research that the young analysts are doing is uncovering the history of psychoanalysis in Germany during the war. Some of the psychiatrists you mentioned in relation to euthanasia were psychoanalysts. There seems to be a self-assigned place for the generation of psychoanalysts that would be the grandchildren, who are doing more than their share of investigating, inquiring, looking into, asking their senior analysts, some of whom were collaborators, asking elders in the society what happened, uncovering documents. It might be interesting to support that in some way and learn more about what they're taking on.

Lifton: Just to continue that, from my own work dealing with what some psychiatrists and analysts did in the Göring Institute,* and to encourage the young analysts to look into their grandfathers or fathers or their own analysts' role. Geoffrey Cocks wrote this book in which he said, in effect, "Wasn't it wonderful that psychoanalysis was maintained under this duress."** Freud had some of that feeling too, but he changed his mind. Jones had to cover it over. So you have two competing value ideas. One is, you maintain psychoanalysis under duress and the other, the deeper truth, is *Gleichschaltung* or coordination, which was ultimately collaboration, because the Institute served the government. Thus relatively decent individual analysts helped individual people. Göring himself had a nice side and would allow the analysts to do Freudian work, even though they didn't call it that. He was also nice to some people. He gave some warnings. Nonetheless, the overall outcome was that the Institute did all kinds of intelligence work. They worked for the military and served the regime.

Margaret Brenman-Gibson: This was a chilling and brilliant presentation and it all goes back, Raul, to your term paper for the course with Rosenberg. I would like to earnestly suggest that you reconsider what Dan Ellsberg calls "the bureaucratization of massacre" by asking yourself why was that impossible for you to pursue, as it was impossible for the German analysts to pursue? Is it because they lacked, as you did, the conceptual tools to do it with? What is missing is a dynamic psychosocial theory, both of history and of human development. Actually, as Erik has offered an elegant one, not yet fully

---

* I.e., Deutsches Institut für psychologische Forschung und Psychotherapie in Berlin, 1936–1945, named after Matthias Heinrich Göring, a cousin of Hermann Göring.

** Geoffrey Cocks, *Psychotherapy in the Third Reich: The Goering Institute* (Oxford: Oxford UP, 1985).

grasped, it seems to me, by psychohistorians. Are we going forever to talk about "individual" versus "group" responsibility? If we are going to ask, for example—as you do—"what is the role of the civil servant in the destruction of the Jews?," a splendid research inquiry, then we must not be stuck with ancient psychoanalytic theory. If we are to ask genuine psychohistorical questions, we must ask such things as "What are shared defenses? How is a group-identity formed? What is the nature of group-identification? What threatens that group-identification? What keeps a person in *any* group?" It doesn't matter what the group is. It can be the American Psychoanalytic Association or the Rand Corporation; it can be the Wellfleet Conference or a group collecting clothes or gold teeth in the Dachau camp. It doesn't make a bit of difference. I would say that the thing Bob brought out in his book *The Broken Connection* is the profound threat of losing that connection. To "break" with the group to which one belongs means that a significant piece of your identity, part of which keeps you feeling alive, feeling that you are a human being with a self-identity, has been lost. That is not to be understood as "individual versus social"; it is all one and the same thing occurring at one and the same moment. The most sophisticated conceptual equipment is crucially needed to study such an important question as "the role of the civil servant in the extermination of the European Jews" or, for that matter, the "bureaucratization of massacre." Dan Ellsberg asked us at one of these meetings what kept everybody else at the Rand Corporation, besides him, from speaking out about a war they knew to be evil? You may recall he added wryly, "Everybody can be as dumb as he needs to be to keep his job." I understood him to mean not simply the practical matter of keeping a job but of maintaining a sense of personal wholeness, a sense of self-identity. He described such a broken connection as like an astronaut leaving a spaceship in orbit and having what they call the "umbilical cord" break. Suddenly you're all alone in the universe. A bleak image indeed.

Hilberg: Well you see, I did ask the question many times. But the way you put it, why the person remains on the job doing what he's doing, obviously the question has been asked the wrong way many times because the Germans themselves have deliberately asked it the wrong way. They say: "Well, you know what the consequences would have been if I had refused orders. I would have been shot." But that's not it. The real answer, as we know, is that he wouldn't get promoted or he might have been transferred.

Brenman-Gibson: But that's all practical. We're talking about something psychological and at the heart of the human necessity to hold on "for dear life" to a "connected" sense of oneself.

Hilberg: That is psychological because you're losing your "identification." This was an avenue that was open. I've talked with Bob Lifton about the strange case of Dr. [Wilhelm] Hagen who was a public health physician and chief physician of the city of Warsaw in 1941 and 1942. His name came up in a document I found when, somewhat surprisingly, he as a physician characterized an attempt to slice off a portion of the Warsaw ghetto as *Wahnsinn*, as insanity, and said "we can't do that." All the other physicians in this area were in favor of ghettoization as a public health measure. I next came across Hagen in some documents relating to a conference for social workers who were being promoted into population experts; in other words, not just doctors changed roles to become killers but the social welfare people as well. There was talk about how to push out the Polish population in order, presumably, to make a reserve for Germans. And while they were at it, they were going to thin it out by eliminating some of them. In other words, they were going to do with the Poles what had been done to the Jews. Hagen then sent a letter to Adolf Hitler protesting against these plans. Needless to say, Hitler didn't get to see it because it was intercepted long before it got there. Whereupon there was a big to-do, the person Hagen had quoted denied ever saying such things and wanted to know what was the matter with this guy? Himmler said: "We've got to send him to a concentration camp." Finally Leonardo Conti, the chief doctor, entered into the controversy and said: "Well, there are some things you have to understand." Hagen's father was a Social Democrat. He just never got over his early education, but he was a doctor. Take him out of Poland and put him back into Germany, where he can be a normal doctor doing his job. That's exactly what happened. He lost his position in Warsaw. He wasn't shot. He just lost his position.

Lifton: There's an addition to that. I happen to know about this case, this Hagen. And in addition to everything that Raul just said, when he was honored later publicly for resisting the cutting down of the ghetto and the killing of tubercular patients and Poles, some voices spoke up in Germany attacking the honor, and revealing another dimension to his case that apparently was also true. He had issued an edict while in charge of health in the ghetto that said that any Jew caught outside the ghetto was to be immediately shot. Other people who knew something about the case and understood the problem spoke to me and said it's a very complicated idea as to why he did this. He might have done it because he wanted to resist the killing of Poles, knowing there was no hope for the Jews. In any case, they were shooting Jews who left the ghetto. It wasn't that he was instituting anything; it was rather that he was formalizing it. Or maybe he was a mean administrator who wanted the Jews to be killed—maybe he was anti-Semitic and not anti-Polish. I don't know exactly. But the point that Raul is making is that he was able to resist to a considerable extent a certain amount of further killing of Poles within the bureaucracy and wasn't, of course, at all punished for it. Again and again I heard situations of not so much direct resistance but avoidance, and sometimes something approaching resistance and never being punished. The only thing they punished you for was a direct assault morally, to say "This is wrong, you're evil," which nobody did.

Brenman-Gibson: Bob, are you saying that there are levels of risk, meaning that there are levels of resistance? Everything you've been saying applies to the nuclear arms race.

Lifton: There are levels of refusal and there are levels of resistance. I would like to ask Gene [Weiner] to respond. I'd like to hear from him.

Gene Weiner: First of all, in being asked to be a respondent to a talk of this quality and depth, fundamentally I think those of you who would find yourselves in my situation would probably just want to say "Bravo!" and leave it at that. I'm very tempted to do that, but you're pushing me on a bit and I think I'd like to respond to that. My comments are idiosyncratic and related to specific issues. First, in regard to that man who came up to you after the talk, Israel's leading writer Amos Oz has a wonderful description of how a kibbutznik passed in front of his window combing his hair because he was afraid of how he was going to appear in Oz's novels. Perhaps the people who come up to you after your talk are concerned about how they're going to appear in your footnotes. I may be belaboring the obvious here, but it is a kind of sociological cliché to say that memory is a social product. In other words, it requires an investment of energy, it doesn't just happen. One of the things that interested me when I first came to Israel was the enormous effort and energy that went into the commemoration of fallen Israeli soldiers. I was absolutely astounded at the money and the energy and the institutionalization that was expended by parents of fallen soldiers to make sure that the memory of their sons remained fresh. In fact, one of the things that really astounded me was the enormous input that went into *Memorbuchen* in terms of commemorating fallen soldiers, a virtual library devoted to dead young people. And of course this has a tradition in Jewish history.

I was witness one time to the hauling of a gigantic stone from Mt. Sinai to the city of Yamit, where it was set up as a monument for a number of pilots who went down in a helicopter. The sociological cliché that social memory requires a tremendous input of energy, I think is underlined in your book. Another thing that is particularly relevant to this context: it requires an enormous identification with individuals who have a great personal stake in making sure that memory is kept. Permit me a personal observation with deep psychological implications. The process of personal identification that you went through, Raul, in terms of seeing yourself linked up to this project, means to me that such a project as the one you have achieved requires the input and energy not only of an institution; it requires primarily an enormous process of identification of somebody somewhere who is willing to take up that project. I think what is so daunting and so overwhelming in this presentation is the fact that it was done at periods when it was, to put it mildly, less than popular and in situations where the resistance that you met on professional grounds (and from what comes through your talk on deeply personal grounds) would have overwhelmed another person who might not have persevered. I think what is so palpable about your talk is, in addition to your erudition and the obvious control of the literature, that strong sense of personal identification and the willingness to risk it. I thank you for exposing us to the richness of this presentation.

Lifton: I'd like to bring the subject back to the question of the Jews' failure to resist. In the same way the Jews set up stages of response to other aspects of the Holocaust, I wonder if there have been stages in response to this subject of non-resistance and where it is right now. I am dealing with that with my work on Korczak. Once someone came up to me at a dinner party as we were putting salad on our plates and said, "That man you're writing about just led children to their deaths."

Hilberg: I think the issue of Jewish non-resistance is dying because something is happening now. In Israel, the people who are in charge of the research apparatus and whose main business is the Holocaust belong to a different generation from those who preceded them. I am struck by the fact that somehow an awful lot of people concerned with writing about and dealing in some aspect or another with Holocaust matters were born in the single year 1926. This is a generation that just saw the war, some more than others, but for all of them, it is a central fixed point in their lives. But they're sober because they were not leaders and so they didn't have to defend anybody, they didn't have to defend the Jewish leadership, they didn't have to defend the councils, they didn't have to defend anybody. Just the opposite. Israel Gutman was a fighter in the Warsaw ghetto and Yitzhak Arad fought as a partisan. Even Rachel Auerbach, who was Ringelblum's secretary, told me once that she's against all this *Gleichschaltung*. She said: "The people who really resisted are not like everybody else." There were a handful of people who "really resisted," meaning shot a rifle or carried a message or did something very tangible. These people think it is absurd to approach victims as though every victim is like every other victim, all martyrs and heroes, everybody resisting by simply living, eating, discussing things, operating schools, healing the sick. They don't buy it. They simply don't buy this reasoning. Yitzhak Arad came up to me one day in Jerusalem back in 1979 and asked me to go for a walk with him. He said he wanted to test out a theory on me. He was writing a book about the death camps, Sobibor, Treblinka, Belzec, and there he deals with uprisings. You can't write a book about anything in Israel without leading to the uprisings. That's the climax, so that if you write a book about the Warsaw ghetto the climax is the revolt, if you write a book about Treblinka the climax is the revolt, if you write about Sobibor the climax is the revolt. But there's a twist. The inmates in the death camps waited and waited and then they discovered in 1943, particularly in Treblinka, the transports were thinning out, they weren't coming anymore because everybody had already been gassed. And then that handful of people, these thousand people that were kept as an inmate force, went hungry because the only way they fed themselves was from the supplies brought in by the deportees about to be gassed. They feared that if additional trains, which they serviced, were not going to arrive, their turn would come. And then they revolted. Now Arad said, "What is your opinion? Does this comport with what you have concluded?" And I said to myself: "Now that is really very interesting. Not only is this man saying mouthfuls, volumefuls about non-resistance, but now he is explaining what the resistance was all about when it took place!" Who is this man? He is the director of Yad Vashem. What else was he? He was a partisan. He joined the partisans at age sixteen, he fought in the war of 1948. He is a typical general. He takes you on a tour and says, "See that bridge? I lost five men taking this bridge in 1948." He's been through all the wars. So he doesn't buy the old arguments. How can you talk to a general in terms of resistance when you leave out what he understands resistance to be? That's why I think the argument has died.

Lifton: You're saying that this generation has accepted implicitly the idea that there really was no more than limited resistance.

Hilberg: I'll give you another example with Israel Gutman who was a fighter in the Warsaw ghetto. If you look at the old books about the Warsaw Ghetto fighting, the old ones, you'll often see a statistic that the Jews killed a thousand Germans in the ghetto, maybe more. Statistics are a subject in and of themselves. We know who fought in the Warsaw Ghetto battle. We know what kind of equipment was available. I know how much ammunition can be shot away before one hits a dog, let alone a man. When I look at the Stroop Report of the Warsaw Ghetto battle, I see he begins the report with a casualty list, with the names of his dead and wounded men. He doesn't hide his losses—quite the opposite—he emphasizes them. Sixteen people killed, he says, eighty-five wounded; that's a lot. See what we had to endure with these Jews! Now you look at Gutman's book. Does he mention three thousand people killed? Not at all. One thousand? Not at all. No figure. But he does say how few the defenders were. And why? He himself fought there. If everybody is supposed to have been fighting, where does that leave him? He really fought. It's as simple as that. Moreover, this man had a son who was killed in the Israeli army, and the book is dedicated to his memory.

Holt: There seems to be here a kind of attempt to indict the Jews for not having resisted, which carries with it the implication that others would have. It would have been possible for there to have been more resistance, so why wasn't there more resistance? Is there something in Jewish character, is there something in Jewish tradition, is there something in the situation—there are many possibilities. All of these really need to be investigated before any kind of moral condemnation is issued. I find it very annoying that there is this constant throwing out of this accusation as if it stands on its own feet and no one needs to justify the charge.

Hilberg: Well, this form of accusation I think surfaced in Israel during the Eichmann trial on the part of younger people who were asking those questions in an accusatory form because they could not understand any situation other than that with which they grew up. They are accustomed to shooting first, and then to discover the facts. But there is a lesson there, you see, that by not resisting one makes a mistake. Even if you resist by killing the wrong person, that is not as bad as not offering resistance against the right enemy. That is a lesson ingrained. Since you raise the question, I suspect something that is extremely sensitive and that underlies everything we talk about, whether we discuss nuclear war or the Holocaust. I see in World War II the collapse of chivalry. I see the totally defenseless person who can't cope with anything anymore and above all cannot protect his wife and his children. So long as warfare was conducted in trenches, where my father fought, it was still the business of soldiers. If a civilian was incidentally killed, too bad, it happens. In World War II, it all changed. The new idea was put forward in the 1920s by the Italian general, [Guilio] Douhet, in his book *Command of the Air*. To win the next war, he said, one must destroy the weakest link of the enemy: his women and children. One does it by bombing them from the air. Wars are not won by taking territory, but by destroying the enemy's morale. Douhet was an original thinker. Now take the Holocaust. In the ghettoes the Germans wanted to kill the Jews, all of them, but they had to make compromises for the sake of the war effort. That means that they killed the children and the old people and left the productive ones. The ghetto leadership also played this game called "productivization." More and more people worked and more and more people paid for the right to live by working. You have to remember that as soon as the ghetto was created, it had an adverse trade balance with the outside world, and it had to have an even balance, or else it became an object of charity, and the Germans were not going to charitably maintain a ghetto. So the children are shipped out. Do you draw the line at age eleven or age twelve? This progression results in something very peculiar. You've got fathers, young fathers, still working, whose wives have been killed, whose children have been killed, whose parents have been killed. The unspoken question is, and no one may ask it, because to ask it is staggering, "Why did you live in that case?" There's a film by Claude Lanzmann: *Shoah*. It is nine and a half hours long. In it there's a barber from Treblinka. He was cutting hair off the women, and he's asked brutal questions. "You saw your own family, your village, you saw your people, you saw, and you went and you worked and you continued in your cutting." As it happened, he's one of the handful that survived. We're talking about a death toll at Treblinka of three-quarters of a million and of a few dozen survivors. And what does he do in Israel? The same thing that he did in Treblinka—he cuts hair. He's a barber. But now we have to face the question as to whether we've lost something permanently. Right now, every woman and every child is on her own. I wonder whether this is sensed by the people at large and especially whether the woman's movement senses it without perhaps realizing it.

Lifton: But maybe you shouldn't put it so starkly. That man, and I interviewed many inmate physicians to whom that happened, whose wife and children and parents were immediately killed on arrival, relates to the question "Why would you survive?" as the psychological question he asks himself. And in the act of asking that question he lives a life of some degree of survivor guilt. It just exists. I don't think we have the right to ask that question with any kind of moral judgment. To be able to survive, after that has happened, is not a sign that the world has lost its moral bearings. The loss is, of course, in placing that person in that position. The struggle to survive has some sort of energy of its own. Their defensive maneuvers involve numbing and adaptation, and of course, they involve a loss. They also involve a gain in the statement of some kind of affirmation in the act of surviving. When I first came into the work of Holocaust peripherally—it was for my Hiroshima work—I met with people who had studied the Holocaust and some survivors. There were one or two analysts who were themselves survivors, and what they had learned and what they said to me was, "It's as though we always feel the accusation, why did you survive?"

Chuck Strozier: Would you comment on the desire to bear witness and how that operates in the psychology of adaptation among a people like that?

Lifton: It's a way of accepting one's own right to live in the face of all those unacceptable dreadful losses. If one bears witness, there's a reparation, one gives meaning to the experience and one serves those people and one serves the future. What has gotten confused here, and Bob Holt raised the question very well, is the terrible truth that there wasn't a great deal of Jewish resistance. But I doubt any group of any ethnic, racial, intellectual, historical background in that position would have acted much differently. If the assault is sufficiently overwhelming, it's difficult to imagine mobilizing a defense.

Strozier: There's an interesting and I think hopeful piece of psychoanalytic history that is relevant to this. It goes back to Bettelheim who actually wrote his first statement on the response of victims in 1943, which was around the same time he created the Orthogenic School in Chicago. Bettelheim said everything in 1943 that he later rewrote in ten books. It's always seemed to me that the Orthogenic

School tried to create a total environment for children, that it turned identification with the aggressor upside down and created a total environment for healing children.

John Mack: I'm struck that we're repeating something that Raul described as the central point of his work, which is to focus on the psychology of the victims and their resistance and not look at how it can be that an entire society can wholeheartedly be complicit in its act of genocide.

Steven Kull: I think that we feel comfortable looking at the perpetrators as the problem. It is easy to explain because the Nazis were conceivably getting something out of it. I think it's harder for us to look at the fact that the Jews in some way cooperated. The image of people cooperating with their executioners is very troubling. That seems to me to be the recurring theme that people resisted about your work. I've been thinking about why it is so crucial. The Jews in that situation were following conventional values, the kind of values that we all follow in a day to day way. Perhaps we can't help thinking, "maybe that's what I would do if I were in the situation like that." That's rather unsettling. We can at least take the perpetrators and say, "Well, they were following more primitive values than the kind of values that I follow on a day to day basis." So there's an effort to repress that image of cooperating with the executioners or to the extent that it comes up, we try to distance ourselves from it by saying, "There's something unique about the Jewish people. That couldn't happen to me, that couldn't happen here." In some way, we might also have the hunch that this image of cooperating in our own execution might apply to our current preparation for nuclear war. We are now following the same kind of values that the Jews followed in their situation. This too suggests why there might be so much collective resistance.

Lifton: This relates to the central point of the presentation, namely that of the ostensible victim of bureaucratic domination gets caught up in the bureaucratic structure. The heads of the *Judenrat* and even the inmate physicians, whom I interviewed and to whom I was enormously sympathetic and with whom I identified—their problem was that to save some people in Auschwitz, they had to make sure that the Nazi doctors, when they did the selections on the medical blocks, at least selected the worst ones who would have died anyhow. So you're into the process of selecting and if they didn't do that, which they didn't want to in many cases, then the ones who had a chance to survive would be chosen by the careless Nazi doctor making the choice in very broad sweeping ways. That is parallel to the problem of the *Judenrat* in many ways. In that sense, one could say that, to a degree, although inmate physicians did save lives, at times they contributed to rendering the killing process more efficient. It's a deeply tragic dimension.

Gene Weiner: Just a follow-up in terms of Israeli society because here we are witnessing reactions to the thesis. I would agree there is a kind of implicit acceptance in Israel of your fundamental thesis, which has been around now for all these years. If you say World War II represents the end of chivalrous behavior in warfare, the Israeli experience would seem to me to add a footnote to that. There you see a kind of eternal return of the need for heroism. In the beginning the response to your argument was a kind of resistance that said "No, you're wrong," and flung in your face the mythology of heroism, which factually was on very shaky grounds. But in Israeli society, at the present time, there is a kind of resurrection of heroism. Whatever you call it in terms of the psychodynamics, the social reality is that large groups of people are incapable of living without the sense of impotence. They have to create for themselves first the mythology even though the mythology is not factually correct, but then they act out in terms of their behavior the very opposite of that. I think this is a key to understanding the Israeli temperament. As an American in Israel, one feels that the Israeli, social-psychologically speaking, defines his own personal identity "in opposition to." There is a tremendous need for exercising and demonstrating oppositional potency.

It's very clear that some politicians are using this to make political capital. It's impossible to understand [Menachem] Begin except in these terms. It's impossible to understand the way in which every visiting person in Israel is taken to Yad Vashem. It's impossible to understand the morale-building in the Israeli army without this. The reason why this exposure to the Holocaust as an issue empowers is because of the negative contrast, here in Israel you have the opportunity not to be bureaucratized and made impotent by a process that you have no hand in. There's a kind of splitting here that's interesting. We have the best of both worlds in Israel. On the one hand, we have the imagery and factual reality of a kind of impotence that comes from an understanding of that bureaucratized process. On the other hand, we've built up, in almost direct contradiction to that, a kind of sense of empowerment, so that we have a choice at all times. We can either see ourselves impotent and therefore deserving of a kind of identification and support and protection by the world out there, but then we also have the benefit of having a very strong powerful image of ourselves. Depending on the circumstances, we have the best of both possible worlds. When the payoff is big enough, we can claim impotence and be believable in our own eyes to a certain extent. On the other hand, when we really want to feel a sense of ourselves, we can just point to the fact that we're very strong. Bringing that issue to the surface in public ways is now going on for the first time in Jewish history. We have a major destructive event, and a person such as yourself is not filtering it through an aesthetic configuration that gives the group some explanation of itself. You are presenting the facts in such a way that it is hard for mythological processes to be worked that are apart from those facts. Your facts will be the raw material, the aesthetic imagination, that reworks facts into meanings that can be lived with and will have to be dealt with for generations to come.

Lifton: But fact doesn't interfere with the aesthetic imagination. I think fact can evoke. But, Gene, the problem is how can the historian describe the Holocaust for aesthetic recreation? The problem is the event itself. Raul and others, late twentieth-century men and women, may try to get some perception of the event in terms of its actualities and some of the larger overviews. But still the event itself defies the aesthetic recreation.

Birnbaum: Bob, I'm not so sure about that because it seems to me that if you look at the greatest of aesthetic recreations, the poetic dimensions of scripture, or the great novels, they create their own order of facts, which contain truths of some kind. Here I'm reminded of the question asked by Adorno: "Is poetry possible after Auschwitz?" Think of the angry reaction of the partisans of preparation for nuclear warfare, their limitless hatred and withering scorn, for the Physicians for Social Responsibility. A book was just published the other day by two Pentagon correspondents. It is an ordinary critique of waste and inefficiency in the Pentagon; such books are a dime a dozen these days. The authors have the affrontery to put in this book: "We're not peace freaks." This is a way of legitimizing their criticism. This panic, this hatred for those who point out that there is a system where we're all not simply potential victims but bystanders and accomplices seems to suggest that the breaking of solidarity, the threat to identity outweighs the fear of victimization. Think of the cowardice of the so-called Defense Democrats in the Democratic Party, the sell-outs. The decline of chivalry you talked about, Raul, is really the destruction of civilization.

It seems to me that the reason for the revulsion for studying the Holocaust is that it makes that all too clear.

Kull: One of the most common rationales that I encountered in my interviews is "If it wouldn't have worked against Hitler, then it's the wrong thing to do." In many ways we haven't answered the question "What could the Jews have done?" Basically, the only answer given is to use force—that they could have had some kind of organized armed rebellion. I think there is a consensus that Gandhi's methods wouldn't have worked. That yes, Gandhi was effective in a very specific situation, but for the Jews in Europe, it's not a satisfactory answer.

Erik Erikson: I want to ask about the historical connection between all of this and the existence of fanatics. The Germans, somehow, were against themselves—and the Jews. The defeat of the Germans in World War I had been devastating. It also mattered that Germany was in the middle of all Europe.

Lifton: When I talk tomorrow about genocide I will try to connect one actual and one potential genocidal event. The issue you mention, Erik, seems to be essential in the sense of total powerlessness of the Germans following World War I and the desperation for corrective assertion of vitality and immortality in whatever way feasible. Yes, that was the Germans, that has been the Jews, but it's anyone. It's a universal potential that different groups may embrace or feel victimized by.

List of Participants

Norman Birnbaum (1926–2019) was a sociologist and professor emeritus at the Georgetown University Law Center, and a member of the editorial board at *The Nation*.

Margaret Brenman-Gibson (1940–2004) was a psychologist in the Department of Psychiatry at Cambridge Hospital at Harvard. She was one of the first women to be appointed as a full professor—Clinical Professor of Psychology in 1982.

Erik H. Erikson (1902–1994) was an Austrian-born developmental psychologist and psychoanalyst, and served as a professor at several prominent institutions, including Harvard, University of California, Berkeley, and Yale.

Robert Holt (b. 1917) is a psychologist who worked in the field of psychoanalytic theory.

Steven Kull is a psychologist and author, and fellow at the Center for International Security and Arms Control at Stanford University.

Betty Jean Lifton (1926–2010) was a writer, psychotherapist, and leading advocate for adoption reform.

Robert Jay (Bob) Lifton (b. 1926) is a psychiatrist and author, chiefly known for his studies of the psychological causes and effects of wars and political violence, and for his theory of thought reform. He was an early proponent of the techniques of psychohistory.

John E. Mack (1929–2004) was a psychiatrist, writer, and the head of the Department of Psychiatry at Harvard Medical School.

Charles B. (Chuck) Strozier (b. 1944) is a practicing psychoanalyst in New York City. He is a professor of history at John Jay College of Criminal Justice and the Graduate Center, City University of New York.

Eugene (Gene) Weiner (1933–2003) was a rabbi and professor of sociology at the University of Haifa.

13

THE DEVELOPMENT OF HOLOCAUST RESEARCH
A PERSONAL OVERVIEW
(2007)

Holocaust research has a history of more than six decades and it can be analyzed from different perspectives. In this overview, I will divide this history into three sections: (1) the early period of research and writing, (2) the period of organized research, and (3) the period in which complexity is acknowledged.

The Early Period of Research and Writing

This period began, in fact, before World War II, when some treatises and articles were already being written, and can be extended to some years after the war. Indeed, some aspects of it are still with us. In that early period—when what we now call "the Holocaust" was not yet at the stage of annihilation—the primary source material available to

---

This is a slightly revised version of the remarks Hilberg presented in the closing session of the 15th International Scholars Conference held by the Yad Vashem International Institute of Holocaust Research in November 2004. That conference was the basis for the collection in which this essay was first published: *Holocaust Historiography in Context: Emergence, Challenges, Polemics, and Achievements*, ed. David Bankier and Dan Michman (Jerusalem: Yad Vashem / New York: Berghahn Books, 2008), 25–36.

anyone interested in what Germany was doing consisted of newspapers, printed laws, commentaries on these laws, and various articles in so-called official journals explaining what a law meant. On the whole, that was all that was available. Needless to say, there were personal reports as well, but one did not think of them as testimony or memoirs.

It was only after the war was over, and still in this early period, that documents began to appear. These were the secret correspondence of German agencies, of Germany's allies, of the satellite states and even of those agencies operating in countries under German occupation that were not German themselves. These documents were found piled up in various archives, sometimes quite unorganized. They were not accessible; they were not available. But in the very early period right after World War II something happened that I can only describe as a miracle, spearheaded by the United States, which wanted to conduct a trial of the major war criminals on the basis of documentary evidence. Assembled for the prosecution were some thirty-six thousand items! That is a pretty heavy load. And it included testimonies. Those were actual documents of the Germans. Some of them, perhaps six thousand, were used in the first trial and the remainder made its appearance at the Subsequent Trials also conducted at Nuremberg.

When the first researchers approached the topic, they started with the documents used in the trials, which were supplemented by the earlier laws that had already been studied; they also made an occasional dip into original documents that were collected by certain institutions. I personally went to YIVO (Institute for Jewish Research) in New York in 1949 and saw an interesting collection of original German documents. They are still there. That was our basic material; it constituted the basis of our research and our knowledge. Yes, some items that we call "testimony," literally testimony in court, were beginning to appear. There were already a few books that were memoirs. But what was the result of this research, of this writing?

Primarily, I believe that it was regarded holistically; there was as yet no word for what had happened. If I went to YIVO, they said this was a *"hurbn"* (the Yiddish/Hebrew word for destruction).* If I looked elsewhere for some word, it was sometimes called the "Disaster" in English. The vocabulary with which to describe what had happened had not yet been developed. One thing that the contents of these collections did reveal was that the entire process had not yet

---

* Also known as *churban*, *churbn*, or *khurbn*.

been grasped, but that the entire process was the result of what the Germans did step by step and not what the victims perceived or suffered. This is what we find when we read the book by Franz Neumann, *Behemoth*,[1] or *The Dual State*[2] by his law partner Ernst Fraenkel (a very fine book, actually written before the war began, analyzing the legal structure of Germany). We also find it in the work of Léon Poliakov, a driving force who collected documents in Paris and who—in some sense—became the founder of this academic discipline that we now call "the Holocaust" when he published the first comprehensive study *Bréviaire de la haine*.[3] If you open it, you will find that its basic sources are Nuremberg documents (though, of course, not all of them; there were too many to be absorbed). But he already had an idea of the whole business, and he even had a thesis, namely, that this was the product of hate. Clearly—whether it is Poliakov or indeed anyone else who utilizes this kind of material—we can characterize it as the "top-down approach."

Why so? The reason is that the Allies were looking for the top war criminals, so obviously they looked at the correspondence of these people, which would constitute the evidence for conviction. After they had taken care of Hermann Göring and other such individuals, they went one step down, looking for the second in command, namely, ministers or top generals. And then they turned to the business sector, and then to other sectors of society, obviously also the Nazi Party. In the subsequent trials, the Allies, meaning primarily the United States, were examining these tens of thousands of documents that had been collected from among piles in relatively unorganized German archives. Some were called EAP documents, meaning *Einsatz Aktionsplan*, some had other designations, like WI for *Wirtschaft*, others were named RKO after *Reichskommissariat Ostland*, and so forth. In the first trial, most documents were labeled PS, meaning "collected in Paris by Colonel Storey." But they were later reorganized, and in subsequent trials documents were labeled NG, meaning that this was something about the Nazi Government; NO—relating to Nazi Organizations; NI presumably meaning Nazi *I*ndustry; then OKW, which stands for *Oberkommando der Wehrmacht* (i.e., the army). Those four designations correspond exactly to Neumann's thesis about how Germany was organized into four hierarchies (*his* four hierarchies). One can see the continuity from Neumann to Nuremberg to the subsequent writing about anything having to do with Nazi Germany, including the Holocaust.

However, there were drawbacks. In looking for the perpetrators the Allies had somehow forgotten certain, rather major players—like the railroads,[4] the Order Police (the *Ordnungspolizei*, which Christopher Browning later described as "ordinary men"),[5] and the *Organisation Todt*, which was heavily involved in the utilization of Jewish labor from the Channel Islands all the way to the Bug River. All of this was overlooked at the trials, at least those that were held in the 1940s and 1950s. Also, the documents that were utilized were given accession numbers, for example, NG 1, NG2, NG3; even though 3 had nothing to do with 2, 4 had nothing to do with 3, and so on. In fact, to use them properly you had to read them all. And that is what they did.

The problem with this kind of source material is that it is extracted from a context, the context being: who is writing to whom, what was the preceding correspondence, what was the subsequent correspondence. And we had to attribute meaning to what we read without knowing the complete background. Who were these people? Most perpetrators were part-timers. Only Adolf Eichmann was full time, and only his corresponding experts in the Ministry of Interior or the Ministry of Finance, etc., concerned themselves almost entirely with Jews. Most others had Jewish matters on their desks amid all sorts of other things. So it was very difficult at that stage even to *identify* who was who. Yes, we had the name; we had the rank; we had the correspondence of what he did when, but we had no full view—no real portrait of any individual.

As far as the victims were concerned, they were a mass of indistinguishable people. In part that is attributable to the fact that the names disappeared gradually in the German correspondence. They were only to be found in the lowest regions of the bureaucracy, and they became numbers. That is how the victims show up: 1; 450; 20,000; 30,000 up and up into the millions. But even the Jews, when approaching this subject, have tended to make all the victims an indistinguishable group of people. Why? Because the victims had the same end: everyone is alike in death. I heard a man, who was for a while the director of the United States Holocaust Memorial Museum, refer to them as *Mekadshei HaShem* (martyrs). That tells you everything. Even today, we have trouble making distinctions between the dead and the survivors. We must remember: most are dead. Even David Boder[6] called his book *I Did Not Interview the Dead*.[7] One can therefore appreciate that we had an incomplete picture of what was happening and that the victims were not properly described at all. In fact, they were not really listened to, even though they spoke in courts or published memoirs. The exception was a single, best-selling diary—Anne Frank's diary. But that too tells you something: the story of a young girl, a teenager, in an attic that became the sole source of knowledge for tens of millions of people!

The Period of Organized Research

We come to the middle period when research became organized. Organized research takes place in archives. I need not tell this audience that the access to archives was very slow.

My view of what an archive looked like was made possible only because I got a job, which I held for a very short time between 1951 and 1952 in a project (Prof. Gerhard Weinberg was also involved in this project, but for somewhat longer). When I entered this building (which we called "the torpedo tube factory" because that was what it had been during the war)—where with American resourcefulness we had German documents standing up in so-called *Leitz-Ordner* (boxes)—we faced ten thousand meters of shelving, and we were let loose. We had to investigate, for instance, what the Germans knew about the Soviet Union—that is, what it amounted to, because we were in an intelligence unit operation. I found very interesting things about the fate of the Jews, but those documents were confidential. I could not cite them. All I was told was that it didn't matter if I used the content of the documents so long as I did not write a footnote about them. You can't tell that to a "documatic" person!

So, you must remember that when we talk about archives, it was a very long and slow process, of opening up the gates to the real thing. This also applies to various centers—some Jewish, some non-Jewish—that were constructed for that very purpose and are the foundations of this gathering. When were they established? Some of them were closed; some were privately owned. One might think that if there are archives and researchers then research will emerge. That is not always the case since some people gathered information but did not like to share it with visitors. As for the Soviet Bloc, we received only very small samples, tantalizing samples. If you consider the enormous damage that was done by Germany in Eastern Europe, then the portion of the Nuremberg documents furnished by the Soviet Union was infinitesimally small. It was much later that I discovered the reason for that. The Soviets could not find the stuff! These materials were scattered—or rather, they had not been collected and stored in a single place—because when the Soviets captured a city they left the documents there. And since the Germans did their damage *everywhere*, the Soviets would have had to look in Minsk, in Dnepropetrovsk, in Kiev, in Krakow and so on. When I arrived in Minsk—and that was before the breakup of the Soviet Union—I was greeted by the archivist with the question: "How do you expect me to find what you want?" That is very revealing. We operated, so to speak, on one leg. We could not walk without the other; we could not totally grasp what went on. There is much that we did not grasp.

The archival period begins with the gradual opening of archives. Microfilms of German documents were made in Alexandria, Virginia. Various other archives in Europe were relatively open; behind the "Iron Curtain" only Polish archives were relatively accessible. One could go there only after West Germany established the *Bundesarchiv* and received back from Alexandria, Virginia, the original documents captured by the United States. One could also go to Ludwigsburg, even though this was a functioning center aimed at collecting materials for the purpose of bringing war criminals to trial.

So, gradually, in the 1960s and 1970s a more in-depth picture began to emerge. At the same time many difficulties started to surface. Naturally one would not choose to use thirty different archives in order to write a book, especially when you don't yet have your doctorate, or (what we call in the United States) tenure. So, you ask yourself: what do I know best? For instance, a particular language will determine the direction. In other words, someone does research on Hungary as a result of having the advantage of knowing Hungarian, or starts researching something that happened in France because he or she lives in France. I once counted the number of languages that can be legitimately called 'languages of Holocaust research'. And, there were twenty! In fact, there are more. At the United States Holocaust Memorial Museum in Washington, DC, there is currently a Chinese scholar who is studying Chinese documents with respect to the Shanghai Ghetto! I had not thought of such a possibility before. Obviously, a language like Lithuanian is important. And a language like Romanian is more important even than French. In other words, the hierarchy of the languages differs from that existing in universities in Western Europe, North America, and Israel. This means that there is a shortage of people able to read some documents and do research on many issues, *other* than those born in the country concerned. When there is such fragmentation, specialization becomes paramount. And that is our situation now. We are highly specialized and becoming more so. The same thing has happened in other fields, such as medicine and physics, so why not here? The problem with specialization, however, is that it engenders a certain degree of isolation, unless one has the opportunity of attending a conference such as this one, with its gathering of experts from many countries (and even these occasions are few). One does not necessarily know what the fellow scholar in a different country or in a different archive, with more or less the same kind of subject matter, is researching. That's the price.

The middle period also generated arguments. Here we see the full gamut of different views colliding with one another. First was the dispute about truth—what tells the truth: a document or a testimony? When you read a German document you will read lies, argued some. If you really want to know what was going on you should listen to the survivor, said others. But how much did the survivor know? To find out you have to read German documents. Now, equally, the Germans knew extremely little—in fact, almost nothing—about the Jews. It is amazing to realize that when they conquered a town they did not have the faintest idea about the occupants, the leaders, or who would be the proper person to head the *Judenrat*. They could not select anyone, because they did not know *who should* be selected from their point of view. They had no knowledge of Hebrew, although Eichmann tried to learn it. And Yiddish -they could hear it, but they could not read it. The Germans had problems with languages anyway. So a rather mutual exclusion exists here: two different streams and infusions of information. And there was a heated discussion of which should be given priority.

Another argument: that raged at the time concerned whether the development of the process of destruction was intended to result in death from the beginning (the "intentionalism" theory), or whether Hitler was merely incidental and did not really decide anything ("functionalism"). That argument was quite heated for a while.

Or take the problem of definition, which hit us hard in the Holocaust Museum in Washington, DC, when an executive order was issued—written by Stuart Eizenstat—in which "the Holocaust" was defined in an official US document as: "the death of six million Jews and five million others." We celebrated that in a special meeting of the Jewish members of the museum's council. But, what now? Well, if you believe that research like this can surface, can become the basis of a museum, of books, of films, of novels, without political overtones, you are naive.

We also make judgments. We sometimes hide them. We praise some people and condemn others. We acclaim some countries and censure others. The Danes are the most righteous nation. Why? Because only fifty-five Jews or thereabouts died, and all the rest were saved. The Poles have a much lesser, lower standing. Why? Because when you look at Warsaw, the percentages are just the opposite. Almost 99 percent died and not many more than 1 percent of those in the ghetto ever survived. That, apparently, tells you something. But when you take a closer look, it gets more complicated. I received a letter from a Danish professor who was sending me a manuscript. In the meantime, the article has been published, but it hasn't been translated, to my knowledge, to any other language. I can tell you: "We Danes are not so wonderful as you believe." The strangest argument took place in an exchange I had with the Danes. They say: "We are not wonderful," and I write back: "You misunderstand something; you really are wonderful." They say: "We are *not* wonderful, because when those rescue boats were sent out to Sweden with Jews on board"—and this is true—"the German Navy saw these boats and did not intercept them; the German Navy would have had the capability of sinking every one of them." So you see, they said, "we are not wonderful at all, because we were in no danger." And I had to ask: "Why were you not in danger? Why did the Germans respect you? Because you are 'Aryans'? Because they did not want to push you? Or, perhaps, because they knew that you were serious about protecting the Jews?" We heard a very good paper about Italy at this conference.[8] Although one may disagree with its conclusions, because if you take ideology as your guiding principle, the Italians should have been just as bad as the Germans and the French just as wonderful as the Danes. But it didn't happen that way. For instance, why in Nice, did Italian troops liberate Jews already arrested by the French police? When I first read this, I could not believe it.

The Period of the Maturity of Acknowledging Complexity

The major arguments of the second period gradually disappeared. Arguments of this sort are not won by any one side. Superficially one might say that the people who hold these arguments get older and die off. The real reason, however, is that the complexity of what happened was recognized more and more as research proceeded. We are now entering the third stage, the stage of complexity. I call this stage "maturity." Maturity means that you know what you are dealing with. We now look for contexts. The fact is that Holocaust research is now in a kind of "ghetto." That is the blunt truth. Connecting it with other evidence, simultaneous events, other occurrences, other conditions, is rare. Researchers at Yad Vashem are aware of it, because you chose Gerhard Weinberg as the opening speaker at this conference, a man who called for context, in this case the actual, obvious context of World War II.[9] How can you divorce the study of the Holocaust from what was going on at the battlefronts? How can you divorce the *Einsatzgruppen* sent to Russia from *Fall Barbarossa*? How can you divorce anything in the Holocaust from what was going on in the war theater—be it on one front or another, be it with a country just trying to get out of the war, like Hungary (which was occupied in March 1944), with the result that they were going to deport the Jews.

But there are other contexts that are not so obvious. Ulrich Herbert demonstrated a very interesting one, with regard to France.[10] There was a hostage problem, and there was an army general who did not feel comfortable shooting a lot of Frenchman. Three Frenchman shot for a dead German was okay, but a hundred? He had to keep the peace. So he suggested the following: how about Jews as substitutes? Who would think of that!? And indeed, the first trains going out to the death camps from the periphery of Germany left the same month, March 1942—one from France and another from Slovakia. Why would France trade so early? Because it was urgent. Somebody lost the argument; somebody won it. The general actually lost it, because Hitler could accept both the shooting of the hostages *and* the deportation of the Jews. The Slovak situation is another fascinating context. The Slovaks made an offer to the Germans before the Germans were ready. They said: "You can have twenty thousand Jews. You say you need a labor force? Here are twenty thousand Jews!" But it was too early for the Germans. Their problem was: where are these Jews going to be received? "What are we going to do with them?" Why did the Slovaks offer them the Jews? I had to figure out the answer by reading literature that was entirely different, completely *divorced* from the Holocaust. Namely, the context in these small countries like Slovakia—where (as elsewhere) there was an economic depression and a great deal of unemployment during the 1930s—was the economy. So the

Germans said: "Okay. We now have a war. You can send us a hundred thousand laborers." And they started sending laborers. Until they suddenly realized that the depression was over and they did not want to send anymore. So they offered Jews as a substitute. And the Jews went—not, to be sure, to any German industry. They went to Majdanek and Auschwitz. But these connections take a while to establish.

Götz Aly presented another context by pointing to population movements of ethnic Germans.[11] He explains what happened in Łódź and other places in the region that were incorporated into Germany (Wartheland) by the phenomenon of population movements. *Volksdeutsche* were coming in from Bohemia and from other areas and the people in charge had to prepare a place for them. It was a matter of housing and other things. So: Jews out, ethnic Germans in.

I do not recommend my method of research. My method involves looking into an archive and asking for nothing. I remember for instance when I was in Lwów, Ukraine, while the Stalinists were still there. The Stalinist lady archivist asked me: "What would you like to see?" I said, "Anything." I could see (even though I don't understand Russian) what she was telling somebody there: "You see this idiot from America, he doesn't even know what to ask for. We'll fix him." So she gave me the files of the fire department of Lwów. And I started to read. I read the fire department files, 1941–1944: a kitchen fire; an electrical fire, and inevitably someone smoking in bed. It could have been the reports of the fire department in Haifa. I went through the whole lot. I closed the last folder and asked myself: now what have I learned? Aha, where's the arson; where's the resistance; where's anything? Nothing. If anything like that happens, the fire department will note it. But that's not all. These archivists offered me the garden department files. So I read the garden department files and what did I discover? It was the garden department that produced the camouflage for the Janowska labor camp! Since I was reading more or less at random, I found that a major problem in Belarus was the diversion of wheat for the production of vodka, because the Germans needed the wheat. Well, what does that tell us? If it is a major problem, then there is a population that is drunk. What does that say about bystanders, what are we learning about their lives? Quite a lot! And it is the same with the movies in Poland. When Jan Tomasz Gross first described the occupation of Poland (which he did not do in terms of Jewish experiences, i.e., from the point of view of the Holocaust), he mentioned that the Poles were flocking to the movies, to see even the worst movies. What does that tell us about the lives of these Poles? We need to know that if we want context. So, what can researchers conclude from this? That you have to look everywhere; that you cannot skip anything; you cannot omit any place or any organization.

I must say, however, that this is not without problems. We push into new territory, but we face taboos. There are still some subjects that have yet to be put on the table. When Yad Vashem published an English translation of a survivor's story of the Warsaw Ghetto, I'm referring to the one by Stanisław Adler,[12] I happened to find the book in a little store. Then I looked for it in the United States, but it was never distributed. So I approached German publishers, but they did not want it (and I can understand why German publishers would not). I also approached US publishers, but nobody would take it. Who was Stanisław Adler? He was a police officer in the Warsaw Ghetto. That book was the most sophisticated memoir of that ghetto or any other that I have ever read. He did not emigrate from Poland after World War II; after the Kielce pogrom, he killed himself.

Take another taboo: Jewish Councils. In Israel, a publisher in Tel Aviv had in his possession a memoir, four hundred pages long, written by Oskar Neumann. The only such memoir that exists—to my knowledge—of one of the chiefs of the Slovak *Judenrat*, the *Ústredňa Židov*. That book was published in German.* It was published in Hebrew. But never in English. English-language publishers refused the request to translate and publish this book. The same story with the diary of Raymond-Raoul Lambert, head of the Jewish Council in France, which was published in French (edited by Richard Cohen, a professor at the Hebrew University):[13] I asked five or six publishers to take Lambert's diary, which is very dramatic. No takers. The taboo has not left us.

To close, only now are we beginning to ask some of the most difficult questions. We must ask them, we must search for the answers, in any sources we can find. We will also have to come to grips with the fact that some of our questions will never be answered. Keep in mind that a copious amount of documents were destroyed. Many things seen by those who survived were never reported. Therefore, we will have to accept the fact that, however great our effort, we will remain with only a partial picture. Nevertheless, I do not believe we have the

---

* Oskar Neumann, *Im Schatten des Todes. Ein Tatsachenbericht vom Schicksalskampf des slowakischen Judentums* (Tel-Aviv: Ed. Olamenu, 1956).

luxury to cease making the effort to restore the fullest picture possible. And, looking back, I am extremely gratified that we are making a far greater effort than I ever imagined possible.

Notes

1. Franz Neumann, *Behemoth: The Structure and Practice of National Socialism* (New York, 1942/44 and London, 1943).
2. Ernst Fraenkel, *The Dual State: A Contribution to the Theory of Dictatorship* (New York, 1969).
3. Léon Poliakov, *Bréviaire de la haine: Le IIIe Reich et les Juifs* (Paris, 1951); English version: *Harvest of Hate: The Nazi Program for the Destruction of the Jews of Europe* (Syracuse, NY, 1954).
4. See Raul Hilberg, "German Railroads, Jewish Souls," *Society* 14, no. 1 (1976): 520–56; German version: *Sonderzüge nach Auschwitz* (Mainz, 1981).
5. Christopher Browning, *Ordinary Men: Police Battalion 101 and the Final Solution in Poland* (New York, 1992).
6. See Alan Rosen, "Evidence of Trauma: David Boder and Writing the History of Holocaust Testimony," in *Holocaust Historiography in Context: Emergence, Challenges, Polemics and Achievements*, ed. David Bankier and Dan Michman, 497–518. Jerusalem: Yad Vashem / New York: Berghahn Books, 2008.
7. David Boder, *I Did Not Interview the Dead* (Urbana, IL, 1949).
8. See Iael Nidam-Orvieto, "Fighting Oblivion: The CDEC and Its Impact on Italian Holocaust Historiography," in Bankier and Michman, *Holocaust Historiography in Context*, 293–304
9. See Gerhard L. Weinberg, "Two Separate Issues?: Historiography of World War II and the Holocaust" in Bankier and Michman, *Holocaust Historiography in Context*, 379–402
10. See Ulrich Herbert, "The German Military Command in Paris and the Deportation of the French Jews," in *National-Socialist Extermination Policies: Contemporary German Perspectives and Controversies*, ed. Ulrich Herbert (New York, 2000), 128–62.
11. Götz Aly, *'Final Solution': Nazi Population Policy and the Murder of the European Jews* (London, 1999).
12. Stanisław Adler, *In the Warsaw Ghetto, 1940–1943: An Account of a Witness* (Jerusalem, 1982).
13. Raymond-Raoul Lambert, Richard Cohen, and Liliane Servier, *Carnet d'un témoin, 1940–1943* (Paris, 1985); and Richard Y. Cohen, "A Jewish Leader in Vichy France, 1940–1943: The Diary of Raymond-Raoul Lambert," *Jewish Social Studies* 43, no. 1 (1981): 291–310.

Bibliography

Adler, Stanisław. *In the Warsaw Ghetto, 1940–1943: An Account of a Witness.* Jerusalem: Yad Vashem, 1982.
Aly, Götz. *'Final Solution': Nazi Population Policy and the Murder of the European Jews.* London: Arnold, 1999.
Boder, David. *I Did Not Interview the Dead.* Urbana: University of Illinois Press, 1949.
Browning, Christopher. *Ordinary Men: Police Battalion 101 and the Final Solution in Poland.* New York: HarperCollins, 1992.
Cohen, Richard Y. "A Jewish Leader in Vichy France, 1940–1943: The Diary of Raymond-Raoul Lambert." *Jewish Social Studies* 43, no.1 (1981): 291–310.
Fraenkel, Ernst. *The Dual State: A Contribution to the Theory of Dictatorship.* New York: Octagon Books, 1969.
Herbert, Ulrich. "The German Military Command in Paris and the Deportation of the French Jews." In *National-Socialist Extermination Policies: Contemporary German Perspectives and Controversies*, ed. Ulrich Herbert, 128–62. New York: Berghahn Books, 2000.
Hilberg, Raul. "German Railroads, Jewish Souls." *Society* 14, no. 1 (1976): 520–56.
———. *Sonderzüge nach Auschwitz.* Mainz: Dumjahn Verlag, 1981.
Lambert, Raymond-Raoul, Richard Cohen, and Liliane Servier. *Carnet d'un témoin, 1940–1943.* Paris: Fayard, 1985.
Neumann, Franz. *Behemoth: The Structure and Practice of National Socialism.* London: V. Gollancz, 1943.
Nidam-Orvieto, Iael. "Fighting Oblivion: The CDEC and Its Impact on Italian Holocaust Historiography." In *Holocaust Historiography in Context: Emergence, Challenges, Polemics, and Achievements*, ed. David Bankier and Dan Michman, 293–304. Jerusalem: Yad Vashem / New York: Berghahn Books, 2008.
Poliakov, Léon. *Bréviaire de la haine: Le IIIe Reich et les Juifs.* Paris: Calmann-Lévy, 1951.
———. *Harvest of Hate: The Nazi Program for the Destruction of the Jews of Europe.* Syracuse, NY: Syracuse University Press, 1954.
Rosen, Alan. "Evidence of Trauma: David Boder and Writing the History of Holocaust Testimony." In *Holocaust Historiography in Context: Emergence, Challenges, Polemics and Achievements*, ed. David Bankier and Dan Michman, 497–518. Jerusalem: Yad Vashem / New York: Berghahn Books, 2008.
Weinberg, Gerhard L. "Two Separate Issues?: Historiography of World War II and the Holocaust." In *Holocaust Historiography in Context: Emergence, Challenges, Polemics and Achievements*, ed. David Bankier and Dan Michman, 379–402. Jerusalem: Yad Vashem / New York: Berghahn Books, 2008.

Index of Persons

Adam, Uwe Dietrich, 59, 82, 94
Adenauer, Konrad, 100
Adler, Alfred, 210
Adler, Hans Günther, 9, 152
Adler, Stanisław, 87–88, 91, 235
Adorno, Theodor W., 102, 155, 222
Altstötter, Josef, 154–55
Aly, Götz, 82, 234
Arad, Yitzhak, 83, 92n10, 216
Arendt, Hannah, 64, 201, 203
Auerbach, Rachel, 216
Auerswald, Heinz, 93n22, 124, 126, 131nn53–54
Azéma, Jean-Pierre, 92n2

Bach-Zelewski, Erich von dem, 40, 45n22
Baeck, Leo, 144, 146n24
Bafia, Jerzy, 163
Barasz, Efraim, 141
Bauer, Yehuda, 130n21
Bebenroth, Erich, 54
Beethoven, Ludwig van, 73
Bene, Otto, 66n18
Bertelsen, Aage, 145n13
Best, Werner, 35
Bettelheim, Bruno, 201, 204, 219
Biebow, Hans, 90
Birnbaum, Norman, 208, 222–23
Bischof, Max, 123
Blobel, Paul, 171
Bockhonn, unk (Reichsbahndirektion), 68n49
Boder, David Pablo, 152
Bomba, Abraham, 153
Braham, R. L., 145n3

Brenman-Gibson, Margaret, 211–14, 223
Brickner, Richard M., 46n32–33
Brill, Friedrich, 67n32
Brockdorff-Rantzau, Ulrich von, 110n12
Broniewski, Władysław, 163
Browning, Christopher R., 4, 82, 228
Bunom, Alice de, 93n28

Cahnman, Werner J., 45n15
Carter, Jimmy, 6, 102, 159, 176
Casdorf, unk (Oberfinanzpräsident), 67n42
Clauberg, Carl, 32
Cocks, Geoffrey, 211
Cohen, Elie A., 201
Cohen, Richard L., 235
Czerniaków, Adam, 5–6, 62, 68n55, 73, 118, 120–25, 129, 130n13, 130nn29–31, 131n34, 131nn42–44, 131n52, 131n54, 137, 142, 163, 168, 176

Daluege, Kurt, 55, 66nn14–16, 66nn21–22
Dannecker, Theodor, 60
Dejaco, Walter, 67n32
Delbo, Charlotte, 102
Deuerlein, unk, 66 Fn17, 66 Fn28
Deukmejian, George, 110n15
Deutscher, Isaac, 3
Dickinson, John K., 91
Dilli, Gustav, 53
Dinur, Benzion, 144

Index of Persons

Dirlewanger, Oskar, 32
Dobroszycki, Lucjan, 93, 152
Dorpmüller, Julius, 53, 67n40
Douhet, Guilio, 218
Dürrfeld, Ernst, 67n45

Eberl, Irmfried, 58, 126, 131n53
Ebner, Karl, 73, 142, 145n14
Eck, Nathan, 9n11
Edelstein, Jakob, 138, 145n5
Edvardson, Cordelia, 149–50
Eggert, Albert, 54
Eichmann, Adolf, 5, 33, 40, 59–60, 64, 65n11, 67n36, 67n38, 68n56, 26, 76, 103, 200, 217, 228, 231
Einstein, Albert, 26
Eizenstat, Stuart, 231
Ellsberg, Daniel, 211–12
Emrich, Ernst, 54
Eppstein, Paul, 138
Erikson, Erik H., 223
Ernest, Stefan, 145n2, 145n15

Fassbinder, Rainer Werner, 72, 182
Ferenczy, László, 65n12
Fischer, Fritz, 110n12
Fischer, Ludwig, 130n29
Fraenkel, Ernst, 227
Frank, Anne, 229
Frank, Hans, 131n54
Freud, Sigmund, 26, 28, 36, 45, 47, 211
Friedländer, Saul, 3
Friedman, Philip, 148
Friedrich, Carl, 199
Fröhlich, Wilhelm, 54
Fromm, Erich, 47n40

Gancwajch, Abraham, 122
Ganzenmüller, Albert, 53, 65n5, 65n8, 68n48, 68n56, 68n58, 186, 191
Geitmann, Hans, 75–76, 185
Gens, Jacob, 129

Gerstein, Kurt, 154
Globke, Hans, 60
Goebbels, Joseph, 29, 45n17, 45n20
Goethe, Johann Wolfgang von, 43, 73
Göring, Hermann, 17, 19, 45n20, 59, 67n37, 198, 211, 227
Goudsmit, Samuel Abraham, 44n5
Grävenitz, Hans von, 107
Green, Gerald, 201
Greenberg, Irving, 168
Grimsted, Patricia, 174
Gross, Jan Tomasz, 234
Groß, Walter, 33
Gurian, Waldemar, 45n21
Gutman, Israel, 85, 86, 93–94, 216–17

Hagelstange, Rudolf, 46n36
Hagen, Wilhelm, 213
Hartl, Albert, 171
Hartmann, Eduard von, 25, 44n4
Hartmann, Ernst, 54
Hausner, Gideon, 5
Hedtoft, Hans, 141
Hegel, Georg Wilhelm Friedrich, 43
Heidegger, Martin, 40, 43, 190
Heim, Franz, 92n17
Heim, Karl, 68n56
Heine, Heinrich, 46n26, 192
Henriques, Carl Bertel, 141
Henschel, Moritz, 144, 146n23
Herbert, Ulrich, 82, 233
Hermanns, William, 147
Heydrich, Reinhard, 17, 19, 55, 59, 67n37
Himmler, Heinrich, 35, 39–40, 55, 59, 61, 66n26, 67n36, 67n43, 77, 92n11, 213
Hitler, Adolf, 3, 23, 36, 38–39, 40, 42, 46n34, 54, 58–59, 67n36, 180, 183, 187, 196, 204, 213, 223, 231, 233

Index of Persons

Hochhuth, Rolf, 154
Hoffmann, Curt, 93n23
Höfle, Hermann, 82n17, 93
Höfler, Wolfgang, 44n5
Holt, Robert, 210, 217, 219, 224
Horowitz, Irving Louis, 128
Höß, Rudolf, 35
Huber, Franz Josef, 142

Jäckel, Eberhard, 202, 204
Jacobi, Karl, 54, 65n9
Jeckeln, Friedrich, 66n25
Jodl, Alfred, 107
John Paul II. (Pope), 168
Jones, Ernest, 211
Jong, Louis de, 35

Kallenbach, Richard, 68n52
Kaltenbrunner, Ernst, 35
Kanfer, Stefan, 172
Kastner, Rudolf, 14
Katz, Jacob, 24
Katz, Robert, 152
Katzmann, Fritz, 84, 92n12
Keitel, Wilhelm, 107
Kelly, Petra, 203
Kempner, Robert, 197
Kermisz, Josef, 5
Kleinmann, Wilhelm, 53
Klünder, Heinrich, 145n7
Kohl, Helmut, 100–101, 104–105, 107, 109, 110
Kohl, Otto, 60
Kompa, unk (Hauptmann), 66
Korczak, Janusz, 215
Korherr, Richard, 84, 92n11
Kovner, Abba, 151–152
Kramer, Stanley, 155
Kreidler, Eugen, 185, 188
Krüger, Friedrich-Wilhelm, 66n26, 92n12, 93n21
Kull, Steven, 220, 223–24
Kumanyov, V. A., 175
Kunska, unk (Treuhandstelle), 68

Lambert, Raymond-Raoul, 235
Langgässer, Elisabeth, 149
Lanzmann, Claude, 153, 218
Laval, Pierre, 20
Leibbrand, Max, 53, 65n8
Leist, Ludwig, 129n9, 130n29
Lerman, Miles, 169
Lerner, Max, 26
Levi, Primo, 89–91
Lewin, Abraham, 86
Lichtenbaum, Marek, 93n22
Lifton, Betty Jean, 224
Lifton, Robert Jay, 6, 195, 206, 208, 210–11, 213–15, 217, 219–20, 222–225
Loeblowitz-Lennard, Henry, 45n13
Lösener, Bernhard, 16, 60
Löwenherz, Josef, 73, 136, 142, 145n5
Luther, Martin (German Foreign Office), 33, 68n50
Luther, Martin (reformation), 196, 200

Mack, John E., 210, 220, 224
Maedel, Walter, 60, 68n52
Mangold, Philipp, 54, 65n8
Mann, Abby, 155
Mann, Thomas, 39
Manoschek, Walter, 82
Martin, Victor, 146n16
Marx, Karl, 26–27, 44n9
Massing, Paul, 45n21
Mathias, Charles, 107, 110n11
Mayer, Josef, 68n52
McAfee Brown, Robert, 172
Mende, Gerhard, 124
Mengele, Josef, 32, 103
Merten, Max, 146n21
Mertes, Alois, 107, 110n11, 111n16
Milgram, Stanley, 74, 76
Mitterrand, François, 101, 107
Mohns, Otto, 129n10
Möhs, Ernst, 145n5
Moll, Otto, 32

Index of Persons

Mrugowski, Joachim, 67n43
Müller, Herbert, 142
Murmelstein, Benjamin, 145n5

Neuendorff, Willy, 61, 68n46
Neumann, Franz L., 4, 13–14, 18, 44n1, 44n9, 45nn18–20, 65n1, 197–99, 202, 227, 236n1
Neumann, Oskar, 90, 235–36
Nietzsche, Friedrich, 44n9, 46n24
Novak, Franz, 65n7, 65nn11–12, 68n58

Ornstein, Hans, 47n40
Oz, Amos, 214

Pemsel, Max Joseph, 107
Petropolous, Jonathan, 79
Petsch, Adolf, 93n26
Petschek, Frank, 199
Pilichowski, Czesław, 163
Pinson, Koppel S., 45n21
Piwonski, Jan, 153
Pohl, Dieter, 85
Poliakov, Léon, 227

Rademacher, Franz, 60
Raphael, Frederic, 74
Rathenau, Walther, 25, 27, 44n3, 45n12
Rau, Werner, 68n53
Reagan, Ronald, 102–05, 108–09, 110n15
Reimer, Georg, 68n57
Reitlinger, Gerald, 3
Richter, Erich, 68n58
Ringelblum, Emanuel, 128, 131n40, 132n59
Robinson, Jacob, 113, 115, 130n21
Rohwer, Jürgen, 202
Rommel, Erwin, 204
Rommel, Manfred, 204
Roosevelt, Franklin D., 176
Rosenberg, Alfred, 35
Rosenberg, Hans, 4, 196–97, 211

Rosenfeld, Megan, 110n15
Rosenman, Gedaliah, 141
Roth, John K., 79
Rottem, Simha, 153
Rückerl, Adalbert, 180–81
Rudenko, Roman, 173
Rumkowski, Chaim, 90, 120, 129, 144
Rustin, Bayard, 168, 170

Sammern (-Frankenegg), Ferdinand von, 67
Samsonov, Alexander, 175–76
Sartre, Jean-Paul, 26, 46
Scheel, Walter, 107
Schell, Paul, 53
Schellenberg, Walter, 19, 66n14
Schmid, Carlo, 109n1
Schmidt, Helmut, 107
Schmige, Fritz, 145n6
Schultz, Johannes, 54
Sears, Edwin, 74
Seidl, Siegfried, 145n5, 209
Sereny, Gitta, 152
Shazar, Zalman, 119
Sheinwald, Zeev, 66n28
Siegert, Rudolf, 68n54
Simon, Alfred, 54
Smith, Bradley, 77
Sombart, Werner, 44n9
Speer, Albert, 53, 61, 65n5, 67n36, 67n43, 92
Spengler, Oswald, 26, 44nn8–9, 49
Stange, Otto, 54, 60, 68
Stangl, Franz, 58, 152
Staron, Stanislaw J., 5, 130, 163, 176
Stier, Walter, 68n58
Strauch, Eduard, 32
Strauß, Franz-Joseph, 107
Streckenbach, Bruno, 42
Streicher, Julius, 46n24
Stroop, Jürgen, 86, 93n21, 217
Strozier, Charles B., 219
Szeryński, Józef, 136

Toynbee, Arnold Josef, 110n14
Trachtenberg, Joshua, 46n28
Treibe, Paul, 68n48
Trunk, Isaiah, 5, 17, 82–83, 113–121, 123–132, 139
Türk, Richard, 67n31
Turner, Harald, 35
Tushnet, Leonard, 129
Tyas, Stephen, 85

Vaganov, Fjedor Michailowitsch, 174–75

Wagner, Edward, 19
Weil, Hans, 36
Weinberg, Gerhard, 229, 233
Weiner, Eugene, 214, 221, 224
Weizsäcker, Ernst von, 68n50
Weizsäcker, Richard von, 107, 111n18
Well, Günther van, 111n16

Wiesel, Elie, 5, 102, 151, 153–54, 161, 165, 168, 172–73, 176
Wigand, Arpad, 129n7
Willems, Susanne, 82
Winkler, Heinrich August, 3, 9n8
Wirth, Joseph, 110n12
Wisliceny, Dieter, 144, 146n19, 146n21
Witte, Peter, 85
Wolter, Ulf, 203
Wulf, Joseph, 3

Yevtushenko, Yevgeny, 173

Zelkowicz, Józef, 146n22
Ziolkowski, Theodore, 148
Zöpf, Wilhelm, 66n18
Zorthian, Barry, 110n16
Zucker, Otto, 145n5
Zundelewicz, Bernhard, 142

Index of Places

Alexandria (VA), 68n57, 105, 146n21, 198, 230
Amersfoort, 35
Amsterdam, 57, 140
Auschwitz, 3, 20–22, 32, 42, 52, 61–62, 65n8, 67n32, 68n54, 75–77, 89–91, 102, 106, 111n18, 137, 141, 143, 150–55, 160–63, 166–67, 177, 184–85, 188, 190, 192, 194, 201, 206, 210, 220, 222, 234
Austria, 5, 53, 180, 189

Babi Yar, 57, 160–61, 169, 171, 173, 176
Baltic states, 22, 56, 103, 125
Basel, 189
Belarus. *See* White Russia
Belgium, 18, 22, 65n8, 106
Belzec/Bełżec, 7, 20–21, 55, 83–85, 216
Bendzin/Będzin, 130n14, 132n59
Bergen-Belsen, 89, 104, 110n8, 209
Berlin, 19, 25, 32, 66n21, 73, 82, 89, 131n54, 138, 144, 150, 171, 179–80, 203, 209, 211n1
East, 180, 209
Bialystok/Białystok, 53, 118, 120, 130n22, 131n42, 132n59, 144
Birkenau, 166–67
Bitburg, 4, 99, 101–11
Bohemia, 234
Bordeaux, 53
Boston, 130n21, 180
Bremen, 46n31

Brest-Litovsk, 57, 66n17
Bucharest, 82
Bulgaria, 20, 65n2, 203
Burlington (VT), 3, 204
Byelorussia. *See* White Russia

Chelmno/Chełmno. *See* Kulmhof
Copenhagen, 141, 169, 176
Corfu, 152
Croatia, 65n2, 67n33
Czechoslovakia, 39, 150, 181
Częstochowa, 90, 118, 125, 132n60

Dachau, 163, 196, 212
Danzig, 35
Demyansk, 147, 192
Denmark, 35, 46n31, 164, 176
Dnepropetrovsk, 53, 230
Düsseldorf, 65n5, 65n11, 88, 147, 186, 189, 191–94

Florence, 189
France, 18, 20–22, 24, 28, 39, 52, 56, 60, 62, 65n2, 65n8, 68n54, 82, 90, 106–07, 111n18, 141, 189, 196, 201–03, 230, 233, 235
Frankfurt am Main, 2, 72, 75, 93n26, 182, 184, 188, 194, 197
Freiburg, 189–91

Galicia, 65, 84–85, 143
Generalgouvernement, 84–85, 122
Germany, 2–4, 6, 13–14, 16, 17, 20, 25, 27–29, 33–34, 36, 38–39, 42, 46n24, 51, 53–56, 62, 64, 68n50, 71–73, 75, 82, 91,

99–109, 110n12, 139, 143–44,
145n2, 149–50, 152, 164, 179–
80, 182, 189, 191–92, 194, 196–
97, 202–04, 206, 209–11, 213,
223, 226–27, 229–30, 233–34
Głębokie, 107
Great Britain, 18, 24, 71, 196
Greece, 20–21, 28, 62, 106

Haifa, 151, 224, 234
Holland. *See* Netherlands
Horodenka, 120
Hungary, 14, 25, 65n2, 137, 143,
161, 165, 181, 230, 233

Israel, 5, 22, 36, 67, 73, 83, 91,
100–01, 104, 119, 142, 150–52,
162, 164, 176, 194, 199–200,
208, 214–18, 221, 230, 235
Italy, 22, 62, 65n2, 106, 189, 203,
232

Janov, 93
Janowska, 234
Jasenovac, 87
Jerusalem, 5, 80, 150, 165, 176,
179, 216
Józefów, 82

Katyn, 75, 184
Kaunas, 131n52
Kielce, 235
Kiev, 57, 170–71, 230
Koblenz, 179
Kolomea, 55, 131n33
Konstanz, 107
Korea, 202, 209
Krakow, 68n58, 93n17, 122,
130n30, 167, 230
Kulmhof, 20, 22, 57, 131, 143, 152
Kutno, 131n33

Latvia, 56, 61, 63, 66nn20–21,
68n59, 129n3
Leningrad, 192

Liechtenstein, 20
Lithuania, 19, 56–57, 66n21, 88,
123, 129n3, 131n54, 140, 162,
206, 230
Lodz/Łódź, 17–18, 76–77, 88, 90,
114, 116–21, 126–29, 130n21,
130n23, 131n52, 152
London, 197
Los Angeles, 197
Lublin. *See* Majdanek
Luboml, 66n28
Ludwigsburg, 72, 180–84, 230
Lwow/Lwów, 65n13, 144, 234

Madagascar, 18
Majdanek, 3, 22, 57, 67n31,
83, 85, 93n17, 118, 120, 123,
130n14, 138, 145nn6–7, 234
Mantua, 189
Milan, 189
Minsk, 20, 32, 68n47, 129n3,
130n22, 144, 230
Monaco, 20
Moscow, 169, 171–74, 192
Munich, 2, 107, 149, 179, 181, 196

Netherlands, 18, 46n31, 62, 63,
65n8, 68n57, 140, 144
New Haven (CT), 74
New York City, 152–54, 167, 224,
226
Nice, 232
Norway, 28
Nuremberg, 14–17, 31, 51, 64,
65n1, 67n43, 81, 107, 109n3,
150, 154, 186, 188, 195, 197–98,
226–27, 229

Oklahoma, 196, 200
Oppeln, 65n8, 68n49, 76, 185, 188
Oslo, 20

Paris, 4, 65n8, 93n29, 107, 141,
202, 227
Pavia, 189

Index of Places

Pinsk-Stolin, 93n26
Poland, 4, 6, 14, 17, 20–21, 32, 54–55–56, 58, 65n10, 83–84, 90, 107, 110n12, 125–126, 129n3, 141, 160, 162–64, 168–170, 179, 181, 184, 187, 193, 213, 234–35
Potsdam, 180

Radom, 132n60, 145n8
Riga, 20, 57, 63, 88, 129n3, 144
Romania, 20–22, 65n2, 82, 91, 129n3, 143, 146n17, 230
Russia, 19–20, 24, 28, 42, 45n18, 140, 172, 192, 233. *See also* Soviet Union

Saloniki, 89
San José (CA), 4, 147, 209–210
Serbia, 35, 106–07
Shanghai, 230
Silesia, 25, 125, 146n16
Sinai, 27, 200, 215
Slovakia, 62, 65n2, 68n50, 140, 143–44, 233
Sobibor, 20–22, 58, 84–85, 92, 106, 152–53, 201, 207, 216
Sosnowiec, 132
Soviet Union, 6, 18–19, 22, 161, 164, 168–70, 172–73, 175–76, 179, 182, 229–30. *See also* Russia
Spain, 24, 80
Stalingrad, 21, 71, 175
Strasbourg, 189
Stuttgart, 72, 107, 181–82, 202, 204, 209
Sweden, 149–50, 176, 232
Switzerland, 4, 13, 46, 172
Syria, 108

Taganrog, 57
Tel Aviv, 205, 235
Theresienstadt, 89, 138, 150, 152, 209
Treblinka, 3, 20–22, 40, 58, 75, 84–85, 92, 126, 127, 131–32n54, 137, 143, 151–52, 153, 160–61, 163, 165–66, 184, 201, 216, 218
Trondheim, 20

Ukraine, 19, 57, 66n28, 103, 125, 175, 234
United States, 2–3, 5–6, 13, 21–22, 71–72, 74, 91, 101–06, 109, 110n12, 148, 159–60, 162, 164, 166, 168, 170–71, 174, 196, 201, 206, 209, 226–28, 230, 235

Venice, 189
Verdun, 101, 107, 147
Vermont, 3, 5, 7, 44n1, 191, 199, 202
Vienna, 5, 25, 63, 68n49, 73, 136, 138, 142, 145n14, 186–88, 196, 209
Vilna, 117–18, 122, 125, 128–29, 130n14, 130n22, 132n56, 140, 144

Warsaw, 5–6, 17–18, 57, 61–62, 67n45, 73, 85–87, 93nn22–23, 106–07, 114, 116, 118, 120–21, 122–28, 129n5, 129n7, 130nn29–31, 131n32, 131n52, 131n54, 132n59, 136, 138, 140, 142, 144, 153, 162–69, 176, 201, 213, 216–17, 232, 235
Warthbrücken, 143
Wartheland, 234
Washington, DC, 2, 151, 153, 161, 176, 180, 198, 231
Weimar, 1
White Russia, 19, 32, 56, 125, 129n3, 170

Yamit, 215
Yugoslavia, 14, 20, 22

Zamość, 120, 130n14

Index of Subjects

Annexation ("Anschluss") of Austria, 5
Antisemitism, 34, 45n18, 55, 81, 164, 195, 203, 214
Archive, 1, 14, 65n8, 85, 91, 151, 160, 167, 169–70, 174–75, 177, 179–81, 186, 188, 192–94, 198, 206, 226–27, 229–31, 234
Archive of the criminal court Düsseldorf, 186
Archive of the German railways Frankfurt am Main, 75–77, 184–186
Archive of the German railways Nuremberg, 186, 188
Bundesarchiv (Federal Archive of Germany), 230
Central State Archive of the city of Moscow, 174
Federal Records Center Alexandria, 198, 230, 68n57, 105
Armenian Genocide, 108, 110–11n15
Aryanization, 16–17, 31, 106. See also condemnations
Assimilation, 25, 172

Bible, 7
Brooklyn College, 196–97
Bundesbahn (German Federal Railway), 75–76, 184–86, 191
Bundeswehr (German postwar army), 105–07
Bureaucracy, 2, 4, 14–15, 23, 30–31, 36–37, 39, 41–43, 50–69, 71, 74–77, 82, 114, 117, 120–21, 123, 131n54, 136–37, 148, 169, 179, 183–85, 188, 196–98, 202–03, 206–07, 211–12, 214, 220–21, 228
Administration, 15, 30, 35, 38–39, 63, 72, 100, 113, 126, 129n3, 138–39, 144, 166, 174, 190–91
Administrative machine, 30, 33, 58, 60, 64, 123, 183
Bureaucratic machine/Bureaucrats, 4, 30, 36–37, 41–42, 52, 59–60, 64, 75, 117, 120, 131n54, 136, 148, 169, 188
Bystanders, 2, 148, 152, 206, 222, 234

Central Office of the Provincial Administrations of Justice for the Investigation of National Socialist Crimes, 72, 103, 180–84
Collaboration, 134–36, 108, 155, 206, 211
Columbia University, 4, 14, 154, 197, 199
Columbia University Press, 199
Commemoration, 4, 7, 101, 163, 171, 214
Concentration camps, 35, 55, 58, 61, 103, 142, 150, 154, 160, 167, 180, 201, 213
Condemnations, 17, 28, 61, 217. See also Aryanization
Contact theory, 28
Cyanide, 20, 61

– 246 –

Death camps, 53, 55, 58, 106, 125, 140, 162, 164, 182, 216, 233
Deportations, 17, 20, 51, 58, 61–62, 82–85, 90, 93n23, 107, 111n18, 113, 118, 124–25, 129n9, 136, 138, 140, 142–43, 163, 168
Der Stürmer (publication), 35, 64
The Destruction of the European Jews (book), 1–2, 4, 9n10, 44n1, 93n18, 195
Destruction process, 3–5, 8n1, 13–16, 19, 23–43, 45n18, 50–52, 55, 58–59, 61, 63, 64, 68n56, 71, 73–75, 77, 80, 89, 106, 11n18, 118, 123, 125–27, 134, 139–40, 144–45, 155, 159, 162, 175, 178, 183, 197–98, 202, 212, 222, 226, 231
Droemer-Knaur München (publisher), 203

Eichmann trial, 200, 217
Emancipation, 28, 52, 101
Escape, 16, 37, 137, 143, 165, 181, 207
Euthanasia, 31, 58, 144, 207, 211
Exile/Emigration, 6, 18, 59, 164, 174

Final Solution, 1, 19, 50, 58, 61, 63, 73, 75–76, 83–84, 127, 131n54, 140, 183
Forced labor, 17, 51–52, 87, 119–20, 141, 162
Footnotes, 3, 22, 102, 155, 214
Functionalism, 100, 231

Gas chambers, 20–21, 39–43, 50, 55, 129n9, 141, 149, 152, 154, 162, 166, 178, 182, 185, 204, 207
Gas vans, 19, 77
General Directorate East (Reichsbahn Generaldirektion Ost), 54, 185

Genocide, 3, 108, 110–11n15, 111n18, 220–23
German Federal Foreign Office, 18, 20, 22, 33, 35, 45n12, 60, 62, 65n2, 66n18, 68n50, 107, 110n12, 111n18
German Red Cross, 88
Gestapo, 21, 52, 55–57, 62, 68n47, 73, 81, 103, 124, 127, 136, 139, 142, 150
Ghetto, 5, 17–18, 28, 52, 57–58, 62, 73, 83, 85–91, 93nn22–23, 106–07, 113–29, 129n9, 130nn21–22, 131n52, 136–45, 150, 153, 162–63, 165, 168, 173, 201, 206, 209, 213–14, 216–18, 230, 232–33, 235
Ghettoization, 123, 134–35, 164, 213

Harvard University, 199, 223
Holocaust studies/research, 2–3, 7, 8n2, 80, 225–236
Hoßbach conference, 39
Hurbn, 226

I. G. Farben, 52
Ideology, 15, 58, 104, 106, 108, 207, 232
Indoctrination, 34–35, 64
Institute for Contemporary History Munich, 2
Intentionalism, 231

Jew (Nazi definition), 15–17, 51–52
Jewish Council (*Judenrat*), 5, 17, 62, 86, 90, 93n22, 113–16, 119–20, 128, 129n9, 130n21, 131n52, 133–44, 163, 168, 176, 220–21, 231, 235
Jewish Order Service, 122, 127–28
Jewish resistance, 5, 106, 119, 125, 128, 136, 154, 163, 187, 200–01, 203, 214–21, 234
Jewish star, 40, 150

– 247 –

Jud Süss, 72, 181
Justification, 38, 35, 71, 217

Korean war, 172, 202

Labor camps, 84

Machine/Machinery of destruction, 4, 32, 41, 51–52, 55, 61, 63, 126, 128, 134, 139, 145, 179
McGill University Montreal, 201
Mitteleuropäisches Reisebüro, 62, 68nn48–49
Mobile killing units/Mobile operational groups (of the SS or Police), 22, 31, 42, 125

NATO, 104, 182
November Pogrom, 5, 31
NSDAP, 14, 30–32, 39, 45n18, 51, 58, 64, 103, 196–98, 227
Number of Holocaust victims, 2, 22, 42, 53, 84–85, 228
Nuremberg Laws, 15–17, 31, 51, 150
Nuremberg Traffic Museum, 64, 188
Nuremberg trial, 14, 65n1, 81, 103, 107, 155, 195, 198, 227
Nuremberg trials (subsequent), 154–55, 198, 226–27

Oberkommando der Wehrmacht (High command of the Wehrmacht), 14, 198, 227
Olle & Wolter Berlin (publisher), 203
Operation Barbarossa, 18, 233
Order Police, 31, 52, 55–58, 60, 65n13, 66n14, 66n16, 88, 171, 228
Organisation Todt, 228

Perpetrators, 2, 4, 15, 30, 34–35, 39–40, 71, 75, 77, 81, 89, 100, 123, 133, 135, 139–40, 148, 152, 201, 206, 208, 220, 228
Perpetrators, Victims, Bystanders (book), 2, 9
Princeton University Press, 199
Prisoners of war, 105–07, 110n8
Propaganda, 34–35, 43, 71–72
Provocation theory, 24, 26, 28–29

Quadrangle Books (publisher), 94nn35–36, 200, 203

Rationalization, 35–36, 43, 71, 140, 208
Records, 5, 14, 16, 68n56, 77, 79, 85, 89, 91, 105, 110n12, 148, 152, 160–61, 169, 170, 172, 177, 179, 186, 191–92, 198, 206
Regression models, 34–37
Reich Main Security Office, 68n54, 106
Reich Ministry for the Occupied Eastern Territories, 60
Reich Ministry of Agriculture, 31, 143
Reich Ministry of Economy, 16, 31
Reich Ministry of Finance, 21, 31, 52, 60–62, 68n52, 68n54, 228
Reich Ministry of Interior, 15–16, 60, 159, 186, 228
Reich Ministry of Labor, 31
Reich Ministry of Transportation, 21–22, 179, 193
Reichsbahn (German railway), 53–55, 60–61, 67n40, 68n47, 68n56, 68n58. *See also* special trains
Reichskommissariat Ostland, 60, 227
Reichsvereinigung der Juden in Deutschland (official Jewish community organization in Germany), 62
Reichswehr, 105

Index of Subjects

Schutzstaffel (SS)/Protection squad, 18–20, 22, 31–32, 35, 40, 52, 55, 58, 60–61, 65n2, 66n14, 66n18, 66n25, 67n45, 68n54, 76–77, 81, 84, 86, 92n12, 93n17, 93n21, 101–08, 125, 129n7, 138, 142–44, 145n5, 149, 154, 163, 167, 170–71, 179, 186, 198, 201, 208
Security service, 17, 103
Security police, 17, 19, 32, 35, 42, 53–57, 60, 63, 66n14, 66n28, 93n26, 128, 166
Special trains, 53, 57, 75, 162, 178–194
Sources, 2, 5, 71, 79–80, 83, 87, 90, 113–14, 127, 148, 150, 152, 175, 179, 185, 206, 227, 235
Sterilization, 29, 32
Survivors, 5, 19, 21, 66n28, 87–89, 91, 100–02, 104, 120, 129n9, 142, 147–51, 154, 160–62, 165, 169, 194, 200–01, 205–06, 218–19, 228, 231, 235

Typhus, 58, 85

United States Holocaust Memorial Council, 2, 102, 109, 206, 231
United States Holocaust Memorial Museum, 2, 151, 206, 228, 230–31
University of Oklahoma Press, 200
University of Vermont, 5, 7, 44n1, 44n5, 202

Vichy-Frankreich, 20, 65n20, 82, 108
Victims, 32, 38, 40, 42–43, 51, 53, 57, 71, 73, 84–85, 87–91, 104, 119, 123, 127, 135, 141, 143, 148, 152, 154, 159, 165, 171, 173, 175, 178, 187, 193, 195, 200, 201, 206–07, 209
Vietnam war, 202

War Documentation Project, 198
War Refugee Board, 21
Warsaw ghetto, 5, 17–18, 62, 73, 87, 106–07, 114, 121–23, 125–26, 128, 129n5, 130n31, 131n32, 136, 138, 142, 153, 163, 165, 201, 213, 216–17, 235
Warsaw ghetto uprising, 106–07, 153, 162, 201, 216–17
Wehrmacht, 5, 13–14, 19, 22, 54, 65n8, 105–08, 110n8, 147, 166, 198, 208, 227
Württemberg Historical Society, 204

Yad Vashem, 5–6, 91, 152, 176, 216, 221, 225, 233, 235
Yale University, 74, 76, 223
Yiddish (language), 130n18, 145n11, 146n22, 153, 161, 172, 226, 231
YIVO Institute for Jewish Research, 226

www.ingramcontent.com/pod-product-compliance
Lightning Source LLC
Chambersburg PA
CBHW072149100526
44589CB00015B/2158